FUTURE CITIES

FUTURE CITIES

A VISUAL GUIDE

NICK DUNN AND PAUL CURETON

BLOOMSBURY VISUAL ARTS
LONDON · NEW YORK · OXFORD · NEW DELHI · SYDNEY

BLOOMSBURY VISUAL ARTS
Bloomsbury Publishing Plc
50 Bedford Square, London, WC1B 3DP, UK
1385 Broadway, New York, NY 10018, USA

BLOOMSBURY, BLOOMSBURY VISUAL ARTS and the Diana
logo are trademarks of Bloomsbury Publishing Plc

First published in Great Britain 2020

Copyright © Nick Dunn and Paul Cureton, 2020

Nick Dunn and Paul Cureton have asserted their rights under the Copyright,
Designs and Patents Act, 1988, to be identified as Authors of this work.

For legal purposes the Acknowledgements on p. ix
constitute an extension of this copyright page.

Cover design: Eleanor Rose
Cover image © Buckminster Fuller, Dome over Manhattan, 1960.
Courtesy, The Estate of R. Buckminster Fuller.

All rights reserved. No part of this publication may be reproduced or transmitted in any form or
by any means, electronic or mechanical, including photocopying, recording, or any information
storage or retrieval system, without prior permission in writing from the publishers.

Bloomsbury Publishing Plc does not have any control over, or responsibility for,
any third-party websites referred to or in this book. All internet addresses given
in this book were correct at the time of going to press. The author and publisher
regret any inconvenience caused if addresses have changed or sites have
ceased to exist, but can accept no responsibility for any such changes.

A catalogue record for this book is available from the British Library.

A catalog record for this book is available from the Library of Congress.

ISBN: HB: 978-1-3500-1164-9
PB: 978-1-3500-1165-6
ePDF: 978-1-3500-1163-2
eBook: 978-1-3500-1166-3

Typeset by Lachina Creative, Inc.
Printed and bound in India

To find out more about our authors and books visit
www.bloomsbury.com and sign up for our newsletters.

For Evelyn and her futures. – ND

To Alana, with love forever. – PC

CONTENTS

Acknowledgements ix
Figures and Tables xi
Preface xix

1. Introduction: Futures, imagination and visions for cities   1

2. Cities of Vision: A visual history of the future   29

3. Rendering Tomorrow: The impact of visualization techniques   55

4. Technological Futures: Optimism, science fiction and infrastructural systems   80

5. Social Futures: Experiments, ephemerality and experiences   111

6. Global Futures: Challenges and opportunities for collective life   143

7. Tomorrow's Cities Today: Conclusions and alternative futures   173

References 181
Index 190

ACKNOWLEDGEMENTS

The purpose of this book is to provide insight into visions for future cities, their history and their role in shaping our collective future. Our attempt to give a comprehensive account of this would be extremely limited without the many visual materials featured in this publication. With this in mind, we would like to acknowledge and express our considerable gratitude to all the individuals, agencies, practices and other organizations that contributed their material or gave permission for it to be included. Visions for future cities have been drawn from a wide variety of sources across different media. However, the Frac Centre-Val de Loire in particular provided access to a significant number of examples used to illustrate this book facilitated by a special agreement between its director, Abdelkader Damani, and the authors. In recognition of this, a further statement follows below.

En 1991, le Frac Centre-Val de Loire oriente sa collection vers un questionnement transversal, un champ de réflexion ouvert sur l'architecture de demain en réunissant art contemporain et architecture expérimentale de 1950 à nos jours : « une collection d'événements, pleinement spéculative, dont le sens est en devenir ». Reconnue internationalement, la collection offre une traversée inédite des expérimentations artistiques, architecturales et urbaines, rivalisant avec les plus grandes collections d'architecture (Centre Pompidou-MNAM à Paris; MOMA à New York; CCA à Montréal; DAM-musée d'architecture à Francfort). Elle est cependant la seule à proposer une cartographie internationale et une généalogie historique de la recherche architecturale et de ses relations à la création artistique depuis les années 1950. La synthèse des arts, l'architecture radicale, la « déconstruction » des années 1980 et les recherches les plus innovantes en matière de technologies numériques sont les quelques repères autour desquels la collection s'est construite. Elle forme un paysage où tout est architecture. En cela, elle est la représentation du rêve né dans les années 1960 d'une création à l'échelle de chaque instant, l'espoir de voir disparaître et l'art et l'architecture au profit d'une vie devenue œuvre est le fer de lance d'une critique du modèle architectural dominant. La collection est dotée de fonds exceptionnels, grâce à de nombreuses donations (Claude Parent, Chanéac, Pascal Häusermann, Günter Günschel, Renée Gailhoustet, J-F. Zevaco, Guy Rottier, Georges et Jacqueline Adilon . . .).

Abdelkader Damani
Directeur du Frac Centre-Val de Loire

FIGURES AND TABLES

Figure 1. Ikiré Jones, Idumota Market, Lagos 2081 A.D., de la série Our Africa 2081 A.D. © Olalekan Jeyfous & Walé Oyéjidé.

Figure 2. Aldo Loris Rossi, Eliopolis, frammento metropolitano eco-compatibile, 1978, Perspective. Encre, crayon de couleur et crayon graphite sur tirage calque adhésivé sur carton 55.7 × 74.3 cm. inv. 011 007 001. Photography © François Lauginie, Collection Frac Centre-Val de Loire.

Figure 3. Superstudio, Le Dodici Città Ideali, 1971. La prima città. Lithograph. Encre sur papier. 70 × 100 cm. inv. 016 117 002. Photography © François Lauginie, Collection Frac Centre-Val de Loire.

Figure 4. Andrea Branzi, Ernesto Bartolini and Lapo Lani, Masterplan Strijp Philips, Eindhoven, model view, 1999–2000. Plastique, acetate, contreplaqué, miroir 40 × 157 × 157 cm. inv. 004 03 01. Photography © François Lauginie, Collection Frac Centre-Val de Loire.

Figure 5. Nikola Mihov, Photograph of Memorial House of the Bulgarian Communist Party, Buzludja 2009–2012, from Forget Your Past, Communist-Era Monuments in Bulgaria, 2nd ed, Janet 45 Publishing, 2015.

Figure 6. Kenneth Garland, David Jefferis, Future Cities, Usborne Books, 1979. Reproduced from *Future Cities* by permission of Usborne Publishing, 83–85 Saffron Hill, London EC1N 8RT, UK. www.usborne.com. Copyright © 1979 Usborne Publishing Ltd.

Figure 7. Eugène Hénard, 'The Cities of The Future', published in *American City*, January 1903–1909. NCSU Libraries.

Figure 8. Pushwagner, *Soft City – There Goes the Sun*. Drawn between 1969 and 1975 but lost until 2008.

Figure 9. Allen D. Albert, 1933, Exposition Bird's Eye View, The Reuben H. Donnelley Corporation. Courtesy David Rumsey Map Collection.

Figure 10. Patrick Abercrombie, Forshaw's London Community map, Social Analysis, Greater London Plan, 1943.

Figure 11. Chan K Q Audrey and Iskm (Studio aVOID), 'Cities For a Flying World' competition, HSE Graduate School of Urbanism, Moscow, 2017 – 'Aerotopia.'

Figure 12. URBED, Uxcester Masterplan, Wolfson Economics Prize, 2014.

Figure 13. Helmut Jacoby, MK in 1990, Aerial Perspective, Graphite, Milton Keynes Main Centre, 1974–1990, 1974. Courtesy of Derek Walker. © Milton Keynes Development Corporation, Crown Copyright. Licensed under the Open Government Licence v3.0. Image courtesy of Milton Keynes City Discovery Centre, reference IMA/SD/2022.

Figure 14. Andrew Mahaddie, City Club, Milton Keynes, early 1970s. © Milton Keynes Development Corporation, Crown Copyright. Licensed under the Open Government Licence v3.0. Image courtesy of Milton Keynes City Discovery Centre, reference DW/1/1/140.

Figure 15. E.P.C.O.T. Masterplan, 1966–1967. © Walt Disney Enterprises.

Figure 16. Lúcio Costa and Oscar Niemeyer, Brasília, Brazil, 1956–1960. The original pilot plan. Image courtesy Uri Rosenheck via Wikimedia Creative

Commons. https://commons.wikimedia.org/wiki/File:Brasilia_-_Plan.JPG

Figure 17. Buckminster Fuller, Dome over Manhattan, 1960. Courtesy, the Estate of R. Buckminster Fuller.

Figure 18. Otomo, Katsuhiro, Akira – Destruction of Neo-Tokyo, 1982–1990, Akira vol. 3 © MASH • ROOM / Kodansha Publishing Ltd.

Figure 19. Minecraft, Markus 'Notch' Persson, 2009.

Figure 20. DR_D (Dagmar Richter) – An Earthscratcher for Century City, Los Angeles, 1991. Métal, plexiglas, bois, résine, peinture 26 × 122 × 255 cm. inv. 998 01 58. Collection Frac Centre-Val de Loire.

Figure 21. Master plan for London based on research carried out by the Town Planning Committee of the M.A.R.S. Group, 1942. RIBA Collections.

Figure 22. Heinz Schulz-Neudamm, *Metropolis*, 1926. © Deutsche Kinemathek – Horst von Harbou.

Figure 23. Egor Orlov, New topography of the future city, Cybertopia. Image © Egor Orlov, 2015.

Figure 24. Ron Herron, Walking City on the Ocean, project. 1966. Exterior perspective. New York, Museum of Modern Art (MoMA). Cut-and-pasted printed and photographic papers and graphite covered with polymer sheet, 11 1/2 × 17' (29.2 × 43.2 cm). Gift of The Howard Gilman Foundation. Acc. n.: 1203.2000. © 2018. Digital image, The Museum of Modern Art, New York/Scala, Florence.

Figure 25. SCAPE, Oyster-tecture / MoMA Rising Currents Exhibition, 2010.

Figure 26. Neil Spiller, Rachel Armstrong and Martin Hanczyc (AVATAR) Future Venice, (Visualizations by Christian Kerrigan), 2009.

Figure 27. Noel Schardt + Bjoern Muendner (Freischaerler Architects), United Plastic Nation, 2017.

Figure 28. Blessed Ambrogio Sansedoni – detail (the city of Siena), Palazzo Pubblico. © 2018. Photo Scala, Florence.

Figure 29. View of an Ideal City, or The City of God, after 1470 (oil on panel), Laurana, Luciano (c. 1420–79) (attr. to) / Galleria Nazionale delle Marche, Urbino, Marche, Italy / Bridgeman Images.

Figure 30. Plan of Mexico, in Hernando Cortés, La preclara narratione di Ferdinando Cortese della Nuoua Hispagna, Venice, 1524 (woodcut), Italian School, (16th century) / British Library, London, UK / © British Library Board. All Rights Reserved / Bridgeman Images.

Figure 31. Island Capital of the Aztecs, Tenochtitlan (mural), Covarrubias, Luis (1919–1987) / Museo Nacional de Antropologia, Mexico City, Mexico / Sean Sprague/Mexicolore / Bridgeman Images.

Figure 32. Mazhar Ali Khan, A Panorama of Delhi taken from the top of the Lahore Gate of the Red Fort, Delhi, Watercolour, 1846. British Library, London, UK / © British Library Board. All Rights Reserved / Bridgeman Images.

Figure 33. Kosmaj Project, The Berlin TV tower, Drone Photography, 2019.

Figure 34. Francesco Colonna, Hypnerotomachia Poliphili, Signature d8 verso and e1 recto (Text; Satyr with Sleeping Nymph). Image Courtesy of the Met Museum. CC. Aq. No. 23.73.1.

Figure 35. Thomas More, *Utopia* (translated by Gilbert Burnet), George Routledge & Sons, 1885, British Library, London, UK © British Library Board. All Rights Reserved/Bridgeman Images.

Figure 36. Jan Jansson, View of Strasbourg from 'Urbium totius Germaniae Superioris Illustriorum clariorumque Tabluae antiquae et novae accuratissime elaboratae', 1657 (engraving), Dutch School, (17th century) / British Library, London, British Library Board. All Rights Reserved / Bridgeman Images.

Figure 37. Jacopo de' Barbari, Bird's eye view of Venice, 1500. Woodcut printed from six blocks on six sheets of joined paper, © De Agostini Picture Library / A. Dagli Orti / © British Library, London, UK/Bridgeman Images.

Figure 38. Yakov Chernikhov, Architectural fantasy. View of the enormous portal cranes with semi-circular corbels, from the series 'Industrial Architecture', 1932–1936, drafting pen, gouache and lacquer, 105 × 105 mm. © Yakov Chernikhov, Courtesy of the Tchoban Foundation.

Figure 39. Giovanni Battista Piranesi, Italian, 1720–1778, The Gothic Arch, 1761, Etching plate: 41.2 × 54.5 cm. (16 1/4 × 21 7/16 in.) sheet: 48.9 × 63.6 cm. (19 1/4 × 25 1/16 in.) frame: 62 × 77.2 × 2.5 cm (24 7/16 × 30 3/8 × 1 in.) Gift of Frank Jewett Mather Jr. x1938-13n Focillon 37; Hind 28; Robison 40; Wilton-Ely 39 Princeton University Art Museum.

Figure 40. Peter Barber Architects, Hundred Mile City, 2016. Images courtesy of Peter Barber Architects.

Figure 41. Plan of Paris, France, c. 1870, showing Georges Eugene Haussmann boulevards superimposed in thick black. Granger/Bridgeman Images.

Figure 42. Louis De Soissons, Architect, Welwyn Garden City Masterplan, 1920, Cachemaille-Day, Nugent Francis artist/photographer, RIBA Collections.

Figure 43. William Blanchard Jerrold, Doré Gustave, *London: A Pilgrimage*. With illustrations by Gustave Dore, 1872. British Library, London, UK © British Library Board. All Rights Reserved/Bridgeman Images.

Figure 44. Westelijke Tuinsteden Expansion Plan. (Western Garden Cities) for the General Extension Plan of Amsterdam as conceived by Cor van Eesteren (President of CIAM) with the help of Th. K. van Lohuizen, 1935.

Figure 45. Walter Burley Griffin, The Silkscreen Plan of Griffith, commissioned by the Department of Water Resources – Lands Administration Branch – Water Conservation and Irrigation Commission in 1913. Town plan designed 1914. Walter Burley Griffin Society Incorporated Collection, courtesy Bob Meyer, State Archives and Records Authority of New South Wales.

Figure 46. Le Corbusier, Ville Radieuse, Not located, 1930, Courtesy of Fondation Le Corbusier / DACS.

Figure 47. Le Corbusier, Photograph of the Plan of Voisin (1925). Oeuvre Complét de (from complete works) 1910–1929, Courtesy of Fondation Le Corbusier / DACS.

Figure 48. Frank Lloyd-Wright, Broadacre City Project (Model in four sections), 1934–1935. The Museum of Modern Art, New York (MoMA) Scala, Florence.

Figure 49. Paul Rudolph, Lower Manhattan Expressway, project. New York City. Perspective to the east, 1972. New York, Museum of Modern Art (MoMA). Ink and graphite on paper, 40 × 33 1/2' (101.6 × 85.1 cm) Gift of The Howard Gilman Foundation. 1290.2000 © 2018. Digital image, The Museum of Modern Art, New York/Scala, Florence.

Figure 50. Arata Isozaki, Re-ruined Hiroshima Project. Hiroshima, Japan. Perspective, 1968. New York, Museum of Modern Art (MoMA). Ink and gouache with cut-and-pasted gelatin silver print on gelatin silver print, 13 7/8 × 36 7/8" (35.2 × 93.7 cm). Gift of The Howard Gilman Foundation. Acc. N.: 1205.2000. © 2018. Digital image, The Museum of Modern Art, New York/Scala, Florence.

Figure 51. Strelka Unsettled. A project by Roel van Herpt, Daniele Belleri, Olena Grankina, Giulio Margheri, Nicolas Moore.

Figure 52. Kenzo Tange, Plan for Tokyo, 1960. Photography: Akiko Kawasumi, Kobayashi Kenji Photograph Office.

Figure 53. V2 Rocket, Launched White Sands, NASA, Johns Hopkins Applied Physics Laboratory, March 7, 1947.

Figure 54. Mega Cities Project, Paris, the mosaic based on data acquired on October 3 and October 11, 2015. Landsat 8.

Figure 55. Hans Hollein, Aircraft Carrier City in Landscape. Project. Perspective 1964. Unbuilt. New York, Museum of Modern Art (MoMA). Cut-and-pasted reproduction on four-part photograph mounted on board, 8 1/2 × 39 3/8' (21.6 × 100 cm). Philip Johnson Fund. Acc. N.: 434.1967. © 2018. Digital image, The Museum of Modern Art, New York/Scala, Florence.

Figure 56. *Altered Carbon*, Scenic Image, © Skydance Productions, LLC, 2018.

Figure 57. AUJIK, Spatial Bodies, 2016.

Figure 58. Squint/Opera Ltd. Flooded London: St Mary Woolnath, 2008.

Figure 59. *High Rise*, Directed by Ben Wheatley, 2016, © RPC High-Rise Limited, The British Film Institute, Channel Four Television Corporation. Christophel / Scala, Florence.

Figure 60. *A Clockwork Orange*, 1971. Real Stanley Kubrick. Malcolm McDowell. © Warner Bros / Hawk films. Christophel / Scala, Florence.

Figure 61. Magnus Larsson, Dune anti-desertification architecture, 2008, Courtesy of LafargeHolcim Foundation for Sustainable Construction, Switzerland.

Figure 62. Bernhard Hafner, City in Space, 1966. Axonometric of the Core. Dessin. Héliographie colorée. 112 × 76 cm. inv. 008 68 07. Photographie: François Lauginie. Collection Frac Centre-Val de Loire.

Figure 63. Chicago Architecture Foundation, *No Small Plans*, Gabrielle Lyon, Devin Mawdsley, Kayce Bayer, Chris Lin, Deon Reed, pp. 39 & 89, 2017. © The Chicago Architecture Foundation.

Figure 64. Moses King, Future New York, circa 1915. © Mary Evans Picture Library.

Figure 65. Anderson Isometric Maps, 1971. David Rumsey Map Collection. www.davidrumsey.com

Figure 66. New York. 1982 Citivues International, Inc. David Rumsey Map Collection. www.davidrumsey.com

Figure 67. Hugh Ferriss, Imaginary drawings, Zoning ordinances, 1922–1924. © Hugh Ferriss architectural drawings and papers, 1906–1980, Avery Architectural & Fine Arts Library, Columbia University.

Figure 68. *Escape from New York*, John C. Wash, Mark Stetson, Hoyt Yeatman, Scott Squires, et al., 1981. Courtesy of John Wash. © Studio Canal.

Figure 69. Rem Koolhaas, OMA, New Welfare Island, 1975. Peinture acrylique et gouache sur papier 40 × 101.5 cm. Collection Frac Centre-Val de Loire.

Figure 70. Hans Hollein, Urban Renewal in New York Project. Manhattan, New York, Aerial perspective. New York, Museum of Modern Art (MoMA). Cut-and-pasted photograph on a photograph, composition: 7 1/2 × 9 1/2' (19 × 24.1 cm). Philip Johnson Fund. Acc. N.: 433.1967. © 2018. Digital Image, The Museum of Modern Art, New York/Scala, Florence.

Figure 71. Manuel Herz Architects 2018. 'City of Things' perspective from the Storefront for Architecture Exhibition. © Manuel Herz Architects.

Figure 72. Mitchell Joachim, Terreform ONE, Post Carbon City State: Rezoned Circular Economy, 2015.

Figure 73. Newton Fallis, Autopia Ampere, 1978, Graphite on Paper, 92*145 cm. Image courtesy of Newton Fallis.

Figure 74. WORKac & Ant Farm, 3-C.CITY: Climate, Convention, and Cruise, Chicago Architecture Biennale, 2015. Photo © Bruce Damonte.

Figure 75. Onyx, Parsec City, 1968–1970, Signature Michaël B. Hinge. Sérigraphie sur papier 73.5 × 58.5 cm. Photography © François Lauginie, Collection Frac Centre-Val de Loire.

Figure 76. Clouds Architecture Office, Analemma Tower, Project Team: Ostap Rudakevych, Masayuki Sono, Kevin Huang, 2018.

Figure 77. Stefano Boeri Architetti. China, A Vertical Forest on Mars?, Shanghai Urban Space and Art Season 2017.

Figure 78a. *Ghost in the Shell*, Ghost in the Shell. ARISE 6, 2018, p. 36. *Ghost in the Shell*. Stand Alone Complex, Chapter 1. Kodansha Ltd.

Figure 78b. *Ghost in the Shell* (2017). Directed by Rupert Sanders. Universal Pictures/Moviestore Collection Ltd.

Figure 79. Shimizu Corporation, Green Float, 2004. © Image Courtesy of Shimizu Corporation, 2014.

Figure 80. Wenzel Hablik, Der Bau der Luftkolonie (Structure of a Colony Floating in the Air), 1908, Pencil, 22.5 × 18.1 cm. © Wenzel-Hablik-Foundation, Itzehoe.

Figure 81. Yona Friedman, Spatial City, project, Aerial perspective, 1958. New York, Museum of Modern Art (MoMA). Ink on tracing paper, 8 3/8 × 10 3/4' (21.3 × 27.3cm). Gift of the Howard Gillman Foundation. Acc. n.: 1189.2000. © 2018. Digital image, The Museum of Modern Art, New York/Scala, Florence.

Figure 82. Eckhardt Schulze-Fielitz, Raumstadt, 1959. Photography © Philippe Magnon, Collection Frac Centre-Val de Loire.

Figure 83. Eilfried Huth and Günther Domenig's Stadt Ragnitz (1963–1969). Bois, plastique, peinture 62 ×

65 × 48 cm. © Philippe Magnon, Collection Frac Centre-Val de Loire.

Figure 84. Kiyonori Kikutake – Stratiform Structure Module, Takenaka, 1972.

Figure 85. Antonio Sant'Elia, The New City (La Citta Digital Nuova), buildings and steps with four street levels, 1914. Private Collection. Black ink on paper © 2018. DeAgostini Picture Library/Scala, Florence.

Figure 86. Raimund Abraham, Universal City, project. Sectional Digitale (1)(A) perspective, 1966. Photomontage, ink and graphite on paper, 19 1/2 × 22 1/4" (49.5 × 56.5 cm). Gift of the architect. The Museum of Modern Art, New York/Scala, Florence.

Figure 87. Paolo Soleri, Babel IIB, Arcology: City in the Image of Man, 1969.

Figure 88. Viewing the World of Tomorrow, Futurama, New York World's Fair, Norman Bel Geddes, 1939. © Courtesy of the Harry Ransom Center.

Figure 89. *Motopia*, Geoffrey Jellicoe, 1961. Illustrated in 1960 by Arthur Radebaugh for 'Closer Than We Think'. © TribuneContent Agency, LLC. All Rights Reserved. Reprinted with permission.

Figure 90. Geoffrey Copcutt, Cumbernauld New Town, 1963. Bryan & Shear, courtesy of North Lanarkshire Archives. © North Lanarkshire Council / Culture NL Ltd.

Figure 91. City of Manchester Heliport near Victoria Station, R. Nicholas, City Surveyor. Drawn by Sidney R. Fisher, 1956. Courtesy of Manchester Archives.

Figure 92. Charles Péré-Lahaille – La Cité Mobile, 1953. Encre, feutre, crayon graphite, crayon de couleur, collage sur papier 64.8 × 50 cm. Collection Frac Centre-Val de Loire.

Figure 93. David George Emmerich, Agglomération (sous une coupole stéréométrique), 1958–1960. Collection Frac Centre-Val de Loire.

Figure 94. Archigram Plug-in City, Plug-in City Max Pressure Area, Peter Cook, 1964.

Figure 95. *Blade Runner*, Ridley Scott, 1982, Warner Bros. Christophel / Photo Scala, Florence.

Figure 96. *Blade Runner*, Ridley Scott, 1982, Warner Bros. Christophel / Photo Scala, Florence.

Figure 97. *Blade Runner 2049*, Denis Villeneuve, 2017. Ryan Gosling. © Alcon entertainment / Scott free productions / Warner Bros. Christophel / Photo Scala, Florence.

Figure 98. *The Fifth Element*, Luc Besson, 1997. © Columbia Pictures/Courtesy: Everett Collection.

Figure 99. *Minority Report*, Dir. Steven Spielberg, 2002. TCD/Prod.DB / Alamy Stock Photo.

Figure 100. Bachir Moukarzel, Dubai, drone photography, 2016.

Figure 101. Paul Tsui, Macau, Southeast China. 2017.

Figure 102. Richard Buckminster Fuller with a model of the United States Pavilion for the Expo 67. Phillip Harrington / Alamy Stock Photo.

Figure 103. Will Wright, Don Hopkins, SimCity, Micropolis, 1985, Maxis. © (1989–2007) Electronic Arts Inc (Open Source).

Figure 104. Cities of the future, extract from *How Cities Work* by James Gulliver Hancock, 1st ed. With permission from Lonely Planet © 2016, Lonely Planet pp. 24–25.

Figure 105. Paris 2050: A Smart City, Vincent Callebaut Architectures, 2015.

Figure 106. Masdar Development, Abu Dhabi, United Arab Emirates, Foster + Partners, 2007 onwards.

Figure 107. Seed Capital Area Masterplan, Amaravathi, 2015. © Government of Singapore.

Figure 108. SHAU Architects, Jakarta Jaya – The Green Manhattan, 2012 onwards.

Figure 109. *Logan's Run*, Michael Anderson, 1976. M.G.M © 2018. Album/Scala, Florence.

Figure 110a. Constant Nieuwenhuys, New Babylon/Paris, 1963. Collection of the Gemeentemuseum Den Haag.

Figure 110b. Constant Nieuwenhuys, New Babylon, 1963. Encre sur papier 40 × 38 × 1.5 cm. Photography François Lauginie, Collection Frac Centre-Val de Loire.

Figure 111. Superstudio, Manifesto New New York (in nero e azzuro), 1969. Photography François Lauginie, Collection Frac Centre-Val de Loire.

Figure 112. Archizoom, No-Stop City, 1969. Archizoom Associati. Bois, carton, verre, peinture, fibre synthétique, plexiglas 54.5 × 52.2 × 51.7 cm. Photography François Lauginie, Collection Frac Centre-Val de Loire.

Figure 113. Günther Feuerstein – Salzburg Superpolis, 1965–1967. Photography François Lauginie, Collection Frac Centre-Val de Loire.

Figure 114. Cedric Price, Fun Palace for Joan Littlewood, Stratford East, London. Project (unbuilt) 1959–1961. Aerial perspective from cockpit. Drawing date: unknown. New York, Museum of Modern Art (MoMA). Cut-and-pasted painted paper on gelatin silver print with gouache, 8 3/4 × 10 1/2' (22.2 × 26.7 cm). Gift of the Howard Gilman Foundation. The Museum of Modern Art, New York/Scala, Florence.

Figure 115. Instant City, Archigram, 1968. Photography François Lauginie, Collection Frac Centre-Val de Loire.

Figure 116a. Haus-Rucker-Co, Pneumacosmic Formation, 1971. Collage sur papier 48 × 67.5 cm. Photography François Lauginie, Collection Frac Centre-Val de Loire.

Figure 116b. Haus-Rucker-Co, Pneumacosm – Leisuretime Explosion, 1967–1968. Impression sur papier 73.5 × 57 cm. Photography François Lauginie, Collection Frac Centre-Val de Loire.

Figure 117. Zünd-Up, Auto-Expander, 1969. Photomontage 61 × 58 cm. Photography François Lauginie, Collection Frac Centre-Val de Loire.

Figure 118. Ant Farm, Dolphin Embassy, 1974. Diazoïque sépia sur papier 46.1 × 56.7 cm. Photography François Lauginie, Collection Frac Centre-Val de Loire.

Figure 119. Walter Jonas, Intrapolis, 1958. © Stiftung Walter und Rosa Maria Jonas.

Figure 120a. Athelstan Spilhaus, 'Our New Age', 1957–1973. Northwest Architectural Archive, University of Minnesota.

Figure 120b. Athelstan Spilhaus, Minnesota Experimental City (MXC), geodesic dome covering city centre, 1966–1973. Northwest Architectural Archive, University of Minnesota,

Figure 121. Justus Dahinden, Radio City (Hill City), 1970. Feutre sur calque 56.1 × 77.4 cm. Photography François Lauginie, Collection Frac Centre-Val de Loire.

Figure 122. Jean-Louis Chanéac and Claude & Pascal Häusermann, Centre Beaubourg Competition Paris, France. 1971–1974. Photography François Lauginie, Collection Frac Centre-Val de Loire.

Figure 123. Léon Krier, Labyrinth City, Aerial perspective and section, 1971. Ink with gouache on paper, 11 5/8 × 8 1/4" (29.5 × 21 cm). Gift of The Howard Gilman Foundation. The Museum of Modern Art, New York/Scala, Florence.

Figure 124. SITE (James Wines) – Highrise of Homes, 1981. Encre sur papier 35.5 × 28.1 cm. Photography François Lauginie, Collection Frac Centre-Val de Loire.

Figure 125. MVRDV, Waste Sector, Metacity/Datatown, 1999.

Figure 126. Zaha Hadid Architects, One North Masterplan, Singapore, 2001–2021. Courtesy of Zaha Hadid Architects.

Figure 127. Hawkins\Brown, Heathrow City, CGI artist: Factory Fifteen, 2014.

Figure 128. 5th Studio, Stour City, 2016.

Figures 129. Sidewalk Labs, Sidewalk Toronto, 2017.

Figures 130. You + Pea, Peep Pop City, 2018.

Figure 131. Guy Debord, Guide psychogéographique de Paris. Discours sur les passions de l'amour, 1957. Tirage sur papier 59.5 × 73.5 cm. Photography Philippe Magnon, Collection Frac Centre-Val de Loire.

Figure 132. Kevin Lynch, Extract from The Perceptual Form of the City, Boston, Massachusetts, 1954–1959. MIT Archives.

Figure 133. Lawrence Halprin, Fort Worth City Walk Map, 1974. © Lawrence Halprin Collection, The Architectural Archives, University of Pennsylvania.

Figure 134. Bernard Tschumi, Parc de la Villette, Paris, 1983. Encre sur papier 29 × 29 cm. Photography Olivier Martin-Gambier, Collection Frac Centre-Val de Loire.

Figure 135. Atelier Bow-Wow, Generations of Tokyo Architecture, Made in Tokyo Guidebook, 2001.

Figure 136. *Back to the Future: Part II*, Hoverboard, conceptual sketch, 1989. © JohnBell Studio © Universal Pictures, Amblin Entertainment, U-Drive Productions.

Figure 137. Keiichi Matsuda, Still from *HYPER-REALITY*, 2016.

Figure 138. Alan Boutwell and Mike Mitchell, Comprehensive City, Domus 470, 1969.

Figure 139. Luigi Pellegrin, Vettore habitat a scala geografica / Vector habitat at geographic scale –

Ricerche su componenti infrastrutturali lineari / Research on linear infrastructural components. 1970. Drawing Cyanotype, collage, pastel, papier, 156 × 116 cm. Photography François Lauginie, Collection Frac Centre-Val de Loire.

Figure 140. OMA/AMO, Eneropa, EuroGrid, Extract from Roadmap 2050: A practical guide to a prosperous, low-carbon Europe, 2010. © Image courtesy of the Office for Metropolitan Architecture (OMA).

Figure 141. BIG, Loop City, 2010 onwards. Project Team; Bjarke Ingels, Andreas Klok Pedersen, Søren Martinussen, Armor Rivas, Daniel Kidd, Daniel Selensky, Kuba Snopek, Lucian Racovitan, Ole Schrøder, Riccardo Mariano, Ryohei Koike, Xing Xiong.

Figure 142. Hassell / MVRDV. Resilient by Design, South San Francisco, USA, Masterplan, 2017. 800 kilometers of shoreline for Resilient By Design – Stage 1 (Collaborative Research Stage). HASSELL+ (HASSELL, MVRDV, Deltares, Goudappel, Lotus Water, Frog Design, Civic Edge, Idyllist, Hatch, Page & Turnbull) MVRDV Design Team: Nathalie de Vries, Jeroen Zuidgeest with Kristina Knauf and Vedran Skansi © MVRDV and HASSELL+.

Figure 143. Dharavi Masterplan, Mumbai, India, 2008, © Foster + Partners.

Figure 144. Iwamoto Scott, Hydro-Net, 2008.

Figure 145. WORKac, Nature-City, 2012. Photo © James Ewing.

Figure 146. EYRC Architects + Tom Wiscombe Architecture, Blockchains City, Sparks, Nevada, 2018.

Figure 147. Robert Graves and Didier Madoc-Jones, Flooded London, Postcards From the Future, 2010.

Figure 148. Thierry Cohen, Villes éteintes (Darkened Cities), Hong Kong, 2012.

Figure 149. Studio Lindfors (Clouds AO), Aqualta, New York, 2009.

Figure 150. Arata Isozaki, Clusters in the Air (Cluster City), Shibuya, 1960–1962. Deutsches Architekturmuseum, Frankfurt am Main; © Arata Isozaki; Foto: Uwe Dettmar, Frankfurt am Main.

Figure 151. John Wardle Architects and Stefano Boscutti, Multiplicity, Melbourne 2110, 2010.

Figure 152. Georgii Krutikov, The Flying City, (VKhUTEMAS diploma project, 1928). © Schusev State Museum of Architecture.

Figure 153. Tomás Saraceno, Biosphere 3, 2015, Collage. Courtesy the artist; Tanya Bonakdar Gallery, New York/Los Angeles; Pinksummer contemporary art, Genoa; Andersen's, Copenhagen; Esther Schipper, Berlin. © Studio Tomás Saraceno, 2015.

Figure 154. Foster + Partners, Mars Habitat, 2015. © Foster + Partners.

Figure 155. Kiyonori Kikutake, Marine City, uncompleted project, 1963 Plexiglas, plaster, glass and metal, 57.1 × 58.5 × 58.5 cm Paris, Centre Pompidou, Musée national d'art moderne – Centre de création industrielle © Centre Pompidou, MNAM-CCI/Georges Meguerditchian/Dist. RMN-GP © Kiyonori Kikutake.

Figure 156. Paul Maymont, Floating Paris, 1965. Map of Paris and its surroundings. 1962. Blueprint, 28.5 × 38.5 cm. Inv.: AM2010-2-869. Photo: Philippe Migeat, Musee National d'Art Moderne, Centre Georges Pompidou, Paris, France. Photo Credit: © CNAC/MNAM/Dist. RMN-Grand Palais / Art Resource, NY.

Figure 157. Charles Simonds, Floating City, an Arrangement, 1978. Photography François Lauginie, Collection Frac Centre-Val de Loire.

Figure 158. CCCC-FHDI & AT Design Office, Zhujiangkou Island, 2012.

Figure 159. Terreform ONE, Future North: Ecotariums in the North Pole, 2008.

Figure 160. Shimizu Corporation, Ocean Spiral, 2014. © Image Courtesy of Shimizu Corporation, 2014.

Figure 161. Oscar Newman, Nukeproof Manhattan, 1969.

Figure 162. Matsys, Sietch, Nevada, 2009.

Figure 163. Stephane Malka, The Green Machine, 2014. Studio Malka Architecture.

Figure 164. Finbarr Fallon, Subterranean Singapore 2065, 2016.

Figure 165. Nic Clear, Chthonopolis, 2017.

Figure 166. Nick Dunn, Paul Cureton and Serena Pollastri, Timeline of principal paradigms, 2020.

Table 1. City categories identified for *A Visual History of the Future*. © UK Government Office for Science, 2014.

PREFACE

Thinking about what futures are, who they are for, why they are desirable, and how and when they are to be brought into being is central to this book. The people with whom we forge social futures and the increasing frequency of extreme weather events occurring around the globe are important reminders of the urgent need for alternative, sustainable, collective futures. Radical visions for future cities are integral to this process in ensuring better futures for tomorrow's world. This book was written before the global crisis around the coronavirus pandemic. Nevertheless, the need and desire for new visions for collective life, which may be shaped by the challenges and opportunities that arise from this pandemic experience, will remain significant. Combined with climatic breakdown and further urbanization, this area of futures work is critically important. Futures are situated and relational. This book is no different, and we, as the authors, have benefitted from the encouragement, creativity and support given by others.

We would like to thank the Future of Cities Foresight Project run by the Government Office for Science, UK, for the original commission to write on future cities. We would like to give huge thanks to all the team at ImaginationLancaster, Lancaster University, UK. This book and our work on futures derive in a more general sense from having been conceived and written in such a stimulating environment alongside brilliant people. In particular, we would like to thank our colleague Serena Pollastri for producing the wonderful timeline infographic at the end of this book. We would also like to thank Richard Morton for the assistance with image permissions.

We are grateful for EPSRC grant EP/J017698/1, Liveable Cities programme directed by Chris Rogers at the University of Birmingham which partly funded this publication. We wish to offer our deepest gratitude to James Thompson, Alexander Highfield and Sophie Tann at Bloomsbury for their excellent advice, considerable patience and understanding, and tireless efforts during the production of this book.

Nick would like to thank Sarah for the unswerving support, love and good humour she has given selflessly during the writing of this book. He would also like to thank his family and friends, whose love, support and understanding made this book possible. Nick is also indebted to Zola and Camion, with whom he was able to creatively explore alternative futures thinking. He would also like to thank his colleagues at the Institute for Social Futures, not least the late John Urry, who gave considerable insight and is very much missed.

Paul would like to thank Tamara Gwilliam for all the days, nights, and continuous fun and excitement during the writing of this book, from flying aircraft to vineyards. He would also like to acknowledge Paul Ringer for helping throughout all the turbulent periods in this process and Gill Clark for the extensive love and guidance she has provided. Paul would also like to thank everyone in his running club, Wellingborough & District Athletic Club (WDAC), especially the ultra-runners, with whom he has formed a special bond and understanding of what it takes.

Chapter 1

Introduction: Futures, imagination and visions for cities

Hello from tomorrow's world . . .

What might your city look like in ten, twenty or fifty years? A question like this immediately gets us thinking; our mind recalls the places we have perhaps been or seen, and in the case of the latter may include real world examples as well as fictional ones. We might start to think of vertiginous architectural styles, spaceship-like forms or something very similar to how a nearby city currently looks. If we think a bit further about this then we may arrive at a somewhat different set of questions concerning the city. What kind of lifestyles may evolve? How will we move around? Where will we live and work? This encourages us to focus on the everyday life of the city, our relationships and interactions within its context, and the aspects of these that it may positively support or provide barriers to. If we zoom out of the city and think of it within the much larger worldwide situation, we may arrive at a very different and perhaps daunting question. How may future cities face global challenges? In just this short space of time, through a few simple questions, we have quickly encountered some of the many issues that are part of the complexity of future cities. That some of these are so intrinsic to how we might survive and thrive in the future highlights the importance of cities and how they will change. Such a large topic and the questions it presents can seem overwhelming and have many different possible outcomes. There are currently lots of different people and organizations across a wide variety of contexts tackling this in diverse ways. It would be far beyond the scope of one book to cover all these different approaches and perspectives. This book focuses on how cities of the future have been visualized [figure 1]. Within visualization there are numerous ways of constructing and communicating ideas. We will be exploring the interface when cities and the notion of the future come together. Through visualization we are able to experiment in ways that would be impractical and potentially hazardous in the real world, though as we shall also see this did not stop some people trying! This book, therefore, aims to contribute towards a better understanding of the power and agency of visualizations for future cities. Furthermore, it provides a framework of critical lenses with which this material may be viewed and in doing so has a dual function. Firstly, it enables us to look back over the history of how future cities have been envisioned and identify important patterns and trends to establish those ideas that have been important and endured over time [figure 2]. Secondly, by revealing the underlying themes and connections of these visions within a much wider body of material, it seeks to inform the production of such visualizations for future cities which have yet to be made by enhancing the knowledge of those who create them. In this introduction we also gain an understanding of how the visualization of future cities fits within the wider fields of both future studies and urban design. It also explains why the subject of cities is fundamental to many aspects of our lives now and how they may evolve in the future. As a way into the subject, we look at a number of examples to gain an overview of the potential of future cities and the history of representing them. From this point we then examine more specific themes and ideas in the subsequent chapters.

Imagining the city of the future has long been an inspiration for many architects, artists and designers. This book therefore explores how cities of the future have been visualized, what these projects sought to communicate and what the implications may be for us now. Although many of these visions for future cities were never constructed or formed the backdrop for a fictional narrative, this does not mean that these ideas are unworthy of attention. Their importance extends in other ways through their questioning of reality. A multitude of climatic, social, economic and cultural pressures for cities around the world mean the way we vision the future has become particularly important. But how best to approach the future? There are lots of different methods and views on how we might explore the future, so to contextualize the subject and approach taken in this book, we discuss them here.

Figure 1.
Informal Cities. Collage City. Ikiré Jones, Idumota Market, Lagos 2081 A.D., de la série Our Africa 2081 A.D. © Olalekan Jeyfous & Walé Oyéjidé. The image is taken from a series produced by the artist Olalekan Jeyfous for The Escape to New Lagos, Autumn/Winter 2013/2014 collection by fashion designer Walé Oyéjidé. By projecting the character of a smart, cosmopolitan man, Ikiré Jones, into Lagos 2081, the label continues to develop its founding myth as part of six illustrated stories that examine present-day African society and its future.

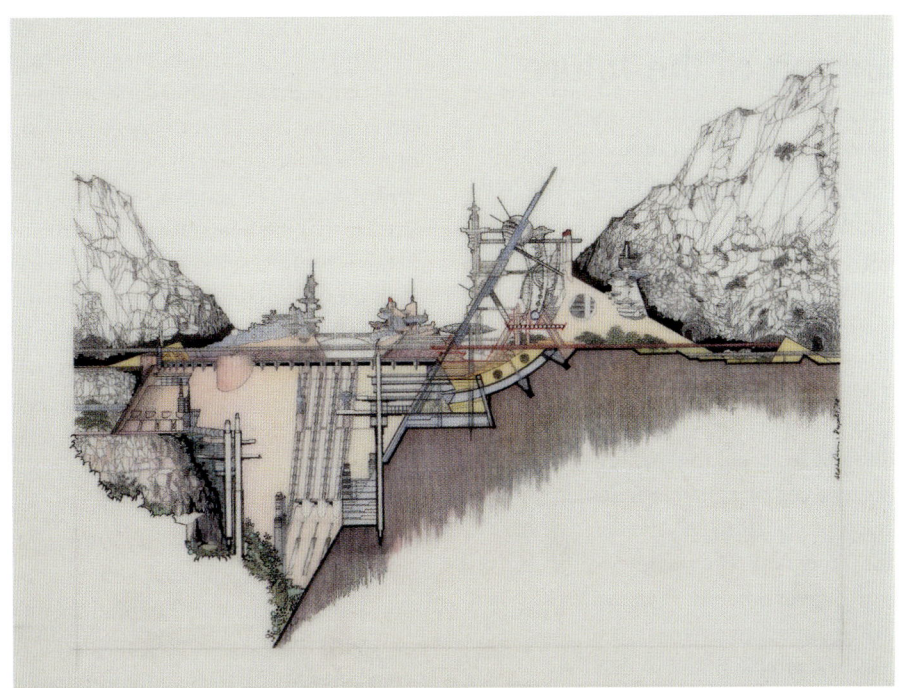

Figure 2.
Layered Cities. Horizontal City. Aldo Loris Rossi, Eliopolis, frammento metropolitano eco-compatibile, 1978, Perspective. Photography © François Lauginie, Collection Frac Centre-Val de Loire. In the early 1960s, Aldo Rossi developed a keen interest in the concept of the utopian city, but within this hypothesis was the motivation to eradicate the traditional criteria for producing urban form. This project proposed urban fragments that combine ecology and economy in order to provide balance between man-made and natural environments, forming an 'eco-politan frontier'.

The beginning of the future

From the start of time we, as humans, have longed to know what is ahead of us. Indeed, for thousands of years we have attempted to predict, control, manage and understand the future. Jennifer Gidley (2017) explains how from using astrology to read the stars, debating philosophically, producing creative visions, and scientifically analysing trends and patterns within data, we have sought to know the future. The ubiquity of the word 'future' reflects the accelerated rate of change that we face as previous apparent certainties such as ecological stability and socio-cultural patterns are becoming increasingly complex, harder to discern and, in some instances, more volatile. This means that how we respond to the future is also increasingly difficult. Faced with its challenges, numerous organizations and societies have become actively engaged in trying to better understand the future so that they may influence it. Many different types of public and private sector groups including corporations, non-governmental organizations, states, universities and even cities themselves are future focused. The future is also the domain of significant business conducted by consultancies, environmental agencies, governmental bodies, military organizations and many others. With such a diversity of different groups and respective interests in the future, it perhaps comes as no surprise that there are a range of methods of working to better understand it. These include anticipation, forecasting, foresight and scenarios, but the general consensus is that these fit within the field of future studies. A common misunderstanding is that studies of the future are typically concerned with prediction based on extrapolation from existing trends, but this is only one approach. It is useful at this point to gain an overview of the different methods to better understand the specific approach used for this book.

Working with the future

There are numerous techniques for thinking about the future, but the majority are founded on the four-stage methodological approach developed by Richard Slaughter (1997). The advantages of this approach are that there is flexibility and choice within each major step and that the methods are integrated into a generic foresight process that can be applied to many different contexts. Given its generous scope, it is perhaps no surprise that the four stages feature many of the futures methods found elsewhere. The four stages are input methods, analytic methods, paradigmatic methods, and iterative and exploratory methods. For the purpose of this book, it is the last category that we focus on. Iterative and exploratory methods include backcasts, scenarios and visioning. Core to this set of methods are imagination and creativity since they all require activism on behalf of the individual or participants involved. Joseph Voros (2003) has described these methods as aligning to prospective methods, which as the name suggests seek to produce future images. Many futurists use visioning as a method not only to forecast but also to encourage potential futures. Visioning involves creating and describing alternative futures, some of which may be preferred. Within the wider foresight process, visioning leads to a plan of action for following through with the ideas generated. The major value of iterative and exploratory methods lies in their ability to uncover new ideas and challenge existing assumptions about the future using imagination and creativity. The role of visualization within these techniques can be essential in enabling those exploring potential futures to capture their ideas and share them effectively. Fred Polak (1973) argued that societies shape themselves partly through the images of the future they construct, and our capacity to visualize entirely alternative futures is essential to this process.

Key to understanding the content of this book is an emphasis on the power and agency of the images themselves coupled with the process of 'futuring'. In a visualization, the ideas and hopes for the future, as well as potential critique of the present or other futures, are loaded within it. Many ideas for future cities are deliberate provocations to question our thinking and encourage us to reconsider prevailing attitudes [figure 3]. These endeavours can lead to extreme and absurd proposals. Considered in this way, the image has an agency and can be powerful, depending on the

Figure 3.
Regulated Cities. Continuous Cities. Superstudio, Le Dodici Città Ideali, 1971. La prima città. Lithograph. Encre sur papier. 70 x 100 cm. Photography © François Lauginie, Collection Frac Centre-Val de Loire. In this example, Piero Frassinelli of Superstudio presented twelve dystopian fantasies of urban planning by taking existing concepts, such as 'zoning' or 'user's needs', and extrapolating them far beyond conventional wisdom to create a series of bleak, domineering visions that reflected the alienation of modern urbanism. This image shows the First City: 2,000 ton City in which, 'Even and perfect . . . All citizens are in a state of perfect equality'.

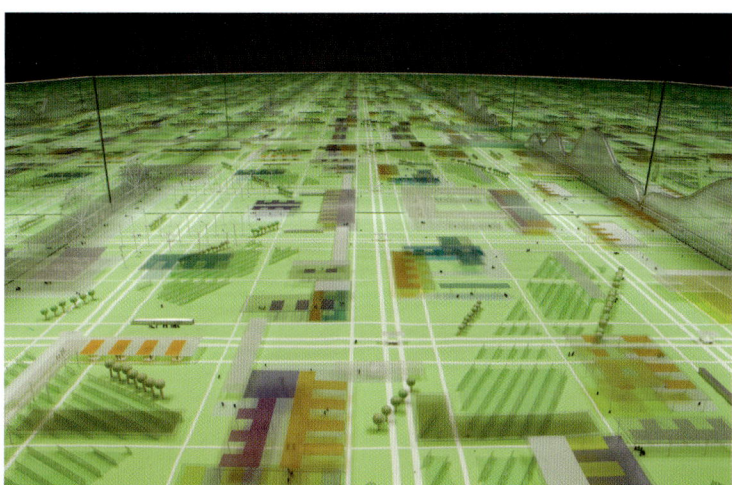

Figure 4.
Regulated Cities. Continuous Cities. Andrea Branzi, Ernesto Bartolini and Lapo Lani, Masterplan Strijp Philips, Eindhoven, model view, 1999–2000. Photography © François Lauginie, Collection Frac Centre-Val de Loire. Through his work as part of the radical architecture group Archizoom, Branzi used the urban project as a social and cultural critique. Over the last four decades, Branzi's examination into failing urban conditions has remained coherent. This project envisions ever-changing typologies for a 'Territory for the New Economy', a natural successor to his earlier work [see figure 112, Chapter 5] and of considerable relevance to contemporary urban culture and theory (Varnelis 2006).

intentions behind it and its purpose. To illustrate this point, let us consider two examples. If we examine a visualization for an entirely imaginary city, its purpose and power come from the nature of its production as an emancipatory utopian exercise. By contrast, if we look at a visualization for a major urban project that is subsequently built, we can understand how the ideology has been applied and its vision is likely to be much more grounded in reality. Visualizations for future cities carry and project the concepts and ideologies behind them [figure 4]. In doing so it is evident they are not neutral or passive since the design of cities and architecture is rarely apolitical. In many cases visions for alternative ways of living are bound up in ideologies and agendas, especially when they seek to promote a radical movement or be symbolic of identity [figure 5]. It is important to remember here that visualizations can also be reductive and what they omit can be as significant, or even controversial, as what they promote.

Figure 5.
Regulated Cities. Divided City. Nikola Mihov, Photograph of Memorial House of the Bulgarian Communist Party, Buzludja 2009–2012 from Forget Your Past, Communist-Era Monuments in Bulgaria, 2nd ed, Janet 45 Publishing, 2015. The project Forget Your Past traces the fate of significant communist-era monuments in Bulgaria. As with many such monuments, these architectural visions were emblematic of progress and national pride, providing an important reminder of the different societies and values that future cities and architecture can represent.

Plurality and diversity of futures

Thus far, we have discussed the future as singular. This idea, that we are all headed towards one common point, has been questioned, particularly since the mid-twentieth century when it became evident that the developments within the military-industrial complex that had promoted the scientific positivist concept of a single future could be usefully challenged (Gidley 2017). Many futurists realized that seeking to predict the future in this way was not necessarily the most useful in thinking about the complexity of our world. This is illustrated by the renowned futurologist Jim Dator (2009: 5–6) when he stated, 'Like many early futurists, I started out with a rather "scientific" and "positivistic" perspective, assuming that there was one, true future "out there" that proper use of good data and scientifically-based models would allow me to predict. I was soon disabused of that notion for many reasons.' As the field developed, Galtung (1982) was one of the first to discuss different kinds of futures, referring to probable futures, possible futures and preferred futures. Probable futures typically relate to extrapolation of trend data and verge towards more negative forecasts. Possible futures by contrast embrace imagination and creativity in the production of alternative visions. Preferred futures relate to and include critical and normative values. A fourth type, prospective futures, was identified by Bjerstedt (1982) which related to activism when confronted with probable futures. Important for us in this context is the overall transition from positivism to pluralism. The former originates from the hard sciences and predicates an empiricist approach to 'the future'. The latter is borne of the social sciences and promotes a diversity of approaches to 'multiple futures'. Indeed, as Law and Urry (2004) observed, there is a plurality of both pasts and futures that are individually constructed to assemble an individual reality. This is particularly resonant with future cities wherein myriad possibilities for how urban life could be have been produced and continue to speculate visually what prospective environments may be possible, desirable, sustainable etc. [figure 6].

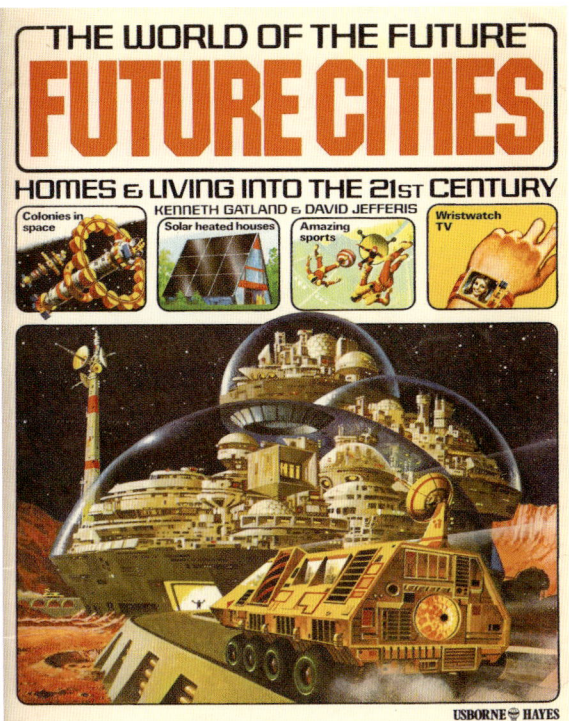

Figure 6.
Hybrid Cities. Space City. Kenneth Garland, David Jefferis, *Future Cities*, Usborne Books, 1979. Reproduced from *Future Cities* by permission of Usborne Publishing, 83–85 Saffron Hill, London EC1N 8RT, UK. www.usborne.com. Copyright © 1979 Usborne Publishing Ltd. Our collective fascination with what the world of tomorrow may bring tends to coalesce around the environments, vehicles and other technologies we think might exist in the future. Encountering speculations for the future from an early age can be very influential on how we imagine the future will be.

What are future cities?

Architecture and design anticipate future possibilities in and of the world, sometimes pushing them to extreme limits in an attempt to show their consequences. One of the most popular ways in which futures are thought about is in the context of a city. This is because cities are symbolic of power, and so future city thinking also crosses metanarratives of capitalist, Marxist and religious canons. Cities also represent major confluences of people, buildings, vehicles and infrastructures etc. alongside numerous other material and immaterial flows. They are therefore suitably complex to warrant speculation since they are interrelated systems in themselves and yet often connect to other cities whether physically or digitally. Therefore, it perhaps comes as no surprise that when it comes to future cities, there have been attempts by a significant number and diverse range of artists, architects and visual designers from various fields to represent them (Fishman 1982; Bingham 2013). 'Future cities' have been speculated and discussed for centuries as urban areas around the world have been imagined, planned, built, adapted and studied. Some future city visions have been successful whilst others have perished. The difficulty of providing a precise definition of a 'future city' is reflected in the many ways the term is ambiguously applied across different disciplines and domains. Its interchangeability with other terms such as 'sustainable city', 'liveable city' and more recently 'smart city' has furthered this lack of clarity. The architect and influential urban planner Eugène Hénard (1910) was arguably the first to publicly discuss 'future cities' in Europe during his address to the Royal Institute of British Architects in London in 1910: 'My purpose is to inquire into the influence which the progress of modern science and industry may exercise upon the planning, and particularly upon the aspect, of the Cities of the Future . . . The Cities of Tomorrow will be more readily susceptible to transformation and adornment than the Cities of Yesterday' [figure 7]. He illustrated the concept of the city having an artificial brain, capable of controlling the organization and management of the urban landscape. This idea has endured, perhaps most evocatively in cinema through Fritz Lang's *Metropolis* (1927) and, though typically less iconic in architectural terms, the principal idea behind many Smart City initiatives.

More recently, a study into the origins and meanings of the term recognized the different variations on it, yet concluded, '"Future cities" has strong appeal throughout the world, and is a common search term in India, Mexico and Brazil as well as in North American and the UK. At the city level, it is notable that "future cities" is of interest in the larger global cities in the West and the East – including Singapore, Mumbai, London and San Francisco. On this evidence, no other term

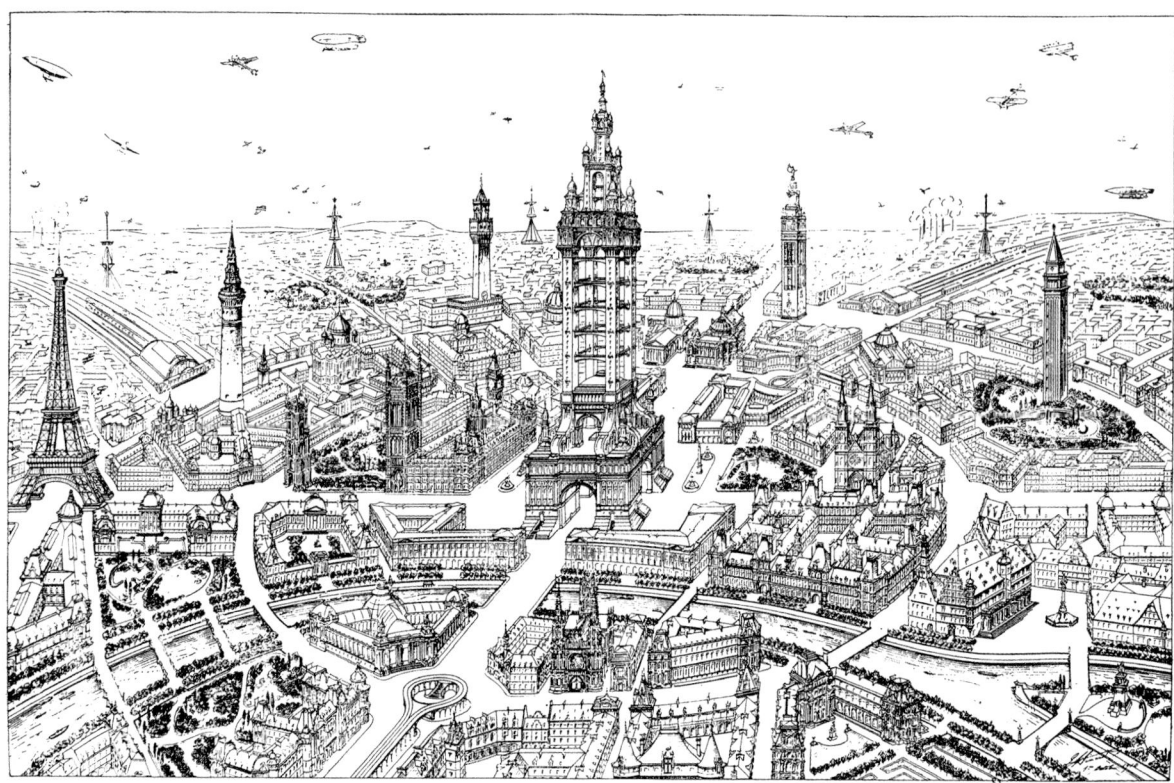

Figure 7.
Layered Cities. Mechanical Cities. Eugène Hénard, 'The Cities of The Future', published in American City, January 1903–1909. NCSU Libraries. Hénard's proposal of a two-tier street system conceives of upper separated levels for pedestrian and vehicular access and underground levels for services and waste disposal. A central super-tower communicates to and coordinates with all the city's zones and arterial routes.

has quite the same multi-lateral appeal' (Moir, Moonen and Clark 2014: 18). The rise in the use of the term also appears reflective of the increasing transition of urban issues into new disciplines. Indeed, current thinking about future cities is more diverse and diffuse than ever, making the definition of the term complicated. Whilst speculation about future cities is not new, today's global context provides major challenges that are focusing attention on the subject through different approaches and from numerous places around the world. For the purpose of this book we define the term to describe those developments which project ideas, whether they are built or remain unrealized, that endeavour to illustrate a change, i.e. a vision, to the contemporary spaces and lifestyles, distinct from the period of their production. The extent of this shift is evident along a spectrum: from radical transformation of the present day to subtler and more nuanced versions of prevalent city conditions [figure 8].

Figure 8. (facing page)
Regulated Cities. Waste City. Pushwagner, *Soft City – There Goes the Sun*. Drawn between 1969 and 1975 but lost until 2008, Pushwagner's narrative follows one day in the life of one family amongst thousands of similar families pursuing the same daily routines. The graphic novel describes the standardized daily patterns within an impersonal and oppressive futuristic city which emphasizes consumerism in all aspects of life within a top-down, Orwellian society.

In addition to responding to the practical issues of how we might all live together on the planet including the many significant global challenges that face us, future cities also require us to explore improbabilities, paradoxes and risks against which we can question the consensual and rationalistic narratives that dominate current debates. Different ways of thinking about cities, their futures, and our relationships and experiences within them are vital. Understood in this way we can view visions of future cities as having transformative power to avoid path dependency (Albrechts 2015). The need to articulate radically alternative futures so that we may better conceive different trajectories and understand their implications finds itself increasingly urgent given our collective responsibility in mitigating planetary consequences and providing a safe and sustainable world for future generations.

One of the key aspects of visualizations of futurity is their duality; many are both allusive and elusive. They typically seek to suggest how people may live, work and move whilst never being able to be fully translated into built conditions [figure 9]. Even in those projects where the design was subsequently constructed in reality, it is not unusual for some of the subtleties and *joie de vivre* to be lost. The power of visualizations of future cities and their ability to capture and remain in our imagination through mainstream media cannot be overestimated (Alison et al. 2007; Goodman 2008). The echoes of such images and their ideas continue to resonate throughout history. World fairs, for example, have proved to be popular and powerful ways in which different futures are promoted and consumed by mass public audiences. Originating from the French tradition of national exhibitions, the first global expo was the Great Exhibition of the Works of Industry of All Nations held in the Crystal Palace in London, 1851. Subsequent world expos until 1938 sought to demonstrate the technological progress and ingenuity borne of industrialization. Visualizations of future cities, meanwhile, contribute to our social imagination, i.e. 'the creative and symbolic dimension of the social world, the dimension through which human beings create their ways of living together and their ways of representing their collective life' (Thompson 1984: 6).

Figure 9.
Flexible Cities. DIY City. Allen D. Albert, 1933, Exposition Bird's Eye View, The Reuben H. Donnelley Corporation. The Century of Progress Exhibition, Chicago World Fair, was a significant event for the centennial celebrations and featured the German Airship *Graf Zeppelin* and the Homes of Tomorrow exhibit displaying modern building and domestic technologies. It is an example of a Technological Future [see Chapter 4] where efficiency and progress are paramount.

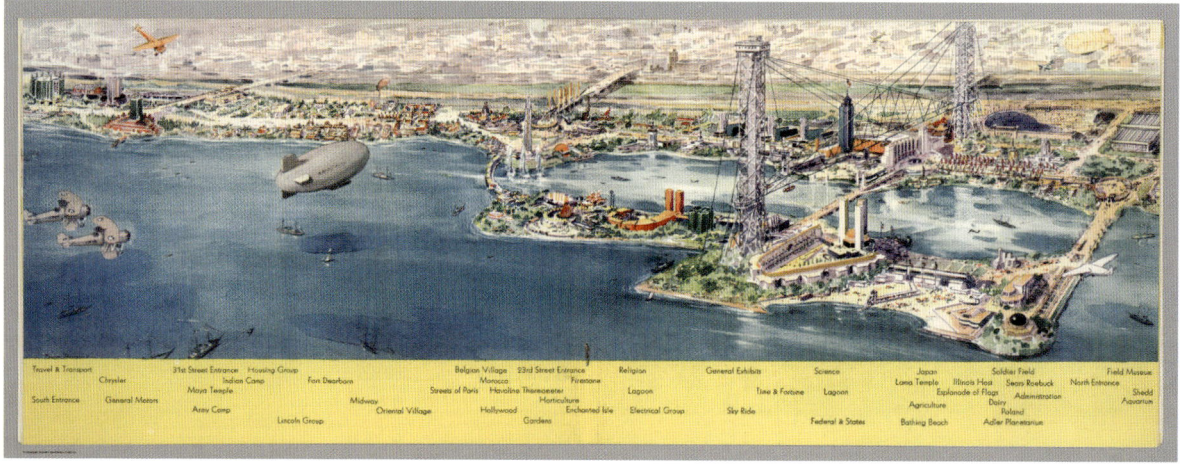

Re-examining the projections made for the future from a historical perspective can provide new insights and greater understanding of the developments and patterns that shape the present and, in turn, their implications for our future (Barbrook 2007). This imagination may be individual, though it also has a social force; the projections often imply a collective or inclusive ability. The visualizations of future cities collected in this book are frequently driven by a strong impulse to transform our relationship with urban space (Mansfield 1990; Eaton 2002). They challenged the prevailing conditions and problems of cities of the time and sought to produce spaces conducive to different ways of living. By identifying the key factors of future city visualizations that have proved most significant and influential, we propose that this analysis will also establish which elements have retained a pervasive presence across different media and over time. The power and agency of the images themselves (Gell 1998; Corner 1999; Ingold 2007), when coupled with the process of futuring, provide a useful resource for understanding how imagination and design can inform the future. Let us next consider why examining visions for future cities might be valuable.

Why study visions of future cities?

Since the publication of the UNFPA's 2007 report, we have been regularly reminded that the future of our planet will be urban as more people around the world move to live in cities than in rural areas. This coupled with the rate of urbanization processes is having profound effects upon our environment, our health and our societies. Cities are complex [figure 10]. Their intermeshing of people, economy and technology is often positioned as positive (Glaeser 2011; Hollis 2013) since they provide the opportunities for us to flourish and transform our lives in positive ways (Montgomery 2013). Yet, it is also a result of the same dynamic forces and interrelationships that many problems arise in urban contexts. Future cities will be complex, diverse and heterogeneous. To understand the scale of this transition, a more recent report by the UN DESA Population Division (2018) projects that by 2050, 68 per cent of the world's population will be urban.

It is also useful to understand the major drivers and shifts in focus that urbanization processes have undergone. From the mid-twentieth century the primary drivers were industrialization and globalization, as urban development sought to maximize productivity and access to labour and resources along with connectivity to markets. However, these drivers have been augmented and in some contexts replaced by those for sustainability and other developments that emphasize people and their environment over profit. As we might expect, the results are uneven (Brook 2013). In the next few decades of the twenty-first century, various nations of Africa, Asia and Latin America will continue to develop towards the Global North across a range of measures. Importantly though, many of these countries do not seek to replicate the old urbanism of half a century ago but instead are exploring new ways of enabling people and planet to flourish in a sustainable manner. Although sustainability is a key goal of this new urbanism, it is challenged and even compromised by rapid growth, especially in those contexts where basic infrastructures cannot be assembled to support it. This has led to the vast number of urban poor, i.e. hundreds of millions of people living in sub-standard conditions with huge health implications (WHO and UN-Habitat 2016).

An important and integral part of how we might respond to the complex situation of future cities is education. If we are able to gain knowledge and understand different alternatives and their implications for our future collective life around the planet, we are more likely to be engaged in it. Earlier we encountered a range of different methods applied for thinking about the future. Whilst there are considerable benefits for each of these, this book is principally concerned with visualization as an iterative and exploratory method with which we may challenge existing assumptions and dominant trends by capturing new ideas. Visions for future cities are able to speculate on possible responses

Figure 10.
Layered Cities. Moving City. Patrick Abercrombie, Forshaw's London Community map, Social Analysis, Greater London Plan, 1943. Following the Second World War, this project proposed a community matrix and series of satellite towns around the periphery of London to prevent urban sprawl. The aim of the matrix was to blend the diverse ethnicities and demographics of the city into a more egalitarian mix and what we might consider to be a Social Future [see Chapter 5].

to global challenges by exploring alternatives to business-as-usual scenarios [figure 11]. The immediacy and accessibility of visualizations for many different people makes them particularly effective at raising awareness of issues and potential ways we might address them creatively and imaginatively. When we are faced with the daunting prospect of many complex, interrelated challenges for our existence on the planet, it is tempting to view the future as one vast, ambiguous shadow stretching forwards within which our path is unknown. Certainly, not much can be changed positively from a position of ignorance. This is where we can contribute to set about shaping a viable and desirable future for all. As Brück and Million (2018: 143) usefully remind us, 'The future is always in the making, and so are cities. Constant reimagining and remaking by citizens and the continuous reconfiguration of the built environment make the urban spaces we inhabit a palimpsest of multiple reimaginations and alternatives.'

The major value of iterative and exploratory methods lies in their ability to uncover new ideas and challenge existing assumptions about the future using imagination and creativity. The role of visualization within these techniques can be essential in enabling those exploring potential futures to

Figure 11.
Flexible Cities. Sky City. Chan K Q Audrey and Iskm (Studio aVOID), 'Cities For a Flying World' competition, HSE Graduate School of Urbanism, Moscow, 2017 – 'Aerotopia'. This vision examines how urban development may evolve when fossil fuels run out and sky travel is no longer feasible. Set in Hong Kong, the concept of 'airport equals the city' redistributes airport infrastructures, flexible devices, and the high intensity of cultural mix that occurs in airports and transplants them around the city to provide a dynamic and diverse urban landscape. It is an imaginative Global Future [see Chapter 6] formulating a local response to a major worldwide problem.

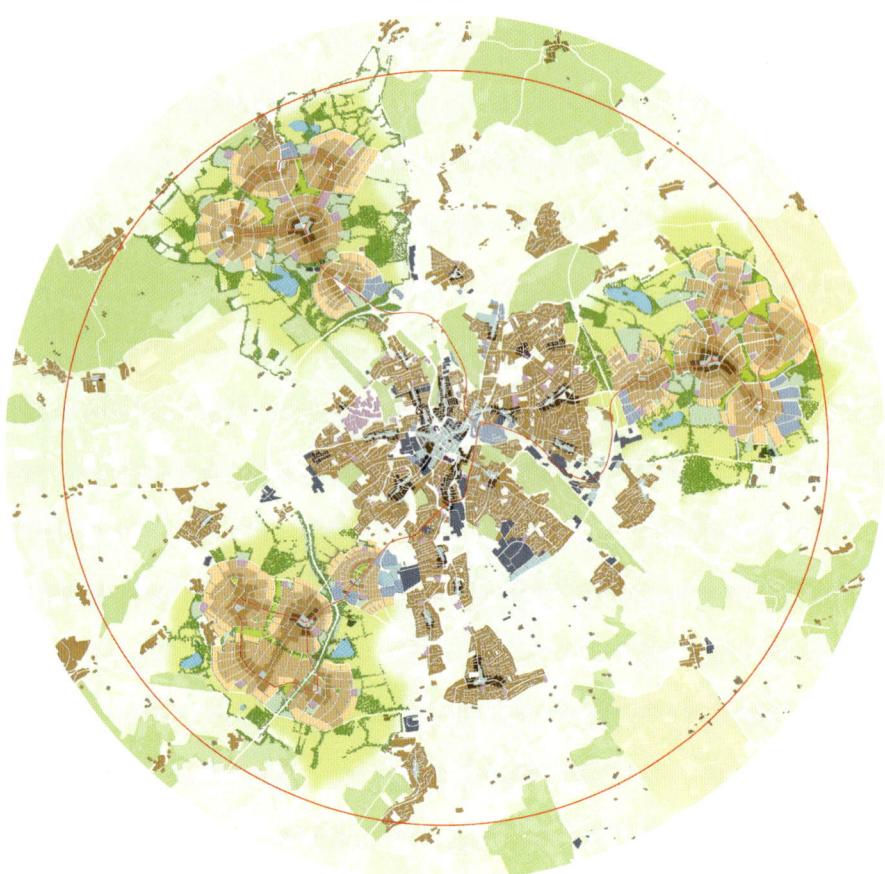

Figure 12.
Ecological Cities. Layered City. URBED, Uxcester Masterplan, Wolfson Economics Prize, 2014. The Garden City concept is an idea that has undergone a recent resurgence. Using a fictional city for 200,000 residents, this design incorporates three large urban extensions that both link to the existing city via public transport and also provide new accessible green space for the city. A jointly owned Garden City Trust comprising local authorities, land owners and central government is envisioned to deliver the scheme.

capture their ideas and share them effectively [figure 12]. This makes the question of how we generate and communicate visions for future cities crucial. Creating visions for future cities has often been marginalized or rejected as being insignificant to the progress of urban development in the real world. However, if as Neuman and Hull (2009: 782) suggest, 'if we cannot imagine, then we cannot manage', the practices of conceptualization, envisioning and performing future cities are essential to our capability to address their increasing complexity.

Underpinning these practices are imagination and creativity which when applied can result in the reshaping of spatial conceptions or provide expressions of alternatives. In his last book, *What is the Future?*, John Urry (2016) explained that the various methods for envisaging futures, visions and the role of imagination can have powerful consequences and are a major way of bringing the state and civil society back into the collective dialogues about futures. More specifically, he believed this to be particularly pertinent where the focus is upon social rather than technological futures. This is where visualization enters the discussion since it provides a highly effective way for designers, planners, stakeholders and the public to develop and share ideas to help guide the forces and complex situations of future cities whilst keeping alternative options possible. Ache (2017: 1) provides further emphasis as he states, 'vision-making processes become very important in such a context, in the best case creating open political horizons interested in becoming and the "midwifing of futures."'

One of the most visionary aspects of built environment professions is that they often create something that does not exist yet [figure 13]. This is a critical dimension to the work of architects, planners and urban designers, amongst others, that tends to get overlooked. It is in moments of significant optimism or huge crisis that designers such as these have returned to the more visionary side of their practices. At their best, these practices explore the potential future as means to explain and respond to present dilemmas. In this manner they address actual needs. Of particular significance is that the visions produced act as conduits for ideas and are able to share and investigate pluralistic possibilities to reconsider the world we live in. In *Envisioning Real Utopias*, Erik Olin Wright (2010: 21) directs us towards the role of the social imagination in constructing possibility: 'what is possible pragmatically is not fixed independently of our imaginations but is itself shaped by our visions'. The expressive and instrumental characteristics of design in future-forming visions make it highly valuable in enabling ideas to travel and have impact for change.

Visions of future cities also represent the cultural conditions under which they were produced [figure 14]. Through such assessment of futurological

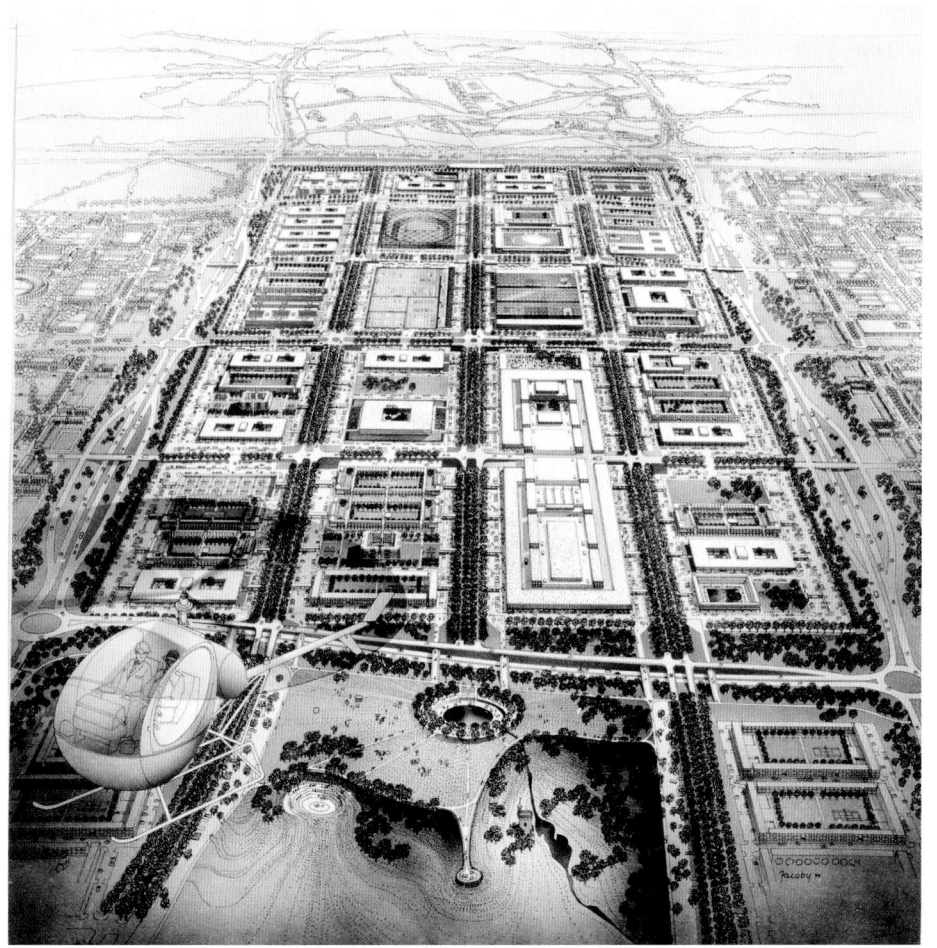

Figure 13. Flexible Cities. Horizontal Cities. Helmut Jacoby, MK in 1990, Aerial Perspective, Graphite, Milton Keynes Main Centre, 1974–1990, 1974. Courtesy of Derek Walker. © Milton Keynes Development Corporation, Crown Copyright. Planned as a thirty-four-square-mile area, the 'Forest City' developed ideas from planner Melvin Webber to establish a grid system (0.62-mile squares) which distributed both transport and building types and would retain 20 per cent green space. The German architectural draftsman Helmut Jacoby depicted the Central shopping area and Campbell Park (base of image) showcasing the grid system (Clapson 2013).

Figure 14.
Flexible Cities. Horizontal Cities. Andrew Mahaddie, City Club, Milton Keynes, early 1970s. © Milton Keynes Development Corporation, Crown Copyright. Featuring experimental ideas including a hydroponic garden, 'mad scientist area', 'mystic gazing', mind chamber and robots, this drawing illustrates an ambitious design for a mixed-used leisure facility. It is reflective of the radical thinking behind many projects of this era though it remained unrealized in this incarnation.

work, patterns emerge, and this book explores the overarching narratives and themes for how urban life has been envisaged and projected. Whilst some of these future cities are familiar to a wide international audience through their exposure in seminal drawings, films, graphic novels, fiction and other media, the impact of such imaginative projections upon the design of our built environment is less well known or understood. How futures are communicated and even experienced is crucial to their ability to endure and influence. Not all future cities are derived from extensive civic projects as some are constructed with other purposes, including entertainment [figure 15]. This area of research is gaining currency across wide audiences as global to local social, cultural and economic changes are shaping cities and their resilience, adaptability and growth. To that end the visions for future cities also require historical reading, an analysis of current ideas and an exploration of future trajectories.

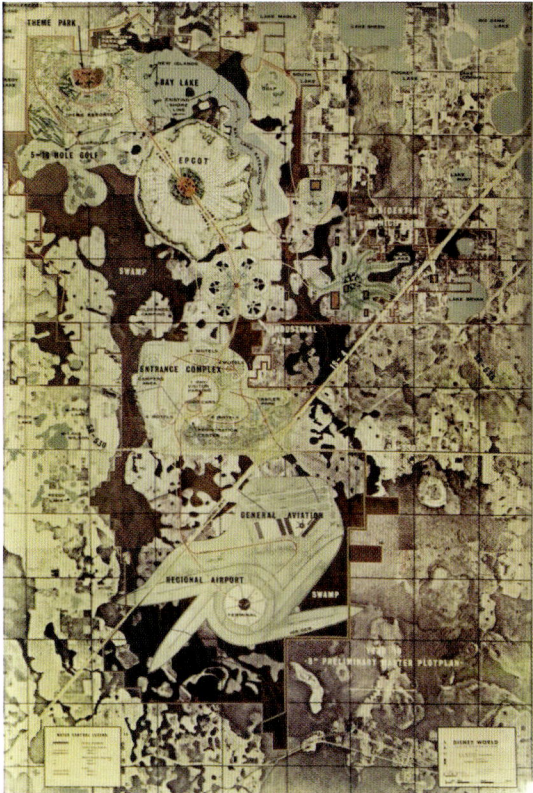

Figure 15.
Hybrid Cities. Divided City. E.P.C.O.T. Masterplan, 1966–1967. © Walt Disney Enterprises. E.P.C.O.T, the Experimental Prototype Community Of Tomorrow, was a long-standing project for a new future city to complement a new Walt Disney Florida World Resort. The use of aerial images helped construct the vision. Although it was unrealized in its full form, some elements were implemented including monorail systems and, briefly, an airport. The cultural impact of these kinds of vision is significant as they are accessible, friendly, and public, and they serve to shape the many visitors' ideas about the future.

How to study future cities

The reason for writing this book is to provide a highly illustrated and insightful text to support those interested in developing an understanding of the built environment – the dreams, ambitions and desires that shaped it from early examples of the ideal society from the sixteenth century to contemporary projected cities envisioned for the rest of the twenty-first century and beyond [figure 16].

The method of our research revolves around selection of visualizations of future cities and clustering these into categories, selecting the most prominent of each area. Such work is an assemblage of speculative and realized cities and points towards the agency of the images. By examining the agency that these visions contain, this book is intended to provide a useful visual resource and guide for catalysing new perspectives on and rethinking the application of future city visions. Visualization of the future city as a whole has long been a utopian desire though typically remains elusive since many of the utopian features evaporate when such schemes are realized [figure 17]. Futurological city images are sometimes bound up from the experience of the city or part of a wider process in which the image reduces other sensory fields, sounds, narratives, materiality and time-based approaches. The images may belong to a wider chain of reaction, as part of an extended design response or social or cultural force. Future city images were not intended as passive creations but are inextricably bound to conceptual thought.

In the contemporary context, futuring process is evident in metabolic studies of cities and urban agendas which map the dynamics of cities through visualized data, whether augmented or virtual. The images project but they also reflect, i.e. they represent wider perceptions; they feedback and also function as critical devices for the evaluation of city form. Such images are often enduring in both the collective imagination and wider cultural context of society [figure 18]. Futuring as a process can also enable participatory and co-creation modes (Pollastri et al. 2018). To that end, engaging as diverse an array of stakeholders as possible in the vision making for future cities is critical to the variety of contemporary projections and histories [figure 19]. However, before we encounter many more future city visions, it is useful to understand the format and structure of this book, the methods of analysis and categorization we have applied, and why.

Figure 16.
Regulated Cities. Vertical City. Lúcio Costa and Oscar Niemeyer, Brasília, Brazil, 1956–1960. The original pilot plan. Image courtesy Uri Rosenheck via Wikimedia Creative Commons , 1956–1960. Designed with ideals and built on an empty plateau, Brasília was a new city of clean lines, rational planning, and space which gave priority to pedestrians, not cars. The city's swooping, streamlined architecture is emblematic of an era preoccupied with air travel, and its zoned organization reflected its primary purpose as a type of office campus for a government.

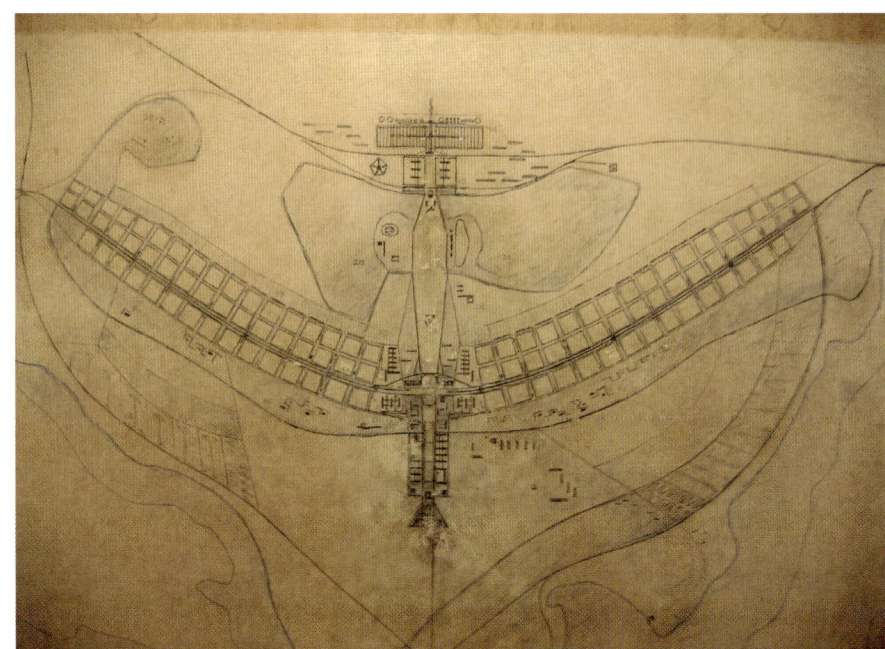

Figure 17.
Regulated Cities. Mechanical City. Buckminster Fuller, Dome over Manhattan, 1960. Courtesy, the Estate of R. Buckminster Fuller. The three-kilometre geodesic dome spanning Midtown Manhattan proposed to reduce cooling costs in the summer and heating costs in the winter by regulating the temperature underneath it. Whilst the technology may not have been available, nor was it deemed desirable by some, the project has endured as a provocation to evolve a better relationship between people and the planet.

Figure 18.
Regulated Cities. Cyber City. Otomo, Katsuhiro, Akira – Destruction of Neo-Tokyo, 1982–1990, Akira vol. 3 © MASH • ROOM / Kodansha Publishing Ltd. Set in 2019, the story begins with a silent mushroom growing in force in Tokyo. The cyberpunk city provides a vision of juxtaposed biological and mechanistic elements of Neo-Tokyo and its genetically modified inhabitants. The monochromatic artwork heightens the sense of atmosphere and tension within the narrative, and led to its status as a seminal graphic novel.

Figure 19.
Regulated Cities. Cyber City. Minecraft, Markus 'Notch' Persson, 2009. Minecraft is an open world video game where players make constructions using textured cubes in a 3D, procedurally generated world. The important aspect here is the level of authorship a player has to create new environments. Different forms of popular media like this have enabled new audiences to engage with future cities, thereby shaping their own imaginations about how the future might be.

The format and structure of this book

The format of the book provides a flow of text with images interspersed to illustrate specific themes and enrich the narrative argument. A key feature of this book is that it illustrates the connectivity between themes rather than offers the material chronologically. Wherever possible we have sought to draw precedents from around the world so that we can examine projects that reflect both distinct and common issues rather than solely from a Western perspective. In reality, around a fifth of the material featured in this book is from non-Western contexts. The recognition of the Global South as leading in many areas of urban innovation is a salient point that is illustrated via some of the selected projects under analysis. However, we acknowledge the discrepancy between the predominantly Western and historical production of visions for future cities and the fact that contemporary future cities are emerging in non-Western contexts, Asia in particular and increasingly Africa. We believe this highlights the urgent need for parallel and counterpoint studies to enable research into this topic to be even more holistic and diverse than this book alone can facilitate. Our aim to produce an authoritative survey of how future cities have been represented throughout history by definition results in glimpses down many avenues that would benefit from specific and deeper inquiries. We hope some readers will be suitably inspired to pursue these, making use of the categories and taxonomy of future cities we present in this book.

This book is subsequently structured into six chapters as follows: Cities of Vision explains the development of visions for future cities throughout history; Rendering Tomorrow explores the influence of different techniques of representation upon future city visions; Technological Futures looks at the optimism of future visions for urban life that have been driven by technology and also how these ideas have formed a major dialogue with science fiction; Social Futures investigates the experimental and experiential visions for future cities that have been led by an impulse to provide for a new society or create novel urban situations; Global Futures takes account of those future city visions that have been produced in response to the significant challenges caused by the effects of climate change and how we might enable collective life to be sustained; Tomorrow's Cities Today provides a summary of the main ideas and themes encountered throughout this book and a discussion on how the future of city visions may evolve.

The format of this book is intended to guide the reader through different ideas in a novel yet practical manner, and, given the visual nature of the material, many of the images included have extended captions that provide a distinct narrative thread through the book rather than merely illustrate the text. This is a deliberate decision to ensure that the relevance of each example is clearly framed and its relationships to others, where appropriate, are evident. As an organizational strategy to aid navigation through such a diverse and broad subject of study, we introduce a taxonomy of future cities to provide critical lenses through which the material may be understood in an original and effective way. These are applied to each image, and a timeline of their relationships is provided at the end of the book. Before presenting the different categories of future cities and taxonomy, it is apparent that any discussion on future cities and how they have been visualized should take account of how architecture is frequently used as an effective vehicle for communicating imaginative ideas about urban life more widely. Indeed, key to understanding some of the material in this book is the significant role architecture plays in its contribution to visions of alternative futures.

Architecture and the imagination

The focus of this book is future cities, and yet not all visions for urban life are as comprehensive as to address an entire city. There are many examples where architecture is the driving force for how a transformation to how we might live, interact and move around is explored. This is because architecture is often able to embody the complexity of issues that concern how we live whilst simultaneously being at a size that is still typically relatable to human scale. Indeed, many of the visualizations of future cities employ architecture as the primary feature of their visions as it serves as a vital gateway into the scenario. Being able to read the image legibly through its elements affords better communication between the designer and those scrutinizing it. Architecture is frequently essential to how cities have been reimagined as we are able to recognize its features and connect with them, even in radical proposals that are very different to the built forms and arrangements we may be familiar with. It is powerful in its ability to convey a sense of building envelope, materiality, enclosure, inhabitation, circulation etc. so that we can understand what we are viewing and how it varies with the existing forms of building we already know.

Architecture is also influential in its capacity to intervene in existing situations and provide radical reconceptualizations of our relationship with our surroundings. The relationship between architecture and the imagination is extremely potent. On the one hand, it connects with a society's deepest social values and expresses them in aesthetic and material form. As one of the most globally recognized cultural practices, architecture is well placed to articulate the complexity of aesthetic, economic, political, social and technical issues it embodies as it responds to context. This is where the power of its representation becomes evident. For on the other hand, it is because of these fundamental connections to architecture as an agent for change and its long history of producing collective meaning and memory that it is able to challenge conventions and offer radical alternatives. Visionary architects are able to articulate through visualization techniques their experimental ideas in order to question how we might live and behave in cities. Clearly, such imagination encompasses a range of possibilities from the purely conceptual to more grounded visions. Across this book, there are various examples of architectural projects. These have been included as they are significant in their expression of how we might envisage collective life in the future [figure 20]. Architecture's ability to intervene in reality and speculate on better worlds and alternative ways of living collectively has ensured it remains at the core of many different visions for future cities.

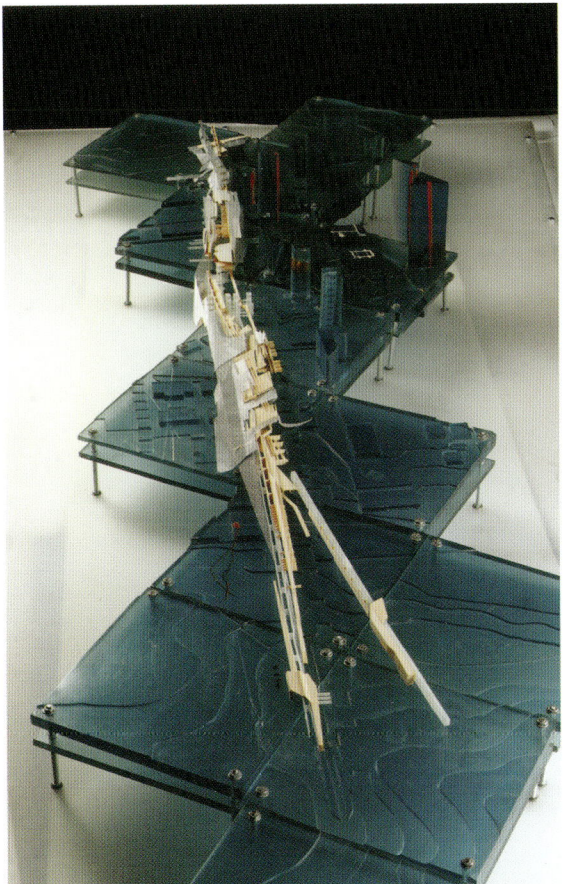

Figure 20.
Informal Cities. Crossing City. DR_D (Dagmar Richter) – An Earthscratcher for Century City, Los Angeles, 1991. Collection Frac Centre-Val de Loire. In this vision, architecture is the motive force for urban transformation as Richter views the city as the sedimentation of interacting 'traces'. Conceiving the city as a media-generated text, it is continuously revised by the city's inhabitants and visitors to simultaneously reflect the palimpsest of its history whilst also continuing to evolve due to contemporary flows and patterns of use.

Taxonomy of future cities

An initial task from the outset is to identify suitable categories of future cities which establish a framework through which they can be better understood. It became quickly evident that there are many different types of future cities. In our earlier work, *A Visual History of the Future* (Dunn et al. 2014), for the UK's Future of Cities Foresight Project, we identified twenty-eight categories of future cities from a wide range of material [Table 1]. It is clear from reflecting on these several years later that many more categories could be added to the list depending on cultural readings and different contexts from

Table 1
City categories identified for A Visual History of the Future. © UK Government Office for Science, 2014.

Cluster City	Cities configured as clustered sets and types
Cognitive City	Cities configured for advanced mental processing
Collage City	Cities as a collection of montaged and collaged features
Connected City	Cities connected to other cities in many forms
Continuous City	Cities that continually expand or have no defined boundary
Crossing City	Cities functioning as crossings both geographical and virtual
Cyber City	Cybernetic cities that are digitally responsive
Desert City	Cities adapted for desert climates
Divided City	Cities layered or separated through transport, zoning or infrastructure
DIY City	Cities that involve temporary or mass construction derived from instruction
Floating City	Cities that float or become airborne
Garden City	Cities based on or derived from the theories of Ebenezer Howard
Haptic City	Cities with overtly sensory features
Horizontal City	Cities focused on landscape aspects and connectivity
Layered City	Cities that sandwich their dynamics through multiple layers
Mechanical City	Cities that have mechanized functions
Media City	Cites developed through extensive mass media communications
Moving City	Cities with mobility able to partially or fully reposition
Sky City	Cities that float and drift in the atmosphere
Smart City	Cities interconnected and responsive through supermassive data sets
Space City	Cities that project beyond earth's atmosphere
Spectacle City	Cities that generate memorable consummative events, primarily visual
Trading City	Cities functioning as trading entities, information and exchange
Underground City	Cities developed below ground level
Vertical City	Cities concentrated on their vertical properties
Vice City	Cities focused on catering to immorality, wrongdoing and misconduct
Waste City	Cities that function through recycling and waste energy capture
Water City	Cities adapted to waterborne environments

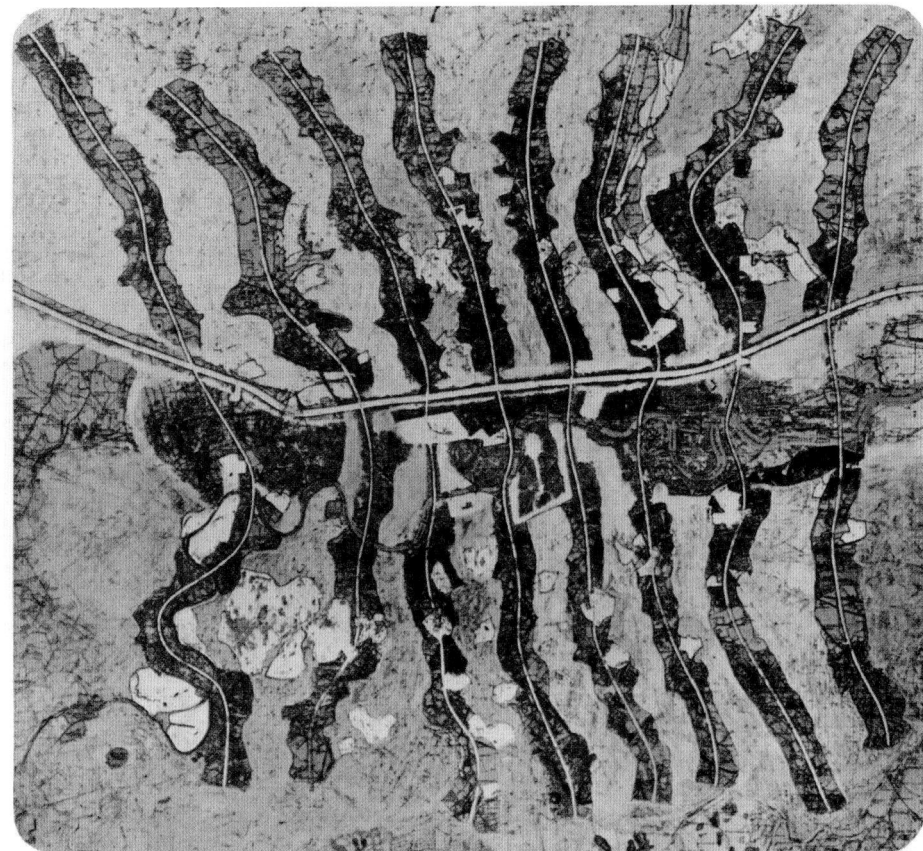

Figure 21.
Regulated Cities. Divided City. Master plan for London based on research carried out by the Town Planning Committee of the M.A.R.S. Group, 1942. RIBA Collections. The M.A.R.S. Group: draught plan giving an impression of what the map of London would look like with ribbons of open country penetrating the city (600,000 inhabitants). As this future city vision seeks to combine urban life with interventions of countryside corridors, it is an ideal example of a Regulated City.

which the material is perceived. However, we believe that further expansion is unhelpful since even if we were able to provide the ultimate, albeit exhaustive, definitive catalogue at this point in time, the nature and dynamics of futures mean it would still be open to extension and revision. Therefore, whilst we retain the use of these categories to signal different ideas throughout history and open up the discussion of them, we believe of even greater value here is the application of the taxonomy we previously developed in our government report that captures the most significant and influential paradigms of visualizations for future cities. These are as follows:

1. *Regulated Cities* – visions that organize or integrate aspects of rural/country/green living [figure 21].

2. *Layered Cities* – portrayals that have explicit multiple but fixed levels typically associated with different mobilities [figure 22].

3. *Flexible Cities* – depictions that allow for plug-in and changes but are still fixed in some manner to context [figure 23].

4. *Informal Cities* – visions that suggest much more itinerant and temporary situations and include walking, nomadic, and non-permanent cities [figure 24].

5. *Ecological Cities* – illustrations of cities that demonstrate explicit ecological concerns, renewable energies, and low- or zero-carbon ambitions [figure 25].

Figure 22.
Layered Cities. Mechanical City. Heinz Schulz-Neudamm, *Metropolis*, 1926. © Deutsche Kinemathek – Horst von Harbou. A seminal cinematic future city is the Weimar dystopian vision of Fritz Lang's *Metropolis* which presented an automated city of hierarchy and control driven by industrialization and its future possibilities. Its iconic images have endured, resonating with current discourse on artificial intelligence and robots. This Layered City of different circulation systems amongst high-rise buildings has been a recurrent motif throughout the twentieth century and twenty-first century thus far.

6. *Hybrid Cities* – visions that deliberately explore the blurring between physical place and digital space, including augmented reality and Smart Cities [figure 26].

These six principal paradigms have, with the benefit of hindsight and further reflection, been checked for their integrity and flexibility. As a means of helping organize the many different examples featured in this book, it is beneficial in three ways.

Firstly, it enables the grouping together of similar species of visions for future cities based on the ideologies and thematic drivers they represent. Secondly, the taxonomy's paradigms represent discrete and robust primary classes that are overarching in their scope and able to accommodate all the categories of city we originally identified and other variations we have been able to conceive of. Thirdly, by framing the six principal paradigms as critical lenses through which the wider topic of future cities can be

Figure 23.
Flexible Cities. Cyber City. Egor Orlov, New topography of the future city, Cybertopia. Image © Egor Orlov, 2015. In this proposal the landscape is able to move in any direction at any time and is conceived as a living organism. Cybertopia is a structure that can mutate in a manner similar to those cities created and altered in Minecraft. The degree of adaptation, flux and interchangeability in this Flexible City connects it back to numerous utopian ideas between the mid-1950s and late 1970s.

Figure 24.
Informal Cities. Moving City. Ron Herron, Walking City on the Ocean, project. 1966. Exterior perspective. New York, Museum of Modern Art (MoMA). Gift of The Howard Gilman Foundation. Acc. n.: 1203.2000. © 2018. Digital image, The Museum of Modern Art, New York/Scala, Florence. Part of the work of avant-garde group Archigram, Walking City continued to explore their core belief that change was integral to how a city worked. The scheme comprises giant roaming pods that could traverse around the planet to wherever they were needed. It is a radical take on the Informal City as the thinking behind it drew influence from both insects and revolutionary machinery.

navigated, the taxonomy enables fresh insights and latent connections to be made through these thematic pathways. Yet, we also recognize that with material that is visually interpreted and potentially understood from many different viewpoints, such classification has to be flexible rather than absolute. We have thus sought to develop and present a taxonomy which aids the reader but accept that further evolution and alternative versions that challenge it is important in shaping the field of future cities, their critical

Figure 25. (facing page)
Ecological Cities. Water City. SCAPE, Oyster-tecture / MoMA Rising Currents Exhibition, 2010. Commissioned by the Museum of Modern Art in 2009 for the Rising Currents exhibition, this vision explores adaptation strategies for New York City as a response to the effects of climate change and sea level rise. Proposing an active oyster reef to improve diversity of marine life and encourage recreational opportunities, the emergent Ecological City is one that prefigures the city's return to the waterfront as a sustainable strategy for the next century.

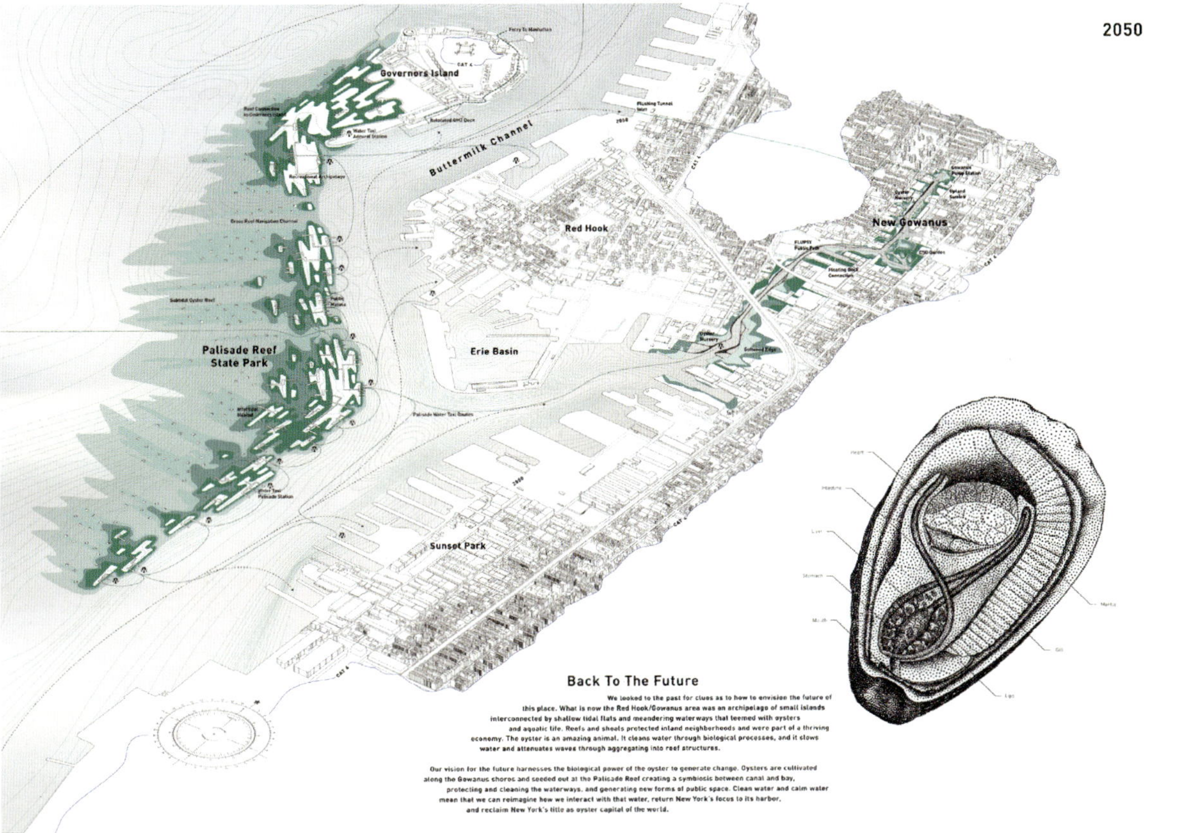

Chapter 1 Introduction: Futures, imagination and visions for cities

Figure 26.
Hybrid Cities. Vertical City. Neil Spiller, Rachel Armstrong and Martin Hanczyc (AVATAR) Future Venice, (Visualizations by Christian Kerrigan), 2009. This project proposes an artificial, programmable, limestone-like reef underneath the historic city in order to spread its weight over a larger area and reclaim the city in a sustainable way. This Hybrid City illustrates the novel opportunities of blurring and combining analogue and digital realms to advance the qualities of our place and respond to future challenges.

investigation and research methods. We establish the taxonomy here so that it may ground the reading of the book and guide the synthesis of prevalent patterns and trends within and across different eras. We then return to it at the end of the book along with a timeline to illustrate how all the examples featured may be connected within parallel themes throughout history [see figure 166, Chapter 7]. In doing so, we hope to illustrate stimulating ideas we have held for our collective future and uncover less familiar ones and explore the connections between them.

Chapter 2

Cities of Vision: A visual history of the future

Imaginary cities

In Buckminster Fuller's optimistic view of our position in 2025, he describes a futurological ability of archaeological researchers to situate themselves at any time point and investigate human occupation on our planet to rebuild lost buildings and cities: 'Research teams can live experimentally at various historical control periods of history thus to elucidate much of the wisdom gained in the past' (1975: 8). This 'ability' of archaeological research is very much the aim of this chapter, to understand and research visions of cities. Future cities are fundamentally attached to the histories and contexts of their production and the values of the society in which they were created. The various artefacts, movements and concepts discussed here sought to challenge the prevailing conditions and problems of cities of the time and tried to produce ideas conducive to different ways of living [figure 27]. These visions of our future urbanism are not fatalistic, as Susan Hagan (2014) has shown in the discussion of future city movement, ecological urbanism and potential to address global climate challenges.

One of the biggest commonalities many of us share, regardless of political, social, economic or cultural backgrounds, is an interest in futures. Future thinking can vary radically from typical questions on weather system forecasts, which only began in 1960, strategic business planning and many other forms of prediction. Responding to the question of 'how we live in the future' concerns many disciplines interested in the built environment, particularly architecture, with a range of methodologies and accepted practices in measuring associated values. Often people have a model in which they conceive the city [figure 28]. Vision is termed in the sense of visual perception, the faculty of sight or powers of observation at ground level, aerial or remote. The process in which visions of future cities are created is therefore critical in helping us decode one facet of our prospects. That is not to say the way we vision is evident, precise or accurate. Visions for future cities and the practices of their making can be manipulative, false and misleading. This is because through the exercise of articulating and promoting certain aspects of future urban life, a vision necessarily has to omit others either

Figure 27.
Informal Cities. Water City. Noel Schardt + Bjoern Muendner (Freischaerler Architects), United Plastic Nation, 2017. The United Plastic Nation questions the concept of the nation-state, which defines itself by the exclusion of the outside via borders and citizenship. This island is instead, by default, inclusive; it has no borders and is part of all continents, and anyone can become a citizen. The island expands, passing all continents, connecting regions of poverty and despair with areas of wealth and prosperity.

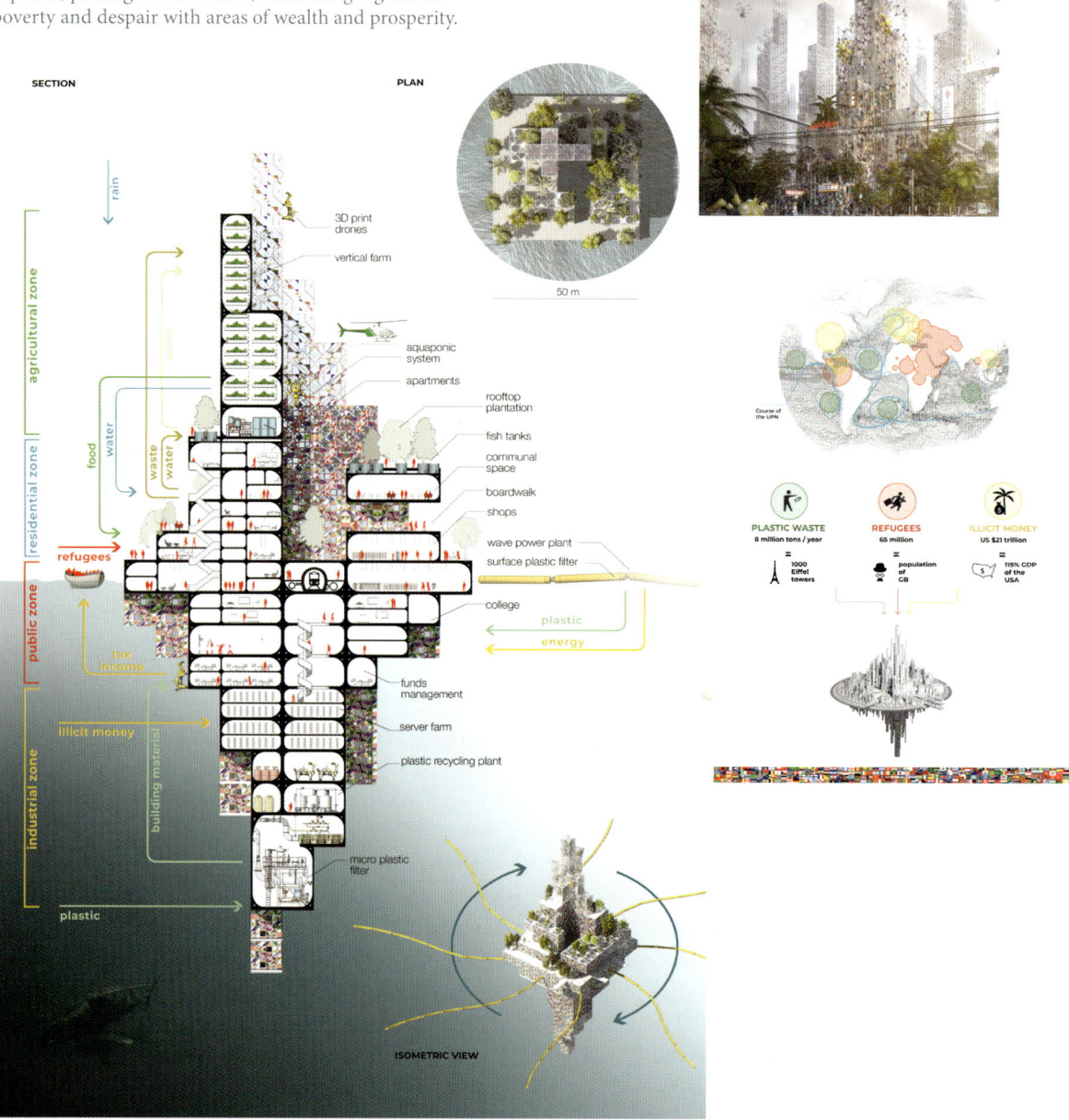

intentionally or subconsciously [figure 29]. In doing so, alternative options are hidden or even discredited through the filtering out of elements that do not fit within the preferred future being illustrated. For example, maps of areas are often conceived as neutral artefacts but inextricably bound or used for political ends often wrapped in Mercator, Anglo-American cartographic bias. In another example, future cities are wrapped up with technological innovation promoted by those very same stakeholders, as evident in Smart Cities, a sort of technology stacking beginning with virtual representations enabling virtual communities (Komninos et al. 2018: 5–6). In a contemporary context, numerous visions for cities are permeated with technological innovation and infrastructure, often pointing towards the notion of Smart Cities whether explicitly or not. However, it is not a recent phenomenon, with the early signs of this development carefully traced historically by Lewis Mumford (Mumford and Winner 2010; Giedion 2013).

We have already outlined the importance of visualizations of future cities and their ability to capture our imagination. In addition, because so many of these visions for what the future may hold for us come from so many different sources and types of media, plus many of us are finding the distinction between our physical and digital lives harder to distinguish, we are now at the point where our dreams are mingled with our daily business. The sources of these visions are numerous, blending fictional cities with built projects; drawing from a gamut of radical alternatives to subtle variations, we encounter many different future cities through mainstream media, subcultures, special interest groups and genres. When we experience them, these visions are the result of mediation between the ideas they contain and the operation of visualization techniques to communicate them. There is an agency at work in this process. This agency is a powerful tool for design and change of current systems and is worth discussing here. Traditionally, architectural drawings project on paper space a physical reality to be transcribed; realized architecture is a projection of ideas (Pérez-Gómez 2000: 4–8). With the development of digital representation techniques and increased blurring between the physical and virtual via augmented reality and virtual reality technologies, the more immersive the experience of these projected futures can be. This is valuable since the more research that articulates and identifies the agency of visions of cities, the more foresight we will gain regarding the methods of visioning futures for built environments (Lustig 2015). Agency in this context is defined as an action or intervention producing a particular effect. Stan Allen (2008) argues these media materials remain instrumental though are particularly expanded through visual culture. Because the agency of visualizations is connected to how we interpret them, this means visions for future cities, while directing us in particular ways towards specific themes and ideas, can also have unintended consequences depending on the context of how they are viewed, when and by whom. When viewed as a body of work, visions for future cities can be seen to have particular themes, and key ideas which had emerged, irrespective of the mode of representation, seem to repeat and endure across different eras of history (Vesely 2006). To help us better understand contemporary speculations, the following section provides a historical framework to explain the development of future visions for cities, starting from antiquity and going through to the present day.

The development of cities over time has seen many physical additions, revisions and geometrical formal patterns, some remaining strictly regulated, such as Beijing's Forbidden City (1420–) from the Ming dynasty onwards (Barme 2012) which was virtualized by the Palace Museum and IBM in 2008 in a $3 million project. Some cities established themselves through geographical exploitation as seen in Tenochtitlán (1325 to 1521) [figures 30 & 31]. What had previously been an island surrounded by Lake Texcoco, now drained, forms Mexico City along with Tlatelolco. Tenochtitlán had a strict and regulated city plan and was released to a European audience via Cortes's letters to Charles V. As a city image, the Nuremberg map of 1524 was endlessly reproduced with all colonial bias. The city was imagined by representation, and Aztec culture was imagined first in Europe before it was actually understood (Mundy 1998; Keen 1990).

Figure 28.
Regulated Cities. Trading City. Blessed Ambrogio Sansedoni – detail (the city of Siena), Palazzo Pubblico. © 2018. Photo Scala, Florence. The city here, presented as a model held by the Dominican friar, is a symbol of governance as indicated by Giorgio Vasari (Parsons 2017).

Figure 29.
Regulated Cities. Layered City. View of an Ideal City, or The City of God, after 1470 (oil on panel), Laurana, Luciano (c. 1420–79) (attr. to) / Galleria Nazionale delle Marche, Urbino, Marche, Italy / Bridgeman Images.

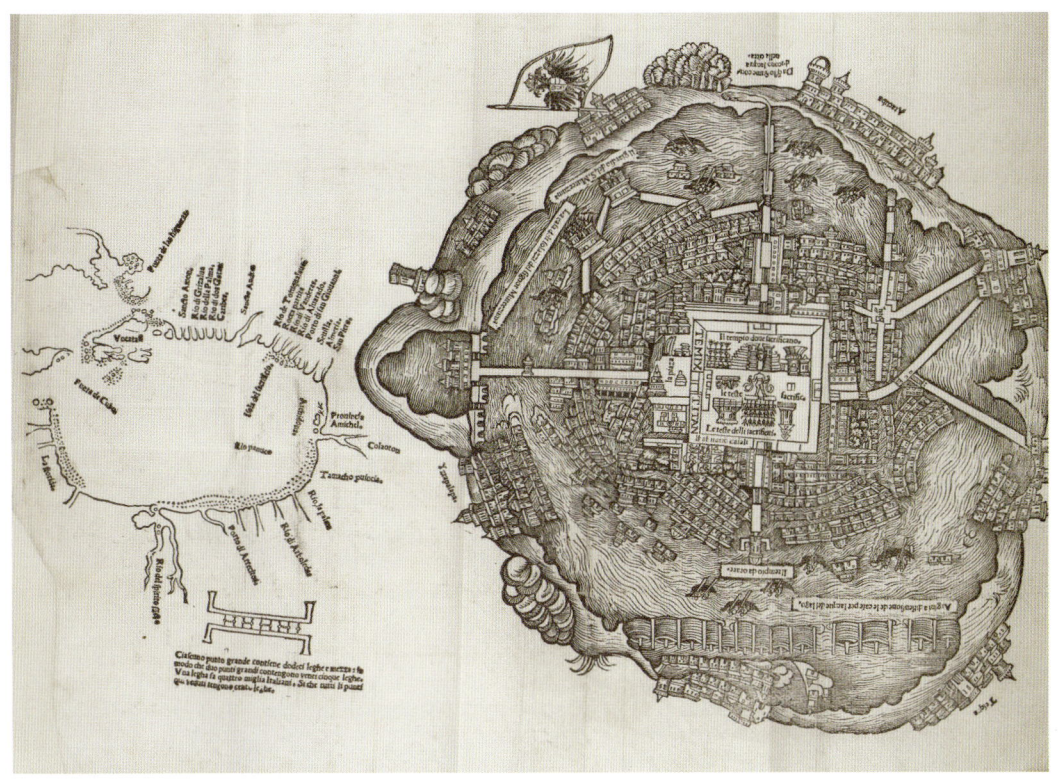

Figure 30.
Regulated Cities. Trading City. Plan of Mexico, in Hernando Cortés, La preclara narratione di Ferdinando Cortese della Nuoua Hispagna, Venice, 1524 (woodcut), Italian School, (16th century) / British Library, London, UK / © British Library Board. All Rights Reserved / Bridgeman Images. This woodcut is divided in two parts, a chart of the Gulf of Mexico (left) and plan view of the Aztec capital Tenochtitlán. The plan morphs into a panoramic bird's-eye view showing the coastal topography and connecting outlying Atacuba, Texcoco and Iztapalapa.

Figure 31.
Regulated Cities. Trading City. Island Capital of the Aztecs, Tenochtitlan (mural), Covarrubias, Luis (1919–1987) / Museo Nacional de Antropologia, Mexico City, Mexico / Sean Sprague/Mexicolore / Bridgeman Images.

Chapter 2 Cities of Vision: A visual history of the future   33

Figure 32.
Layered Cities. Trading City. Mazhar Ali Khan, A Panorama of Delhi taken from the top of the Lahore Gate of the Red Fort, Delhi, Watercolour, 1846. British Library, London, UK / © British Library Board. All Rights Reserved / Bridgeman Images. A section of a 360-degree panorama of Delhi spanning five metres, the overall work is of historical importance as much was demolished in the Siege of Delhi (1857) (Dalrymple and Sharma 2012). Its relevance here is as an example of topographical studies in a fast-paced climate of social, political and industrial change.

Such accounts of cities via maps and topographical description varied between the cosmological, the symbolic, a desire for fidelity for military necessity, as in the case of the panorama of Delhi in 1846, a form of collated media out of a changing geographical and architectural understanding [figure 32].

Various media suited architectural imaginaries, more than half of the romantic novel *Hypnerotomachia Poliphili* (*The Strife of Love in a Dream*) (1499) was devoted to architectural description; the next largest part was devoted to designed landscape and gardens. The text is indicative of the multiple genres and forms in which visionary architecture appears. This form of architectural symbolic imaginary resonates in the contemporary age, for example in the case of the Berlin TV tower realized in 1969 to which this structure could well be another page in the novel [figure 33]. As Liane Lefaivre (2005: 8–9) states, *Hypnerotomachia Poliphili* is as much an architectural encyclopaedia or 'tractate' [figure 34]. The plausibility of many visions is one character of these future city forms – in the case of literature an important mode of utopian exploration, usually located on islands or fictitious geographies in order to justify radical politics: Thomas More's *Utopia* (1516) [figure 35], Francis Bacon's *The New Atlantis* (1627) and Henry Neville's *The Isle of Pines* (1668) are just a few examples. The three texts explore the utopia 'good or no place' as a literary device to make a political comment while also locating the islands at the forefront of geographical discovery and exploration. Fictional literary descriptions such as these were intrinsically

Figure 34. (facing page)
Regulated Cities. Underground City. Francesco Colonna, *Hypnerotomachia Poliphili*, Signature d8 verso and e1 recto (Text; Satyr with Sleeping Nymph). Image Courtesy of the Met Museum. CC. Aq. No. 23.73.1. Liane Lefaivre describes the woodcut as 'Part Temple, part triumphal arch, part pyramid, part obelisk, part sphere, part labyrinth, part propylaeum, part cave, part mountain' (Lefaivre 2005, 47–8). *Hypnerotomachia Poliphili* is a celebrated and enigmatic book, characterized as a commentary on Renaissance architectural thinking with references to Alberti throughout.

Figure 33.
Kosmaj Project, The Berlin TV tower, Drone Photography, 2019.

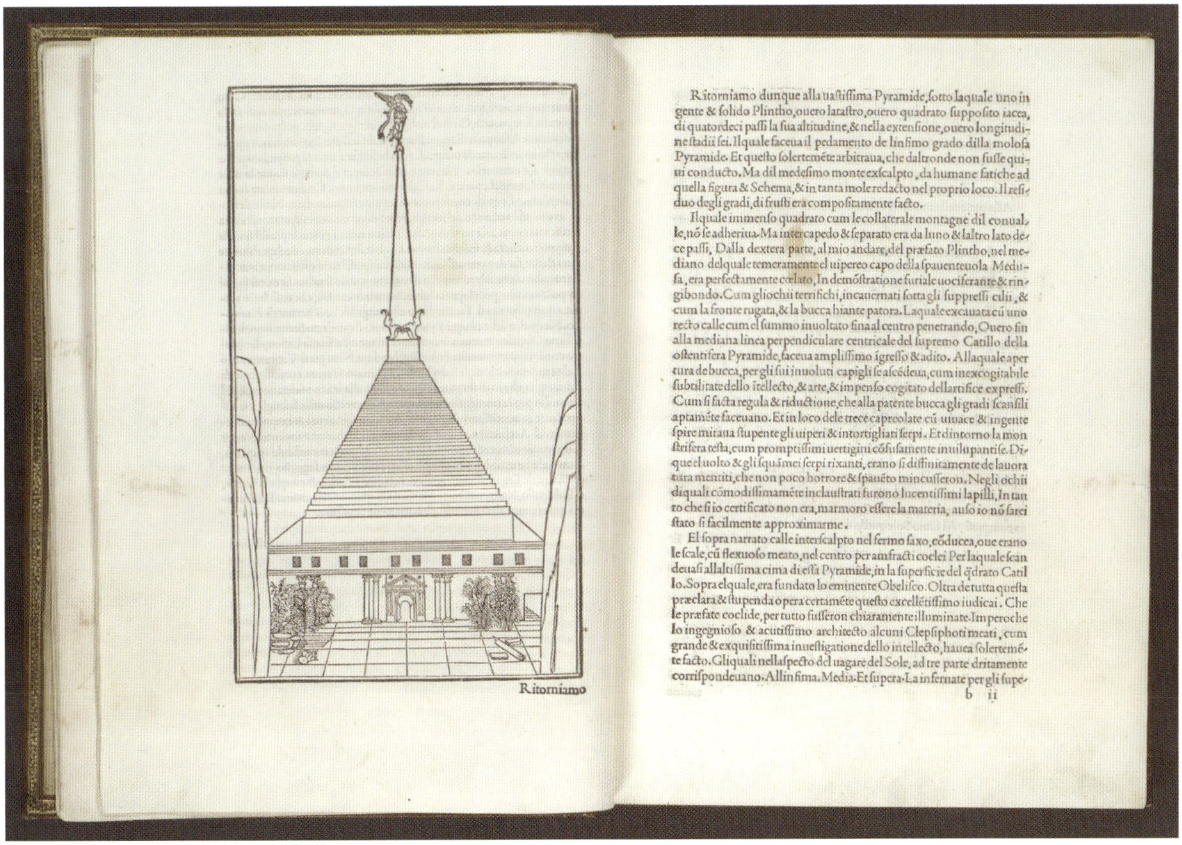

Chapter 2 Cities of Vision: A visual history of the future

12 VTOPIAE INSVLAE TABVLA.

Amaurotũ vrbs.

Fons Anydri.

Ostium anydri.

hythlodaeus.

Figure 35. (facing page)
Regulated Cities. Continuous City. Thomas More, *Utopia*, (translated by Gilbert Burnet), George Routledge & Sons, 1885, © British Library, London, British Library Board. All Rights Reserved/Bridgeman Images. The first text released in 1516 setting out 'utopia: a 'good' 'no place' – '200 miles broad, with 54 cities in the island, all large and well-built around 24 miles between each (or a day's walk). Amaurot is the capital centre. The island has a bay, though a great harbour, requires careful navigation at its mouth' (More 1516: II).

Figure 36. (below)
Regulated Cities. Moving City. Jan Jansson, View of Strasbourg from 'Urbium totius Germaniae Superioris Illustriorum clariorumque Tabluae antiquae et novae accuratissime elaboratae', 1657 (engraving), Dutch School, (17th century) / British Library, London, UK / © British Library Board. All Rights Reserved / Bridgeman Images. This volume was a series of printed works – a 'Books of Cities' capturing urban life. Most prominent are the cathedral with its 466-foot spire and fortifications which the French military engineer Sébastien Le Prestre de Vauban would later transform.

linked to political and social commentary on cities and society in which the author was situated, as further illustrated by Jonathan Swift's *Gulliver's Travels* (1726).

City imaginaries were not restricted to book media; city visions were often realized with brute political force and their geometries linked to the heavens. Lewis Mumford (1968: 69) writes in *The City in History*, 'the ancient city would emerge as a sanctuary, be secure, defensive, ordered, stretching itself to the countryside and or coastline, but enshrine itself in symbolic and monumental forms and images as a simulacrum of heaven'. Rudolf Wittkower's *Architectural Principles in the Age of Humanism* (1998) demonstrates that Renaissance architectural thought realized through symbolic forms would mediate between the micro and the macro in particular central plan churches as in the case of Jan Jansson's topographical study, and the cathedral's central prominence for Strasbourg [figure 36].

Chapter 2 Cities of Vision: A visual history of the future 37

Venice was crucial to maritime trade, in the case of the sea city; became a city-state from the ninth century onwards but with the much earlier settlement; and was a place of significant power. Jacopo de' Barbari's mural-sized wood block Venice study according to the detailed work of Jurgen Schulz (1978: 464) 'was to represent the concept "city", to illustrate the idea of a given place [figure 37]. Faithfulness to a particular model was only secondary, a refinement.' However, the precise reason for Barbari's work, its utilization and rationale for its commission remain a puzzle. Many visual media depicting histories of cities oscillate between faithful reproduction using the latest technological surveying apparatus and cultural and symbolic representation imported to a place. Thus, the imaginary of a city may begin from the point of the draughtsperson. Discussion of future cities often fails to comprehend the operative intention of the production of the image fully, or such information has been lost. However, what is certain is that the city imaginary is intrinsically linked to human settlement.

Cities to Mumford were organic histories. Representations of places are relational and have a similitude of 'being in the process of' and 'being placed to' – we attempt to semiotically order the identity of a place through its materiality [figures 38 & 39]. According to Kevin Hetherington (1997) representations function between networks of agents. Following Latour (1986), one notion of agency that is particularly important here is phrased as 'immutable mobiles'. In this case, representations of places shown here in this very book contain truth claims. Having been assembled from a cultural point, the image, film, or architectural model contains fixed knowledge and facts (immutable) but nevertheless is transportable via agency, making knowledge of a place (mobility). Developing from this, actor-network theory (ANT) has been deployed as a useful tool to map the urban imagination as well as design and planning (Farías and Bender 2011; Latour 2007; Rydin and Tate 2017).

Figure 37.
Flexible Cities. Trading City. Jacopo de' Barbari, Bird's eye view of Venice, 1500. Woodcut printed from six blocks on six sheets of joined paper, © De Agostini Picture Library / A. Dagli Orti / © British Library, London, UK/Bridgeman Images. This bird's-eye view by Jacopo de' Barbari displays Venice, shown from the southwest, at the height of its power.

Figure 38.
Layered Cities. Underground City. Yakov Chernikhov, Architectural fantasy. View of the enormous portal cranes with semi-circular corbels, from the series 'Industrial Architecture', 1932–1936, drafting pen, gouache and lacquer, 105 x 105 mm. © Yakov Chernikhov, Courtesy of the Tchoban Foundation. Chernikhov created 101 composition drawings for his *Architectural Fantasies* book of 1933 (Černichov 2009).

Figure 39.
Layered Cities, Underground City. Giovanni Battista Piranesi, The Gothic Arch, 1761. Gift of Frank Jewett Mather Jr. x1938-13n Princeton University Art Museum. Piransei's carceri, celebration of Roman architectural magnificence, via imaginary prisons are what Richard Wendorf (2001: 161) states as vision of 'a past so present that contemporary sensibility must accommodate rather than attempt to obliterate it'. Piranesi's etchings like Superstudio [see figure 3, Chapter 1] are continuous monuments, infinite spaces which are palimpsest to assembled Roman ruins and antiquity and thus symbolic of a city.

Chapter 2   Cities of Vision: A visual history of the future

Industrial cities

The onset of the industrial revolution from the sixteenth century paved the way for the generalized modern urban definition of cities of millions of inhabitants (Williams 2014). Boroughs, towns, inner cities and suburbs as well as other classifications all define city terminology as opposed to rural settings. Urbanization and our understanding of cities, as well as the documentation of radical environmental changes, are therefore rather new phenomena in a global public context (Iossifova et al. 2017). Discussing how cities and visions of cities have materialized also requires a sensitivity to the various historical and cultural meanings of the term [figure 40]. Many future city visions that are regulated have their origins in strict military necessity, especially in early settlements, or visions of urban changes are in response to military technology such as the ideal ports of Simon Stevin (Kostof and Tobias 1999). This is a route towards some futures that remains significant – for example the work of the European Union's Institute for Security Studies, the National Intelligence Council in the United States, and the Global Strategic Trends programme by the Ministry of Defence in the UK. The history of cities contains numerous examples such as Imola by Leonardo Da Vinci (1502), Avola by V. Amico (1693 to 1757), Palmanova by Giulio Savorgnan (1593), Sébastien Le Prestre de Vauban, Citadel of Lille (1667) in which the city as a defensive space is enabled by military engineering which required strict geometries (Baillie-Hislop 2016). Topology is subservient to the regimental grid streets and defensive walls unless laid out to resist natural catastrophes. These Regulated City forms were driven by the practicalities of defence, commerce, and city administration but also as symbolic

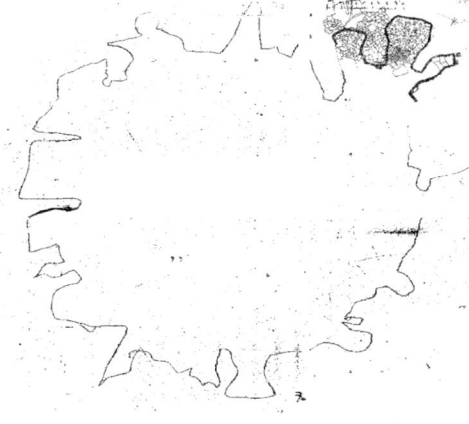

Figure 40.
Flexible Cities. Collage City. Peter Barber Architects, Hundred Mile City, 2016. Images courtesy of Peter Barber Architects. Responding to pressures in housing and density, this linear city is 100 miles long, 200 metres wide and 4 storeys high, and proposes to contain London's sprawl. Filming at one-mile increments, the studio recorded the inefficiency of suburbia and car-based urbanism alongside sketches and models. The work references Patrick Keiller's *Robinson in Space* (1997) and D. A. Pennebaker's visual-jazz montage *Daybreak Express* (1953).

forms, which in combination are values that have established the Regulated City as a dominant paradigm. Robert Bruegmann (2005) discusses the history of sprawl and rightly points out that the development of living beyond these city walls, via the suburban or exurban, would create systems of urban patterns supportive of the city settlement exacerbated through industrialization. The Regulated City defined not only its inner workings but also the system and network beyond. Of these industrial cities, housing would form a critical factor in city demands as seen in New Lanark, Lanarkshire (1786) and Saltaire, Shipley, Bradford (1851) in the UK.

Figure 41.
Regulated Cities. Divided City. Plan of Paris, France, c. 1870, showing Georges Eugene Haussmann boulevards superimposed in thick black. Granger/Bridgeman Images.

Mechanized life

Industrialization caused rifts on the urban fabric when implemented for example in the work of Baron Georges-Eugène Haussmann [figure 41]. His public works gentrified the city core beginning from 1854, transforming the urban experience for a variety of its citizens from flâneurs to petty criminals (Jallon et al. 2017). The reality of swelling cities and the negative effects of industrialization would require radical visions, analytical descriptions and policies. It was an industrial urbanism that would be the material for antithesis in late Victorian utopian literature in Edward Bellamy's *Looking Backward: 2000–1887* (1888), William Morris's *News from Nowhere* (1890) and H. G. Wells's *A Modern*

Figure 42.
Regulated Cities. Garden City. Louis De Soissons, Architect, Welwyn Garden City Masterplan, 1920, Cachemaille-Day, Nugent Francis artist/photographer, RIBA Collections. In transport terms, Fredrick Osborn, a member of the UK Garden City movement and chairman of the Town and Country Planning Association, continued Ebenezer Howard's vision, ensuring landscape wedges segregated traffic and pedestrian movement in the sketch proposal of 1919. Courtenay Crickmer developed the second sketch design layout, though De Soissons's plan here was preferred and realized.

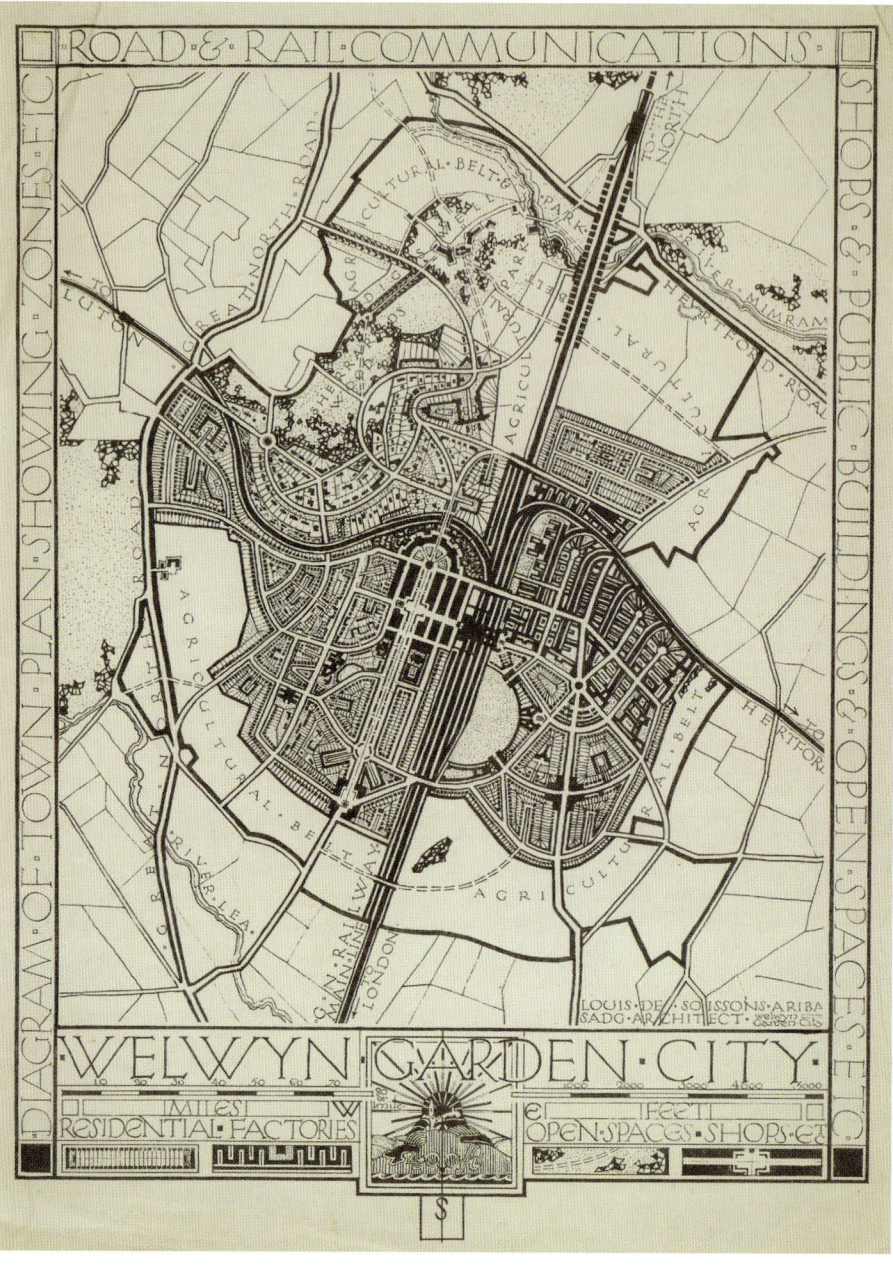

Utopia (1905). This industrial urbanism would also provide stark societal commentary on the conditions of everyday life in George Gissing's *The Nether World* (1889).

Such blight and poverty decimating London would provoke urgent visions for reimagining suburbia as in the case of the Garden City movement [figure 42]. Garden Cities are unique visions, but there is less recognition that the Garden City owes much to near historical events which provided the unique impetus for these urban prototypes. Gustav Doré's 'Over London by Rail' plate from *London: A Pilgrimage* (Jerrold 1872) is

42 FUTURE CITIES: A VISUAL GUIDE

often cited as a pivotal representation in an industrial turn with remedial action from the British Royal Comission of 1885 amongst others [figure 43]. In the UK, the producers of city visions wanted to morally reform, remake or reshape terrain and its populace. Indications of this drive were found in the work of Ebenezer Howard and his publication *To-morrow: A Peaceful Path to Real Reform* (1898), which proposed agrarian change which would become a primer for the Garden City movement. Howard's book is a strategic business plan with a much-reproduced settlement pattern that made an economic case for Garden Cities. The Garden City would surface as the next iteration of a Regulated City and be one of the UK's significant and longest standing models of urban development exported throughout the world (Miller 1989, 2008, 2010; Henderson et al. 2017). Howard projected a concentric moralistic urban spatial form that contained various zones of activity from low-density housing and industrial areas to recreational facilities intersected with green corridor routes and surrounded by green

Figure 43.
Informal Cities. Vice City. William Blanchard Jerrold, Doré Gustave, London: A Pilgrimage. With illustrations by Gustave Dore, 1872. British Library, London, UK © British Library Board. All Rights Reserved/Bridgeman Images. In 1869 the journalist Blanchard Jerrold (1826–1884) together with French artist Gustave Doré (1832–1883) produced an illustrated record of the 'shadows and sunlight' of London. They spent many days and nights exploring the capital, often protected by plain-clothes policemen, and visited night refuges, cheap lodging houses, and the opium den described by Charles Dickens in the sinister opening chapter of *The Mystery of Edwin Drood*.

belt. Each Garden City would hold an optimum population of thirty-two thousand with fifty-eight thousand for the central city and be connected by inter-muncipal railways. These principles filtered into the New Town movement which began after the Second World War (Buder 1990; Hardy 1991). The legacy of these diagrams could arguably be seen in the division of town functionality of Welwyn Garden City, the second Garden City [figure 42], and its recent popular resurgence for the Wolfson Economics Prize (2014) and in particular URBED's winning submission [see figure 11, Chapter 1]. Satellite towns drawn by Ernst May would define the UK form with outlying towns and suburbs in the case of Wythenshawe, Manchester, and the significant Greater London Plan led by Patrick Abercrombie (1945) [figure 10]. Regulated satellite towns would emerge from many strands from New Delhi to the Netherlands and become a global vision in which cities would materialize in the later twentieth century (Srivastava 2014; Wakeman 2016; Vanstiphout and Provoost 2007) [figures 44 & 45]. A geographical-economic interpretation of these systems also emerged

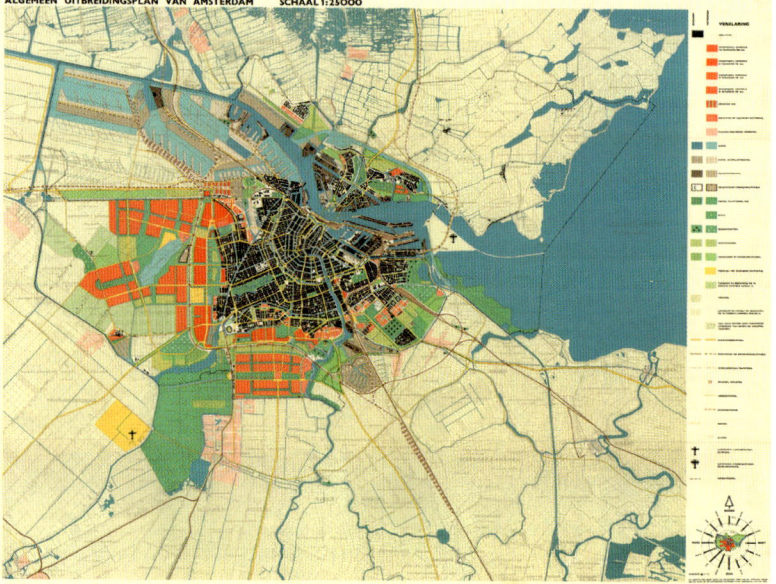

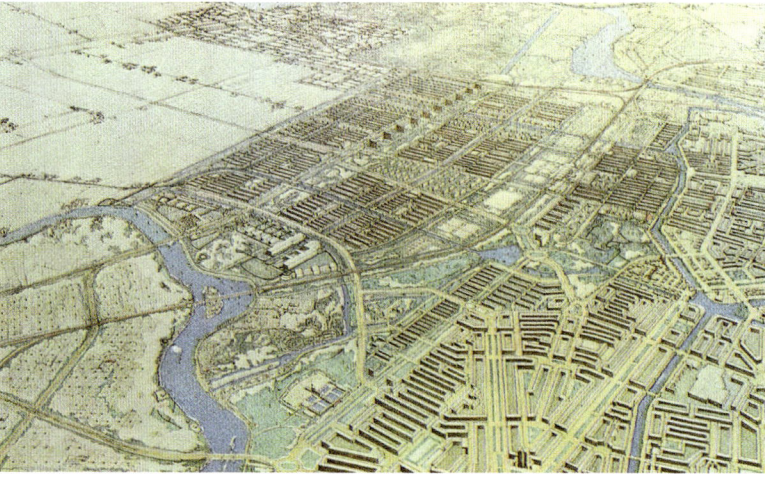

Figure 44.
Regulated Cities. Garden City. Westelijke Tuinsteden Expansion Plan. (Western Garden Cities) for the General Extension Plan of Amsterdam as conceived by Cor van Eesteren (President of CIAM) with the help of Th. K. van Lohuizen, 1935 (see Riedel 1906). The Western Garden Cities represented a development of Garden City ideals with the emergence of modernist architectural rationalization (Demerijn 2013).

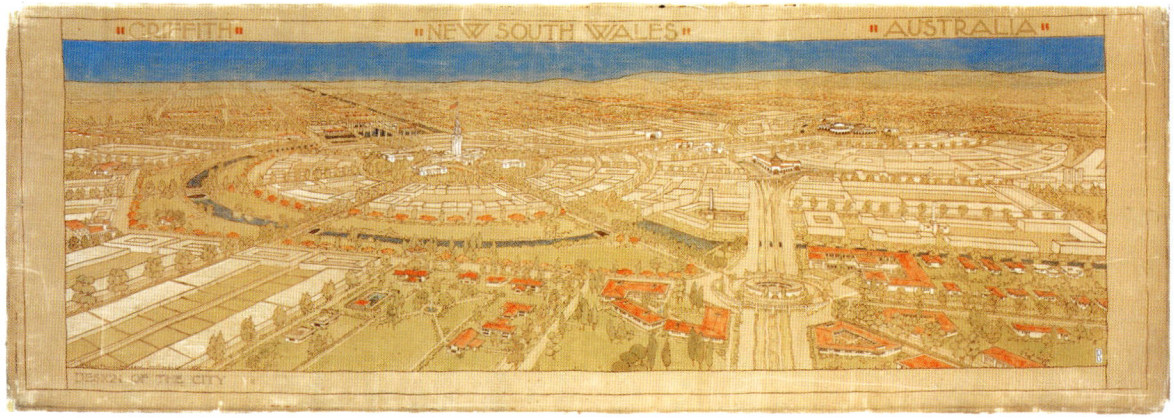

Figure 45.
Regulated Cities. Garden City. Walter Burley Griffin, The Silkscreen Plan of Griffith, commissioned by the Department of Water Resources – Lands Administration Branch – Water Conservation and Irrigation Commission in 1913. Town plan designed 1914. Walter Burley Griffin Society Incorporated Collection, courtesy Bob Meyer, State Archives and Records Authority of New South Wales. A city of 30,000 people named Griffith after Sir Arthur Griffith, Minister for Public Works. Courtesy of State Archives and Records Authority of New South Wales. The Grand Circle formed important structures of the city, commanding the commercial axis and dominating vistas in every direction.

in 1933 through the work of Walter Christaller (1933) and central place theory and later was considered as a system in Christopher Alexander's *A City Is Not a Tree* (1965).

With burgeoning cities across the world and an increasingly global perspective, Great Exhibitions and World Fairs were the ideal vehicles to display new technologies and outputs of national capitalism (Mattie 2000). Visionaries composited attributes from various regions, such as the work of Fritz Lang (Minden and Bachmann 2002) in the film *Metropolis* (1927) showing a future city set in 2026, using city miniatures [see figure 22, Chapter 1]. Such poetically constructed film sets echo with the vertical sketches of Hugh Ferriss in *The Metropolis of Tomorrow* (1929) in which Ferriss (1929: 124) renders existing skyscrapers, considers zoning regulations and then projects a medium-height city layout, bar large mass municipal towers and glass walls, 'Buildings like crystals. Walls of translucent glass . . . A mineral kingdom. Gleaming stalagmites. Formed as cold as ice. Mathematics. Night in the Science Zone.' Such monuments also appeared by Vladimir Tatlin in Monument to the Third International (1919 to 1920) and via photomontage in Dynamic City (1919) by Gustav Klutsis.

Congrès Internationaux d'Architecture Moderne (CIAM), founded in 1928 and run until 1959, formulated a modern architecture and gathered case studies of thirty-eight cities to which architecture would be presented as a radical force of urban planning. CIAM sought to address deficits in each of the cities based in large part on criticism of medieval city layouts (van Es et al. 2014; Mumford 2002). One of its chief protagonists, Le Corbusier, presented his own work, Ville Radieuse (The Radiant City) (1924) [figure 46] and The City of Tomorrow and Its Planning (1929), at CIAM and developed his ideas of the city as a highly centralized and densely populated landscape with infrastructures to enable rapid traffic flow and significant zones of parks and playing fields [figure 47]. The notion that harmony could be found within industrialization was not specific to his work but formed a preoccupation for various leading architects and urban designers of the era. The dominant paradigm of a Regulated City moved to embody or work interchangeably with another dominant paradigm, the Layered City which involved subsurfaces and vertical separation of people, resources and transportation

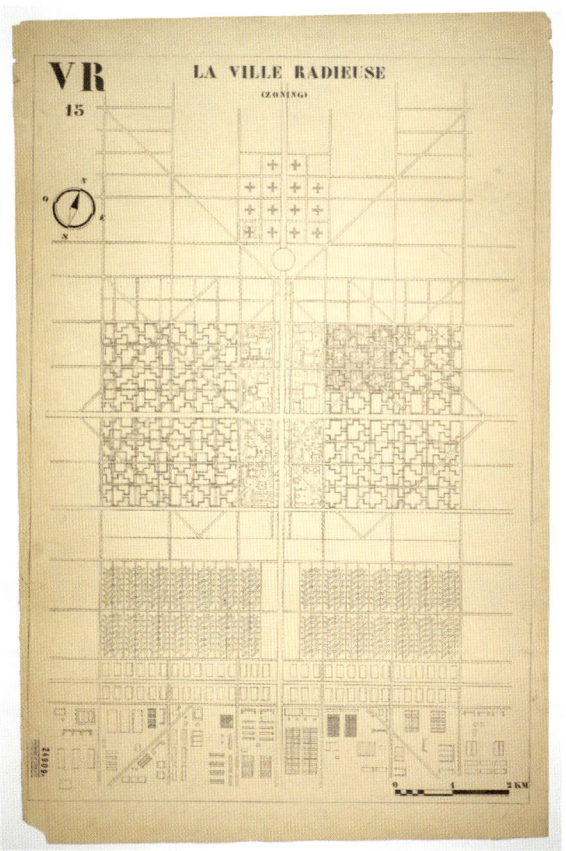

Figure 46. (left)
Regulated Cities. Divided City. Le Corbusier, Ville Radieuse, Not located, 1930, Courtesy of Fondation Le Corbusier / DACS. The buildings rest on ground floor columns, thus putting all of the land area at the disposition of pedestrians. The project is notable for its establishment of new dwelling *unités*, further emphasized by the clear separation of the automobile from pedestrian.

Figure 47. (below)
Regulated Cities. Divided City. Le Corbusier, Photograph of the Plan of Voisin (1925). Oeuvre Complét de (from complete works) 1910–1929, courtesy of Fondation Le Corbusier / DACS.

46   FUTURE CITIES: A VISUAL GUIDE

(Tafuri 1976). Technological advancements in building technology, coupled with political motives of architects to become central in planning processes, delivered radical proposals as in the case of Frank Lloyd Wright's Broadacre City (1932). As the antithesis to the verticality of Hugh Ferriss and Le Corbusier, Broadacre City proposed a decentralized, car-based, low-density settlement (Hall 2014: 341–6) [figure 48]. As Robert Fishman (1982: 163) has commented, Le Corbusier and Wright were destined for comparison in their opposite visions, but both shared a profound belief that industrialization was the agent for separating the city past into a fundamentally new configuration. In Wright's vision for the future city, citizens would have access to all required divisible services within a 150-mile

Figure 48.
Ecological Cities. Horizontal City. Frank Lloyd-Wright, Broadacre City Project (Model in four sections), 1934–1935, The Museum of Modern Art, New York (MoMA) Scala, Florence. The city and countryside through de-urbanization, decentralization which would provide a new democracy.

radius as part of a Usonian vision (1945: 65–6). In this scheme a twelve lane/level highway forms the primary infrastructure in which a city and its mobility will be formed implemented by the 'aerator', the equivalent of a contemporary quadcopter transporting passengers. Broadacre was a vision that required complete realization; city airspace and existing climate and topological conditions are glossed over in this vision, ideas that were subsequently developed further by Mikhail Aleksandrovich Okhitovich in the Soviet OSA group (Levine 2015).

Urbanism from the road and beyond

As part of the technological first wave, car-led urbanism would be one of the most influential factors of future city thinking in the early twentieth century. This future car urbanism can be seen in Geoffrey Jellicoe's *Motopia* published in 1959 with drawings from Gordon Cullen (Jellicoe 1961). With the increasing ownership of motor vehicles and the expansion of London, Jellicoe suggested a separation of transport through elevated auto ramps [see figure 89, Chapter 4]. The domination of the motor car on the American landscape was synonymous with the promotion of this future as a preferred vision of mobile, consumer-orientated, sophisticated lifestyles as depicted in Norman Bel Geddes's Futurama exhibit with architect Albert Kahn in the General Motors pavilion at the New York World's Fair in 1939. With parallels to Le Corbusier and Frank Lloyd Wright, the scale of the vision was breath-taking, with the thirty-six thousand-square-foot exhibit transporting five million visitors over a huge diorama of a future city of 1960 and its surrounding landscape which included over half a million individually designed buildings and fifty thousand miniature vehicles design by nearly two hundred craftsmen. The idea of an independent, car-based future and its implications on the urban landscape were inspiring and provided a blueprint for what would come, perhaps taken to its more extreme conclusion in cities such as Los Angeles. In retrospect, it is also possible to see that the wider ambition of the fair in presenting the 'World of Tomorrow' was a vision of hope to the Depression-weary nation of America where an end to economic hardship was on the horizon and the very real threat of escalating tensions in Europe seemed extremely distant. It was a transportation optimism that was not without criticism, as seen in the work of Jane Jacobs, *The Death and the Life of American Cities* (1961) and her urban activism in favour of high-density living, quality streets and neighbourhoods. Here visions clashed with abundance with visions of gentrification and urban renewal, most famously those of Robert Moses and his radical proposals for clearance of large swathes of New York City (Ballon and Jackson 2008) [figure 49].

In the late nineteenth and twentieth centuries, mobility through industrialization and regulatory urban forms coupled with increasing layering in the city, whether pedestrianized or car-based, led various attempts to try to explain and diagnose the complexity of cities and at the same time present their remediation, i.e. the city had to be rationalized for living in the future. The issues of how we might move around are often intrinsic to visions for future cities, more recently illustrated by either walkable, green-orientated depictions that promote well-being and active travel or the seemingly frictionless, sci-fi-style renderings used to communicate degrees of 'smartness' through integrated infrastructure and information communication technologies. The need for such bold visions was arguably welded to the devastation of the Second World War and the subsequent reconstruction and clearance of many cities that defined much of modernist planning and architecture (Ammon 2016; Klemek 2011). This need for radical proposals following periods of turmoil has led to numerous schemes including those responding to the effects of conflict [figure 50] and those which examine the role of architecture and political identity [figure 51].

This urgent need for visions to accommodate collective life was embraced by numerous figures around the world, not least Richard Buckminster Fuller in the United States. Fuller's geodesic structures were the realized form of his world view philosophy and comprehensive design science. He experimented with triangular stem structures to form a spherical dome

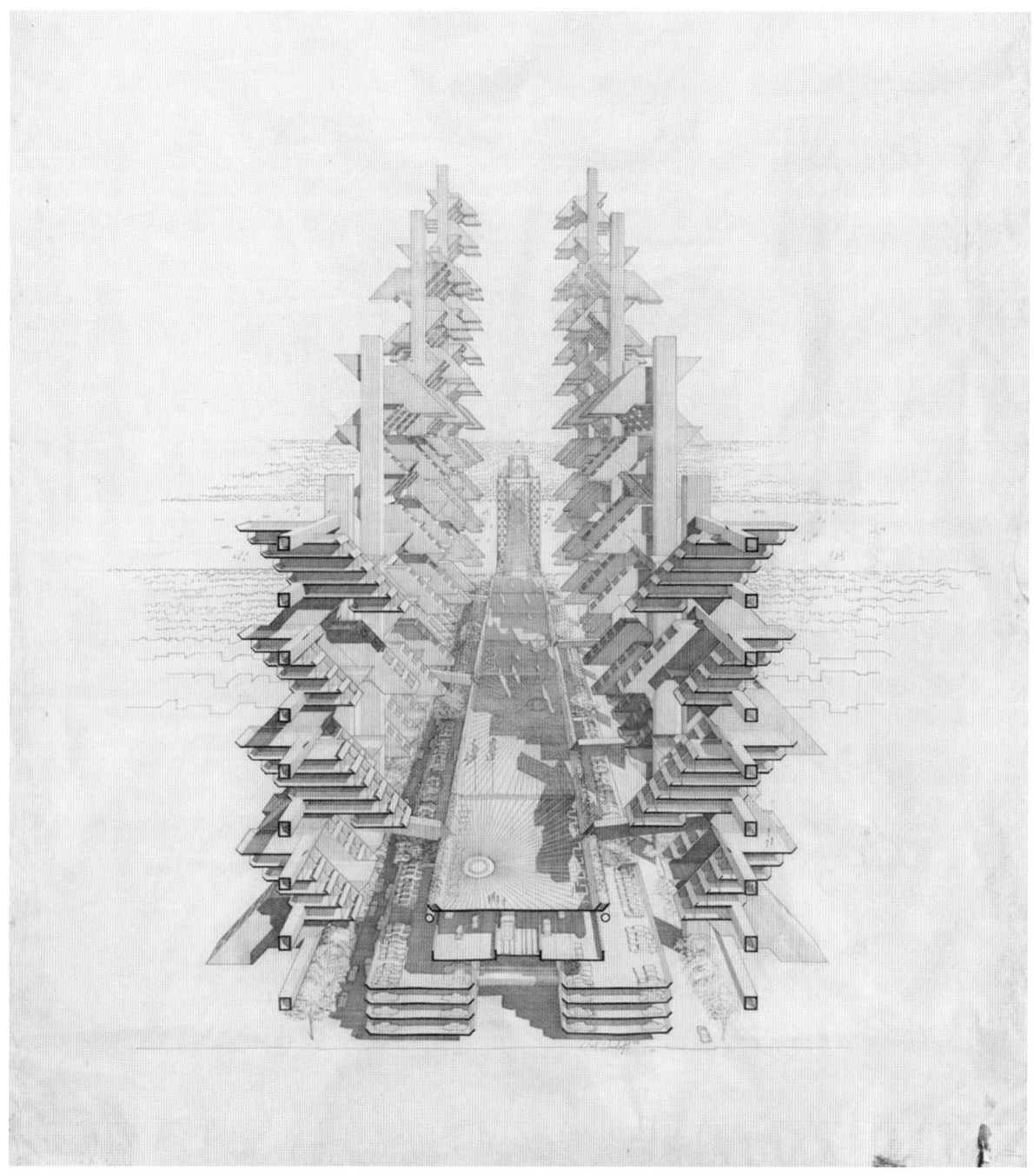

Figure 49.
Layered Cities. Horizontal City. Paul Rudolph, Lower Manhattan Expressway (LoMex), project. New York City. Perspective to the east, 1972. New York, Museum of Modern Art (MoMA). Ink and graphite on paper, 40 x 33 1/2' (101.6 x 85.1 cm). Gift of The Howard Gilman Foundation. 1290.2000 © 2018. Digital image, The Museum of Modern Art, New York /Scala, Florence. Rudolph's drawing for the LoMex proposes to integrate transport infrastructure with more socially connected higher levels of monorails and people movers.

Figure 50.
Layered Cities. Collage City. Arata Isozaki, Re-ruined Hiroshima Project. Hiroshima, Japan. Perspective, 1968, Museum of Modern Art (MoMA). Ink and gouache with cut-and-pasted gelatin silver print on gelatin silver print, 13 7/8 x 36 7/8" (35.2 x 93.7 cm). © 2018. Digital image, The Museum of Modern Art, New York/Scala, Florence. Isozaki Arata's montage projects new megastructures on the atomic plains of Hiroshima (Oshima 2009).

which provided increased strength and resilience and upscaled the geodesic dome to provide a proposal for a stabilized and protective environment. The efficiency of the material was indicative of Fuller's design philosophy and proved a key future vision of how we might live (Buckminster Fuller and Snyder 2009: 241–300) [see figure 17, Chapter 1]. During the same period over in Japan, a country recovering from the devastation of war and entering a phase of rapid economic growth, an increasing need for ideal cities to provide better communities became urgent and led to much spectacular exploration and proposals.

Figure 51.
Layered Cities. Collage City. Roel van Herpt, Daniele Belleri, Olena Grankina, Giulio Margheri, Nicolas Moore, Strelka Unsettled, 2014. Following a competition for the relocation of the Strelka Institute, the winning scheme proposes new scenarios for the disputed yet immense architectural legacy from the late Soviet period. Building on this architecture's powerful symbolism as 'an unpleasant reminder of the recent past', the project is a critical inquiry into ideology and its representation.

Most notably, the visions of Kisho Kurokawa, Kiyonori Kikutake, Fumihiko Maki and other architects who coalesced under the influence of Kenzo Tange formed the Metabolists around their ideas concerning organic biological growth intertwined with megastructures to produce a dynamic architecture and manifesto for future cities [figure 52]. Metabolism was deeply engaged with exploring new concepts for urban design and derived from a vision for architecture and cities that shared capabilities of living organisms to grow, reproduce and respond to their environments. The manifesto *Metabolism: The Proposals for New Urbanism* was published at the World Design Conference in Tokyo in 1960 and consisted of four essays: 'Ocean City', 'Space City', 'Towards Group Form', and 'Material and Man'. Their designs included proposals for huge floating cities and plug-in towers that could incorporate organic growth (Banham 1976; Lin 2007: 76–80). Following their influential work at the Osaka Expo in 1970, the Metabolists shifted their focus away from Japan and towards Africa and the Middle East.

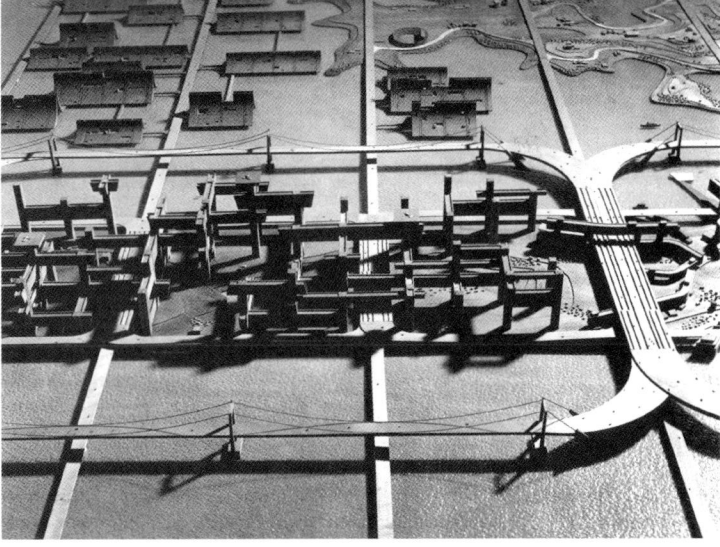

Figure 52.
Regulated Cities. Water City. Kenzo Tange, Plan for Tokyo, 1960. Photography: Akiko Kawasumi, Kobayashi Kenji Photograph Office. This vision for the future of Tokyo included floating residential cities, axial development linking to Fuji City and concentrated urban centres. The project took growth processes of biological organisms as a metaphor for urban futures, and the design was developed from photographs from a helicopter in 1956 (Kuan 2012).

This optimism and experimental research were also reflected back across the Pacific Ocean and seen in the desert town Arconsanti in Arizona by Paolo Soleri (1970) intended to house 1,500 inhabitants. Arconsanti is based on the principles of arcology – a portmanteau of 'architecture' and 'ecology', in which Soleri proposes megastructures that minimize land use and offer a living organic system as architecture supports and develops human ecology. These projects signalled an important era for visions of future cities. From Fuller to Tange and Soleri, an optimism of markedly different architectural intervention to radically shape the fragmentation of cities and bring about collectivity in a burgeoning city populace was increasingly framed to global and environmental understanding.

Visualizations are powerful media – for example, the understanding of the 'whole' earth as an environmental organism was a recent event which was communicated through media. Using V2 rockets which photographed the planet from one-hundred miles in space and later Cold War spy satellite documentation of cities from 1960 to 1972 to the 'Blue Marble' whole earth composite picture from Apollo 17 of 1972 [figure 53] enabled us to gain views of the world that had previously only existed in the imagination and artistic representations. Such photographs appeared in the countercultural 'Whole Earth' (1968 to 1998) catalogue by Stewart Brand which promoted early forms of art, design and ecology and had a profound effect on readers and designers (Brand 2010; Maniaque-Benton

Figure 53.
Hybrid Cities. Smart City. V2 Rocket, Launched White Sands, NASA, Johns Hopkins Applied Physics Laboratory, March 7, 1947. The rocket calibrated by engineer Clyde T. Holliday took the first photographs of space, and these appeared in 1950 in the National Geographic, a technological sublime (Edgington 2012).

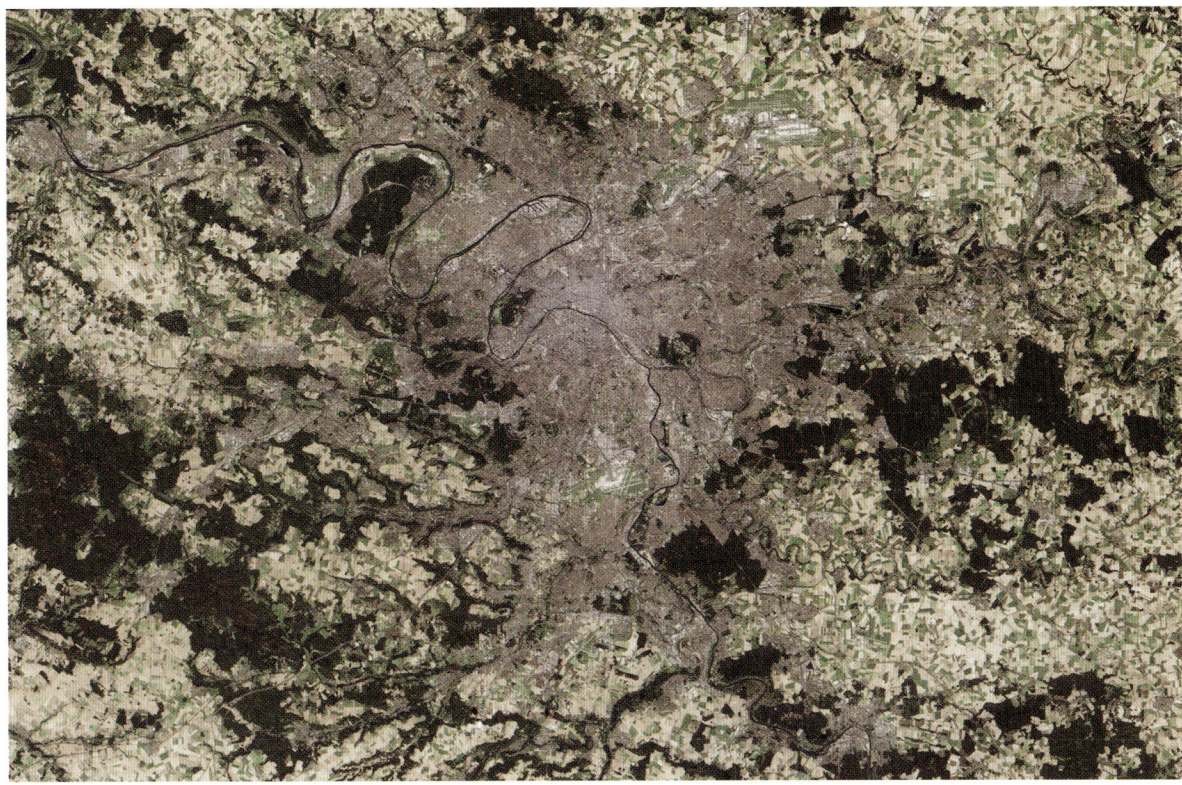

Figure 54.
Hybrid Cities. Smart City. Mega Cities Project, Paris, the mosaic based on data acquired on October 3 and October 11, 2015. Landsat 8. The aim of the project is to develop a global urban carbon monitoring emissions system. Pilot activities have already begun in the megacities of Los Angeles and Paris that build on existing research infrastructure there and collaborations between the teams involved. Discussions are also underway regarding inclusion of a third sister city, Sao Paulo in Brazil.

et al. 2016; Turner 2006). Urbanization as a profound force was also evidenced from 2000 through nighttime photography from the Defence Meteorological Satellites Program. Satellites offer a vision of our urban condition *now* or enable comparison with the relatively recent historical views of urban landscapes from the earliest remote sensed images of the 1960s. They help provide a scientific basis for the understanding of cities through visual material that has been critically evaluated (Jazairy 2011) [figure 54]. This form of material is very different from speculative and imaginary visions. But it does not mean that drawing or other media material can be discounted since, like satellites, drawings and other representational techniques were once the best technology available to describe topographies and cities and plan their future from the period of their creation. Satellites provided technological solutions to century-old concerns of making sense of a city and its full primary area, as seen in topographic studies of Venice, New Delhi and Strasbourg amongst countless others, but the extensive scale of their coverage is able to place cities in the context of conurbations, megalopolis, regions, nations and a more globalized world.

Visions for future cities exist because of a need or desire to project an alternative to how our built environment might be. The urban imagination is a powerful tool in directing this future [figure 55]. Architecture plays a key role in such visions, often working as a radical intervention to suggest new ways of living, moving and interacting in urban settings.

Figure 55.
Regulated Cities. Mechanical City. Hans Hollein, Aircraft Carrier City in Landscape. Project. Perspective 1964. Unbuilt. Museum of Modern Art (MoMA). Philip Johnson Fund. Acc. N.: 434.1967. © 2018. Digital image, The Museum of Modern Art, New York/Scala, Florence. From Hollein's series Transformations, 1963–1968. In the series, an agricultural or urban landscape, often barren, is the site for a monumental industrial object. Hollein used machine technology – sparkplug, boxcar and, here, aircraft carrier – to create a pure, absolute architecture with no identifiable architectonic style. The provocation confounds common understandings of what it means to build in the contemporary landscape.

Cities of vision can range from the complete and holistic reimagining of a new environment for the complexity of urban life to smaller scale projects that seek to address specific areas or aspects of it. Many of these visions arose from intense periods of conflict, rapid urbanization, social and political tension, or environmental destruction. It is also possible to see that a number of these visions for cities are driven by a specific context and set of local issues, whether cultural, political, social or environmental (or a combination of these), whilst others are more utopian in their approach and intended to potentially be sited in different situations. In this chapter we have encountered a range of ideologies embedded in visions for future cities and how in promoting certain elements, others by definition are obscured, discredited or less obvious. However, we have not examined how the technique through which the visualization is produced, i.e. the mode of representation, contributes to this process. It is also interesting to investigate whether different representational techniques have been attached to particular ideologies and what the motivations behind these relationships might be. This naturally leads us to the next chapter where we will consider the various media employed to create visions of future cities.

Chapter 3

Rendering Tomorrow: The impact of visualization techniques

Representing the future city

The representation of cities is intrinsically linked to the type of media used and its context within wider culture and society (Allen 1999; Brooker 2002; Marcus and Neumann 2008). The translation from image to edifice is partially borne of the way in which the image is constructed and how it codifies information to draw in the viewer and enable him or her to connect to various visual cues within the image to make it legible. As such, even the most radical future visions typically reference an element of geospatial information or built form – future cities present archaeology of concepts and existing conditions from which they have sprung. For example, *Altered Carbon* (2018), Netflix's cyberpunk series, presents a neo-Tokyo super-city set in 2384 which draws on a notable lineage including *Blade Runner* (1982), *Ghost in the Shell* (1996) and many other sources whilst also echoing contemporary technological developments through its evolved architectural forms and techno-projections such as autonomous vehicles, personal devices and artificial intelligence [figure 56]. Film media translates well from literature with works such as Aldous Huxley's *Brave New World* (1932) and George Orwell's *1984* (1949) amongst many others which provide rich sources for social and anthropological science fiction. Such dystopian sci-fi is reliant on a critical rendering of a plausible environment, which contains the grit and realism of our perceptions of hyper-developed cities in the age of global capitalism. This plausibility has enabled writers to employ fictional narrative devices to enhance public understanding of key scientific issues concerning the built environment (Billing 2011), produce insightful nonfiction (Anderson 2015), or combine this approach with factual information as a creative and effective method of speculation (Frase 2016).

This is the difference between the visualization of future cities and pure abstraction; there is an element of mining our past in the rendering of futures. Future urban life has been envisaged across a range of media, yet there is not an immediately identifiable pattern between image content and the method of production. Methods of production might be in place for differing purposes such as establishing narrative and atmosphere

Figure 56.
Hybrid Cities. Cyber City. Altered Carbon, Skydance Productions, LLC, 2018. Set in 2384, the dense Vertical City depicted here is a dystopian future city. It draws on cyberpunk and hacker cultures with its grim street level of peculiarities, vices and violence wrapped in AIs and noir tech. The majority of the inhabitants are segregated from the city's oligarchy who reside in Aerium, literally beyond the clouds above.

in cinema (Gold 2001). The composite process for creating future cities in film may draw on a variety of techniques including pre-built or digital procedural models of cities, buildings, people, and places which are brought together in time-lapse footage. Individually these elements in themselves have symbolic meanings and when composed together form powerful urban rubrics of plausible city environments.

Within these rubrics, images reflect broader attitudes towards society, and architecture's position within it, and thus draw in contemporary ideas about transportation, density, and social life and have specific identifiable qualities. In 1953, Ivan Chtcheglov's Formulary for a New Urbanism proclaimed, 'architecture is the simplest means of articulating time and space, of modulating reality, of engendering dreams' (Knabb 2007: 3). This proclamation raises issues that are fundamental to this book. Through imaginative projection, Chtcheglov sought to explore the possibilities and nature of what cities were and how they might be envisioned through radical spatial reconfiguration, across time, coupled with behavioural transformation. In Vladimir Tatlin's quest to find a suitable expression for his Monument to the Third International, the medium was a critical decision, and he developed full-scale laboratory material models for the infamous exhibition of 1917. For Alexander Rodchenko, it was graphic methodologies of juxtaposition and composition through photomontage that provided the constructivist manifesto for the contemporary call for the 'organisation of life' (Rodchenko 1921). Futurism as Franco 'Bifo' Berardi (2011: 17) states during the twentieth century in both Italian and Russian forms 'was the leading force of imagination and project, giving birth to the language of commercial advertising . . . and to the language of political agit-propaganda'. Berardi defines the epoch in three imaginative futures: a modernist utopian imagination from the 1900s, a predominant dystopian imagination from the 1970s, and cyberculture and then a return to an imaginative malaise from geo-political, hyper-mobilized and techno-saturated future shock

2000s; this affirms his belief that the future is over. While Bifo is concerned with global capitalism and the socio-political landscape and futures or meta-utopias, much of this agency has derived from avant-garde movements and individuals using representational tools. It is therefore worth examining the different modes of representation and their impact on the way in which future cities have been visualized – the agency of media is a critical factor in our 'reality tunnels' (Wilson 2016). Reality tunnels as a theory suggest that through an abundance of sensory input, a mental filtration scheme operates from beliefs and experiences to make sense of these inputs, resulting in a construction of reality; these are often different and malleable. By comparison George Lakoff's work and his writings on the use of metaphors are a conceptual construction, and as Sonja Hnilica has shown, metaphors are often used in the understanding and design of cities (Hnilica 2012; Lakoff and Johnson 2003).

The legibility of urban space and cities has been explored through various mapping practices (Brook and Dunn 2011; Lynch 1995, 1960; Sadler 1998) as well as through an understanding of the relationship between branding and city image (Klingmann 2007). This chapter also discusses the failure of the future, in the translation of media. For example, the demolition of Minoru Yamasaki's Pruitt-Igoe, St Louis, Missouri, in 1973 was cited by Charles Jencks as the failure of architectural modernism. Futures such as Pruitt-Igoe did not translate well into built form due to construction complexities, cost-cutting measures by the Public Housing Authority, and large variations and critically omitted elements. Such a project would be ideally suited as a model for criticism of utopian modernism even though the circumstances around this much-publicized collapse are far more complex than Jencks's signposting suggests, as explored in the documentary *The Pruitt-Igoe Myth* (2011). Likewise, Bijlmermeer, a housing estate on the outskirts of Amsterdam in 1966, became the victim of autocratic management and suffered from a lack of cohesion over its modernist design (Vanstiphout and Provoost 2007). The construction and rationales of future city proposals require investigation, but the transition from speculation to the lived experience of realized designs also needs to be taken into account, alongside the falsehoods and myths written about such projects in the search for scapegoats of a failed future (Gyure 2018).

The various recent spins of urbanist agendas – New Urbanism (CFTNU and Talen 2013), Landscape Urbanism (Waldheim 2006, 2016), Tactical Urbanism (Gadanho and Lowry 2014; Lydon and Garcia 2015) and Lean Urbanism (Duany et al. 2010) – as many before them, seek planning and design solutions for cities' urban ills. These various movements and ideas have been executed at different scales with various governance structures each with their own successfully realized projects. Although they may signal wider applicability for future cities, it is important to recognize their specificity as each is seeking different, radical or incremental methods to deal with modern city complexity.

Digital faith and the forgotten fingertips

The draftsperson according to Oliver Regan in the journal *Pencil Points*:

> should be, in a real sense, a part of himself, an extension of his hand. It seems as through one of the first things a draftsman should make an effort to acquire is an acute sense of the feel of his pen or pencil on the paper, a delicacy of touch that is unlike that of a skilled surgeon who is said to be able to almost 'see' with his fingertips (Hartmann and Cigliano 2002: 6).

Visions of cities have been attached to the media in which they are created. The pencil so often attached to fine motoring skills in academic and play-based activities can be seen as an extended tool in the visualization of concepts. As Oliver Regan alludes, the act of drafting is a sort of interplay between responding to the haptics of the surface being inscribed. In addition to this action of drafting, the late architectural historian Robin Evans (1996: 165) has stated the principle of the reverse directionality of drawing – 'the subject matter (the building or space) will exist after the drawing, not before it'. A drawing in the creation of future cities, therefore, is the primary source of much of the visual history of future cities. It is the point of emergence and has an alluring poetic in this very agency. For example, the static nature of grid city layouts due to their intensely regulated form through planning covenants and conservation, more often than not, in the reality of inhabiting these places, closely resembles the urban form of its drawn plan from its inception. Whether residents believe that utopian vision after residing there is another matter! The concept agency flows towards inscription and authorship on a paper surface and following Evans's principle is realized. The agency of visualizations of future cities is of course complex, even more so as generative systems of design have come more to the fore, as William Mitchell's (1979) early text on computer-aided design (CAD) discusses the contemporary possibilities of CAD in the late 1970s and attempted to plot its future possibilities. Technological developments in visual architectural production have developed dramatically; that does not mean to say that earlier renderings of cities have become redundant, but many contemporary works have various levels of immersion, virtualized or augmented as in the case of the nature/tech cult AUJIK and its Augmented Graffiti projects in Eindhoven (2018) [figure 57].

Increasingly the city is computational in everyday life and in its design (Greenfield 2017). Sketchpad (1963) by Ivan Sutherland is poignant in computer development history. Sketchpad, based on the idea of napkin sketches which required refinement to more finished engineering drawings, formed the idea of the invention of the programme. Working with a light pen, predecessor of the mouse, the user could point with the pen and interact with lines displayed

Figure 57.
Layered Cities. Cyber City. AUJIK, Spatial Bodies, 2016. Spatial Bodies depicts the urban landscape and architectural bodies as an autonomous living and self-replicating organism in Tokyo and Osaka, Japan. It is domesticated and cultivated only by its own nature with vast concrete vegetation, oscillating between order and chaos.

on the screen (Sutherland [1963] 2003: 3). In 1966/8 Sutherland and Bob Sproull also developed a head-mounted display called The Sword of Damocles, one of the first functional augmented reality (AR) and virtual reality (VR) machines following earlier prototypes by Morton Heilig (Kipper and Rampolla 2012; Azuma 1997). These early prototypes gave rise to parametric architecture, virtual modelling reliant on constraints and calculations which computes a form, with early proponents such as Greg Lynn (1997, 1998) and later Patrik Schumacher and the Architectural Association school in 2008. Experiments in cyberspace such as Marcus Novak's liquid architectures from 1995 onwards, alongside contemporaries such as Nox (Spuybroek 2004, 2016), played a significant role in developing the potential of computational design techniques. These sources and projects were part of a new digital faith, which had implications for future city generation enabled through generative and digital design establishing a dominant paradigm of architectural visualization and production.

Writing cities

The depiction of future city scenarios has also been a strong, recurrent theme in utopian and dystopian fiction, including the highly influential Bellamy's (1888) *Looking Backward* and Forster's (1909) 'The Machine Stops', via Zamyatin's (1921) *We* and Gibson's (1984) *Neuromancer* and the various environmental and technological apocalypses of J. G. Ballard such as *The Drowned World* (1962) [figure 58] and *High Rise* (1975) amongst many others. Respectively, city futures has a continuous presence through to early twenty-first-century literary works that have examined the relationship of digital code and physical place (Perng 2016) or the rebuilding of cities as cut and paste urbanism in an age of ecological disaster (Boudinot 2012). As Murray Bell and Goodwin (2012) have observed, the power of creative writing and its relationship with the built environment is perhaps stronger than it has ever been. Recently, it has been used to innovative effect by Porritt (2013) to describe

Figure 58.
Informal Cities. Water City. Squint/Opera Ltd. Flooded London: St Mary Woolnath, 2008. This project displayed five images of 'Flooded London' in 2090, depicting the inhabitants' adaptations to a near-deserted city where an office block in Canary Wharf is a place to go fishing. The images are reminiscent of Ballard's *The Drowned World* in which main character Keran's psychotic 'time jungle dreams' emerge from the habituation of the Ritz in London and his viewpoint of a series of lagoons and a glaring Triassic sun.

an imaginative yet viable post-carbon future. Oldfield Ford (2011), meanwhile, has revitalized the practice of urban walking through her series of graphic novellas describing the socio-spatial remnants of late capitalist Britain. Indeed, the adaptation of Ballard's *High Rise* into a recent film directed by Ben Wheatley (2015) [figure 59] resonates with London's ever-congested skyline and critical debates about segregation in housing developments (Legeby 2010). The cinematic experience of *High Rise* is a sort of nostalgic turning over of post-war utopian visions and architecture, which simulates their apparent failure, recast into strong dystopian scenarios. This post-modernist version revels in retro and pastiche readings of architectural history, in a relativistic manner distorting the time and experience of any audiences who have experience of the everyday life of New Towns or the resettlement programs (Mittner 2018). Ballard's original novel and the post-war optimism of modernist concrete via Brutalism, Alison and Peter Smithson and the criticism of Reyner Banham are a strong set of sources for multimedia comparisons between literature and the moving image. As Jameson (2007) has carefully marked, writings on utopias are heavily intertextual – it's the genre requiring comparison. Like all utopias, these cities of tomorrow were naturally imbued with the biases, values, and priorities of their creators, and not necessarily those of the people who would ultimately inhabit them. The process of embedded values and experiences could be reflected in Stanley Kubrick's (1971) adaption of Anthony Burgess's *A Clockwork Orange* (1962) [figure 60], which was filmed on the Thamesmead Estate, Woolwich, Wandsworth and Aylesbury in the UK amongst other locations. The film's locations were endemic of the UK's post-war brutalism and material technological devotion best evidenced by the singular scope of *Concrete Quarterly* from 1947 and its material obsession, but also the environment in which Burgess would write a city of ultraviolence, youth culture, and state psychiatry and totalitarianism. The writing about cities and its relationship with architecture and design concepts is important to understand as essential to their reading. The ideas of cities as they translate into their respective outputted media act as memory call, compress and or hold time these very concepts (Pallasmaa 2011: 78).

Figure 59.
Regulated Cities. Vice City. *High Rise*, Directed by Ben Wheatley, 2016, © RPC High-Rise Limited, The British Film Institute, Channel Four Television Corporation. Christophel / Scala, Florence. Here the supposed concrete utopia is a Brutalist Vertical City of two thousand residences, with its main protagonists beginning as a suburban middle class, journeying and degrading to primitives who resort to violence, factions and gangs. *High Rise* was inspired by the Balfron Tower, London designed by Ernő Goldfinger (1963) as well as the theories of Oscar Newman.

Figure 60.
Layered Cities. Vice Cities. *A Clockwork Orange*, 1971. Real Stanley Kubrick. Malcolm McDowell. © Warner Bros / Hawk films. Christophel / Scala, Florence. The narrative presents a dystopian view of social upheaval and gang violence and delinquency. The backdrop of political and psychological rehabilitation of the gangs after a series of crimes sits between Huxley's (1932) *Brave New World* and Orwell's (1949) *1984* control narratives.

The intrinsic relationship between factual writing on cities and architectural concepts that are developed in fiction is reciprocal and often powerful. For example, marine biologist and conservationist Rachel Carson's *Silent Spring* (1962) and its scientific discussion of negative ecological, human impacts and biocides would influence the writing of *Dune* by Frank Herbert (1965). Herbert's series of science fiction novels dealt with planetary ecology and dryland environments and a complex political power base of competing for institutional houses and corporate forms that was later produced in a film in 1984 by David Lynch and then as a series of computer games beginning in 1992. Such a conceptual legacy appears in Magnus Larsson's Anti-desertification 6000km Green-wall to constrain the Sahara (2011) [figure 61] as well as Matsys [see figure 162, Chapter 6]. In renderings of tomorrow, complex projected visions contain rich streams and develop ideas with both artistic and scientific bases [figure 62] and/or associations that resonate or sometimes compare, develop or pay homage.

The portrayal of future cities in graphic novels has also proved to be a rich seam of illustrative speculations on urban living and built form (Ahrens and Meteling 2010) as well as a vehicle for the retelling of the social history of a city (Talbot 2007). The Chicago Architecture Foundation programme *No Small Plans* (Lyon and Lin 2017) sought visions of Chicago's future

Figure 61.
Ecological Cities. Desert City. Magnus Larsson, Dune anti-desertification architecture, 2008, Courtesy of LafargeHolcim Foundation for Sustainable Construction, Switzerland. The project explores innovative solutions to combat desertification in the Sahel region of Africa where moving sand dunes ruin the land and make inhabitation of the landscape highly challenging. The structure is made out of the desert itself, sand-stopping devices made of sand: a poetic proposal that simultaneously works in a sustainable way with local materials and assets.

through consultation with schools and community groups over five years [figure 63] and was based on *Wacker's Manual* (1911), written by Walter D. Moody, a classroom text explaining Daniel Burnham and Edward Bennett's 1909 Plan of Chicago. The outputs from the Chicago Architecture Foundation were redistributed to learning providers to allow a real discussion about the new possibilities of its future form. Likewise, in Pushwagner's *Soft City*, dystopian car urbanism becomes a pervasive force as everyday life is conducted from within the confines of vehicles [see figure 8, Chapter 1]. Fiction has shown itself to be a critical medium in the rendering or plausibility of future city visions having a profound influence on the construction and design of visual media. While printed fiction has a unique influence on future city proposals, writing has of course also rendered the theoretical framework in which to understand the city.

Manhattan, Manhattan, Manhattan!

Emerging from Chicago and New York, technological developments and industrial progress led to the first skyscrapers creating the symbolic power of cities

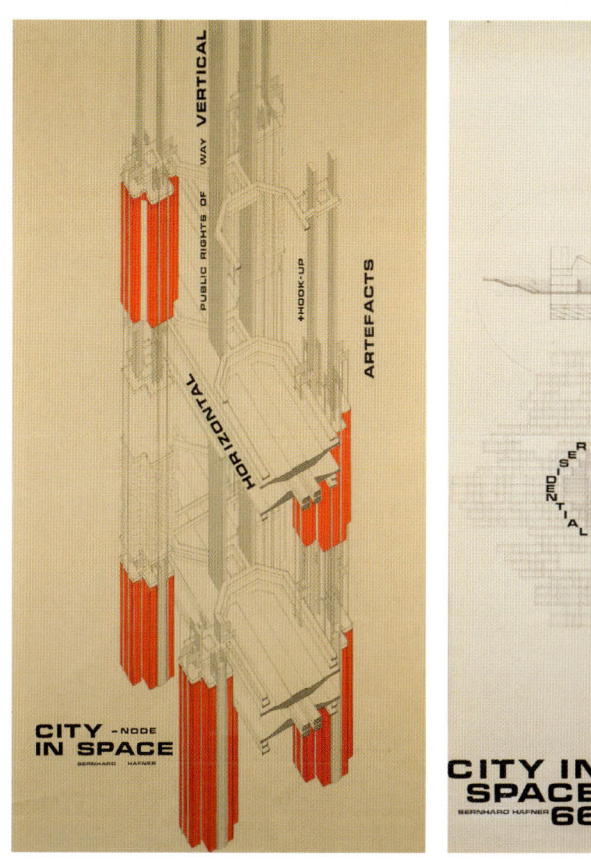 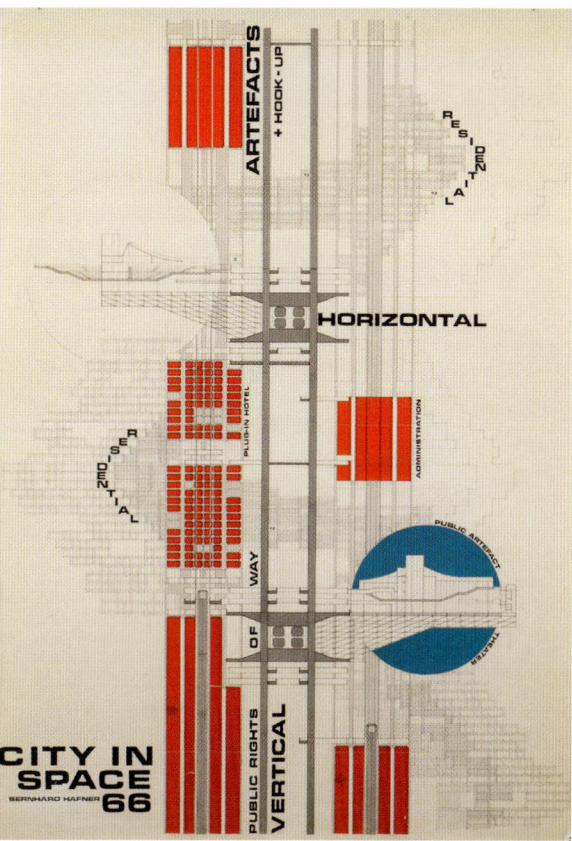

Figure 62.
Layered Cities. Sky City. Bernhard Hafner, City in Space, 1966. Collection Frac Centre-Val de Loire. Hafner's Space City sought networked infrastructures of interlinked communication nodes. A central vertical core offshoots the public, and residential spaces are axonametically floating in space, which can be continuously expanded. Hafner influenced Huth and Domenig for Städt Ragnitz (1963 to 1969) [see figure 83, Chapter 4] and contributed to the emergence of the TU Graz School, Austria.

[figure 64]. Manhattan today is the second city in the world with the highest skyscrapers; it is an excellent case study in which to chart various visions over a century and the changing formal, social, and functional configurations of designers and how they foresee this environment [figures 65 & 66], from the haunting charcoals of Hugh Ferriss [figure 67], tied with the American Institute of Steel Construction, to popular cultural works from *Just Imagine* (1930) via *Escape from New York* (1981) [figure 68] and Tim Burton's *Batman* (1989) to the post-apocalyptic *I Am Legend* (2007) or 'found footage' of its destruction in *Cloverfield* (2008). For such a small area of New York, Manhattan has generated a century of fascination into the verticality and symbolism of a modern Western city. When appearing in popular culture, such environmental projections are critically attached to narrative and context in which its characters perform, concretizing the future. Borne from new industrial techniques in skyscraper production, Louis Sullivan's column-frame and functionalist skyscrapers, amongst others, would mark a burgeoning modernist verticalism (Cruickshank 2018). Skyscrapers

Figure 63.
Informal Cities. Haptic City. Chicago Architecture Foundation, *No Small Plans*, Gabrielle Lyon, Devin Mawdsley, Kayce Bayer, Chris Lin, Deon Reed, pp. 39 & 89, 2017. © The Chicago Architecture Foundation. *No Small Plans* is a graphic novel that traces the journeys of teens in three phases: Chicago's past, present and future. The teens attempt to shape the future of the city in their needs. The graphic novel has been distributed across classrooms today. It was based on *Wacker's Manual* (1911), by Walter D. Moody, a classroom text explaining Daniel Burnham and Edward Bennett's 1909 Plan of Chicago with a series of aerial and perspective renderings.

Figure 64. (facing page)
Layered Cities. Mechanical City. Moses King, Future New York, circa 1915. © Mary Evans Picture Library. Future New York will be pre-eminently the city of skyscrapers – and of noise, what with the elevated railway passing your window and the aircraft flying low overhead.

64   FUTURE CITIES: A VISUAL GUIDE

Figure 65.
Layered Cities. Crossing City. Anderson Isometric Maps, 1971, Pictorial map of Manhattan with the buildings rendered as a bird's-eye view in separated isometric perspective. David Rumsey Map Collection, www.davidrumsey.com

benefitted from both the efficiency of the footprint of a building and also the elevation and detachment of its occupants to street level cultures as well as the corporate iconography. The natural move to build on a Z-axis catered to a new density in a burgeoning city. The island's geographical position and grid layout between the Hudson and East Rivers over a century would see continuous change, one of a variety of factors that lead to why Manhattan remains a compelling motif. In *Delirious New York*, Rem Koolhaas ([1978] 1994: 10) [figure 69] states that Manhattan is the product of an unformulated theory – 'Manhattans whose program – to exist in a world fabricated by man, i.e. to live inside fantasy – was so ambitious that to be realized, it could never be openly stated.' Manhattan led Koolhaas to assert that it is the retainer of global models of cities and precedents. The Commissioners' Plan of 1811 of a street grid provided Cartesian freedom of movement and mobility but at the same time led to criticism that architects became limited by block systems and zoning. From this tension, the fight for the future materialized in the Copenhagen method, scenario planning with

Figure 66.
Layered Cities. Crossing City. New York. 1982 Citivues International, Inc. Bird's-eye view pictorial map of Manhattan from above 5th Avenue and 59th Street, looking towards the southwest and lower Manhattan, with many landmarks, elevated railroads, streets and buildings. Includes text and inset of the global depiction of the Western Hemisphere. David Rumsey Map Collection, www.davidrumsey.com

Figure 67.
Regulated Cities. Divided City. Hugh Ferriss, Imaginary drawings, Zoning ordinances, 1922–1924. © Hugh Ferriss architectural drawings and papers, 1906–1980, Avery Architectural & Fine Arts Library, Columbia University. Ferriss sketched the volume and height attributes, giving mass to the legal frames in which architects would subsequently sculpt the future city. Massing studies and zoning continue to be fundamental tools in planning and architectural dialogues.

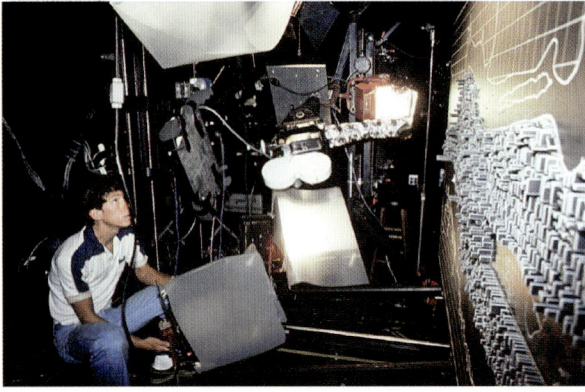

Figure 68.
Regulated Cities. Divided City. *Escape from New York*, John C. Wash, Mark Stetson, Hoyt Yeatman, Scott Squires, et al., 1981. Courtesy of John Wash. © Studio Canal. In this film, directed by John Carpenter, the protagonist initially navigates a glider over Manhattan, which has become a prison colony enclosed by the Hudson and East Rivers, with its access bridges fortified. A captivating sequence provides a topographical overview of Manhattan's grandeur. The ingenious visual effects by John Wash created a wireframe pilot's display by filming a physical model of Manhattan.

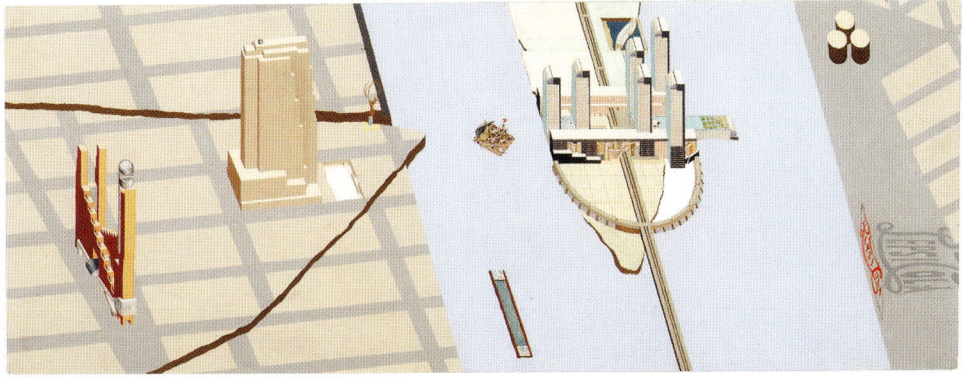

Figure 69.
Regulated Cities. Crossing City. Rem Koolhaas, OMA, New Welfare Island, 1975. Collection Frac Centre-Val de Loire. Featured in the text Delirious New York ([1978] 1994). The theoretical New Welfare Island Project is for the southern half of Roosevelt Island (once called Welfare Island).

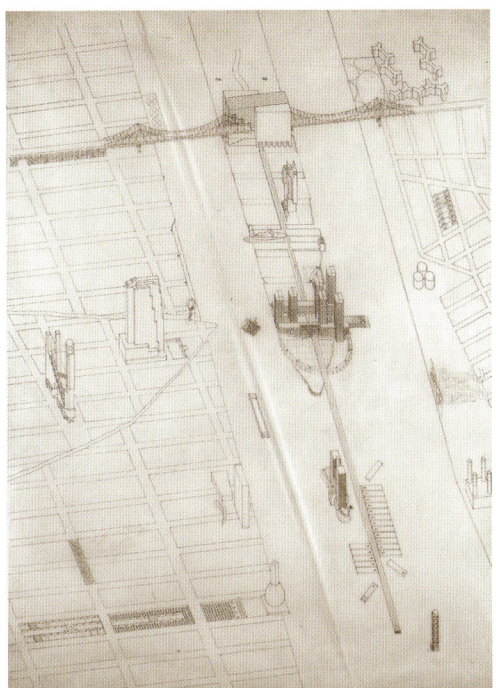

Figure 70.
Layered Cities. Mechanical City. Hans Hollein, Urban Renewal in New York Project, New York, Aerial perspective, New York, Museum of Modern Art (MoMA). Cut-and-pasted photograph on a photograph. Philip Johnson Fund. Acc. N.: 433.1967. © 2018. Digital Image, The Museum of Modern Art, New York/Scala, Florence. Photomontage as a form of speculation and experimentation, as well as Hollein's draftsmanship, created stark juxtapositions of material and industrial material.

dialogue- and collaborative-based approaches which led to the pedestrianization of Times Square based on NYC Department of Transportation data modelling (Mumford 1968: 425; Montgomery 2013: 228–32). While this particular case speaks more of urban governance, the inhabited space is the result of competing embodied urban ideas that materialize both its global precedents and influence. The architectural model has a rich history, and in Manhattan's case, its prototype is tested in theory [figure 70] and reality as many projects have illustrated through to the present day [figure 71].

Figure 71.
Ecological Cities. Crossing City. Manuel Herz Architects 2018. 'City of Things' perspective from the Storefront for Architecture Exhibition. © Manuel Herz Architects. Drawing on Bruno Latour's concept of 'Parliament of Things', Herz declares the future of Manhattan where all things, animate and inanimate, are given a right to be represented. Cars are not used anymore, freeing up an additional 50 per cent of space for novel use. It provides a habitat for a new fauna and flora to develop.

Techno clarity and the off-world future city

The role of architectural representation of cities has changed. In part, these toolsets have awakened some future off-world projections, often drawing influence from the growth of ecological awareness alongside new cybernetics. Future city visions are often part of a colonial impulse packaged with technological speculation as in Marshall T. Savage's *Millennial Project* (Savage and Clarke 1995) in which a series of steps towards off-world habitats is established starting with aquatic cities, new methods of space launch, orbiting habitats, moon ecospheres, terraforming Mars and the solar system. It is an interesting exploratory engineering text packed with scientific and futurist references; the first stage of Savage's book concerning marine inhabitation has found some basis of development in work of the SeaSteading Institute (SeaSteading n.d.). Floating Cities are not just containers for architectural exploration, as Phillip Steinberg et al. (2012: 1541) has stated:

> Seasteading seeks to rework these unstable and contradictory relationships between notions of individual sovereignty, state

sovereignty, and territorial inviolability by designating marine space as 'aquatory', an epistemic connector that builds on the lineage of social and political-economic reformers who have sought to use the liminal political, geophysical, and cultural status of the sea to construct heterotopic societies that are partially inside, but partially outside the structures of the state system.

Artificial islands have popularly surfaced as a reoccurring theme in which to explore new governance structures, ideologies and ways of life [figure 72] as Jackson and della Dora (2009: 2097) observe: '[artificial] island utopias today are explicit both in their efforts to territorialize themselves as parts of wider global complexes and in their promises to bring a future promise to fruition'. The renderings of Floating Cities seek to provide plausibility of a floating habitat, sometimes regardless of incredible technical challenges (Barker and Coutts 2016; Olthuis and Keuning 2010), and many seek to disguise that floating habitats have mainly derived from military intervention in the creation of floating fortifications such as the Maunsell Forts (Turner 1996).

One ecologically driven vision for an aquatic future city was Autopia Ampere (1978) [figure 73]. This proposal by the late seascape architect Wolf Hilbertz with the coral scientist Dr Thomas Goreau invented Biorock™, a mineral accretion technology which fast grows coral and repairs damaged reefs (Goreau 2005). Given the technological potential, Autopia Ampere was seen as a city grown from the sea which utilized cybernetics to evolutionarily expand and support its inhabitants. The Aquarian city was rendered utilizing ocean thermal energy conversion (OTEC) energy converters. Biorock was used as a superstructure material and also its key city export alongside algae farming and novel synthetic food production. Biorock sites have been tested in various locations including the Caribbean and Thailand. Such a genus of sea-based city visions appear, and ways of engaging with marine habitats also appeared in Ant Farm's Dolphin Embassy (1974 to 1978) [see figure 118, Chapter 5], a radical proposal to explore two-way dolphin and human communication. Many of Ant Farm's drawings were destroyed in a fire, but their influence and ideas have been revisited, most recently as 3-C. CITY: Climate, Convention, and Cruise by WORKac (2015) [figure 74] which amalgamated Ant Farm's most well-known projects – House of the Century (1971 to 1973), Dolphin Embassy and Convention City (1976) (Lewallen and Seid 2004). Much of the collective's work sought alternative architectural and graphic expressions as they fully embraced the new media technologies of their era to simultaneously convey their ideas in typically excessive fashion and also question the prevailing consumerist culture of the United States.

Beyond our oceans and the planet's surface, the colonization of outer space has also provided considerable inspiration for future cities [figures 75 & 76]. Literal translation of sci-fi tropes can be seen in the drawings and the thirteen realized biomes of the RMF FM Media Complex near Krakow, Poland, a film production site with the exterior and interiors of a degraded space station, a sort of realized *Silent Running* (1972), the post-apocalyptic environmentalism dystopian film. These off-world spaces and sealed ecological environments such as Biosphere 2, Oracle, Arizona (1991, 1994) all sought to conduct scientific experiments and speculations of future ecosystem services. Many of these sources form a dominant paradigm of the Ecological City and emerged from a burgeoning environmental awareness in the late 1960s from Leopold, Carson, and Tansley and in Landscape Architecture from Ian Mcharg which later formed from the early 1990s to specifically focus on urban ecology (Grove et al. 2017). This ecological awareness emerged in architecture through John Frazer's *An Evolutionary Architecture* (1995) amongst many other sources. In some projects, the challenges of how our species might survive and thrive off-earth have been explored through speculation on how to recreate favourable ecological conditions on other planets [figure 77].

Figure 72.
Ecological Cities. Waste City. Mitchell Joachim, Terreform ONE, Post Carbon City State: Rezoned Circular Economy, 2015. This project illustrates a future Manhattan that is partially submerged by rising sea levels due to climate change, with a new city built in the surrounding East and Hudson Rivers. New bulk/use zoning envelopes maximize solar exposure, regulate population size and optimize resources.

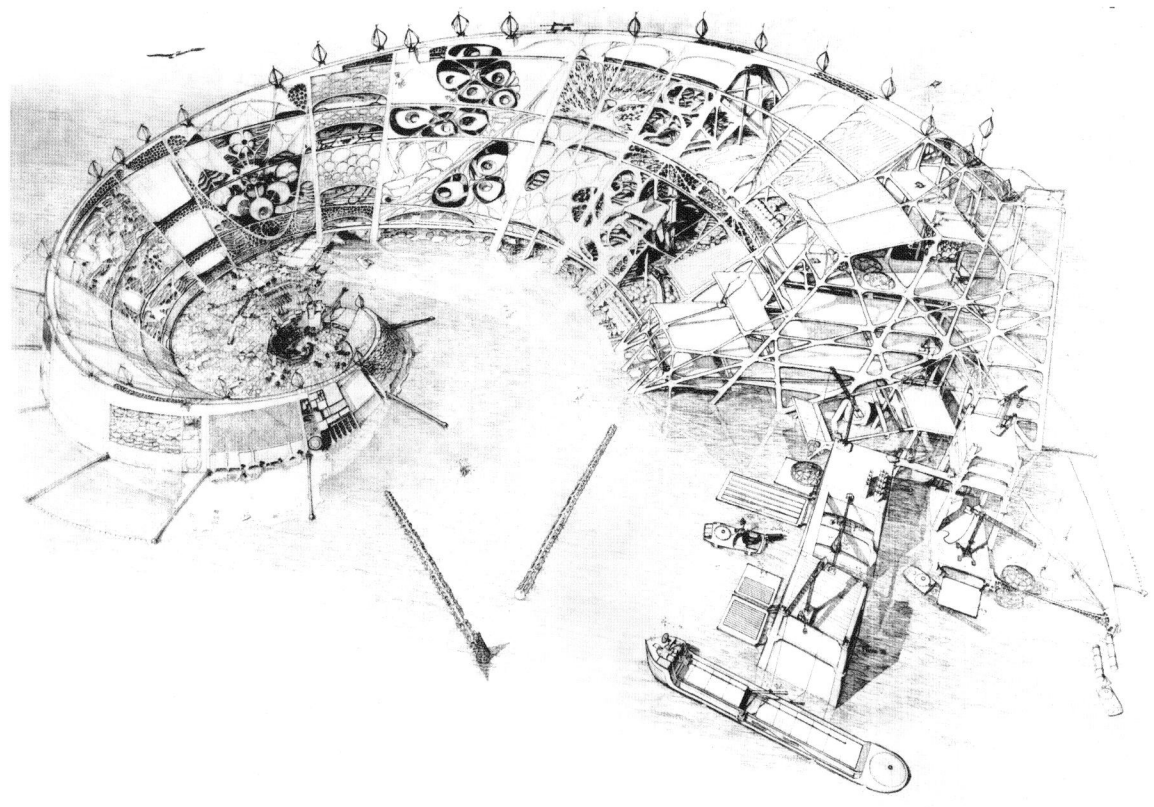

Figure 73.
Ecological Cities. Water City. Newton Fallis, Autopia Ampere, 1978, Graphite on Paper, 92*145 cm. Image courtesy of Newton Fallis. Based on the idea of the late seascape architect Wolf Hilbertz, with the coral scientist Dr Thomas Goreau, who invented Biorock™, a mineral accretion technology which fast grows coral and repairs damaged reefs (Goreau 2005), the project was seen as a city grown from the sea which utilized cybernetics to evolutionarily expand and support its inhabitants. Similar principles have re-emerged in the concept for Future Venice [see figure 26, Chapter 1].

Global urbanized surfaces

The UN's 2018 world urbanization prospects state that 68 per cent of the world population will live in urban areas by 2050. At the same time Isaac Asimov predicts a totalized urban surface called Trantor which, as Andy Merrifield writes, has clear parallels with Henri Lefebvre in *The Right to the City* and *The Urban in Question* (Merrifield 2013). William Gibson's Sprawl triology of *Neuromancer* (1984), *Count Zero* (1986) and *Mona Lisa Overdrive* (1988) is in fact based on the Boston-Atlanta metropolitan axis. The near future of an urbanized surface is nearly upon us, and media which render these impending realities are vital, ever-blurring the boundaries between fact and fiction [figures 78a&b].

Wider issues of global futures are explored later in this book, but new megaregions and megacities are the contemporary formal order. Our collective quest to find new forms and contexts for future cities is epitomized by Shimizu Corp's Green Float [figure 79] with its attempt to urbanize the oceans of our planet. However innovative such projects may appear, it is often possible to detect a lineage throughout history as imaginative floating or flying cities [figure 80]. These forms have projected what seemingly is impossible but now are evidence for many of the past visions of cities. In the chapters that follow we examine visions for future cities through three critical lenses: technological futures, social futures and global futures.

Figure 74.
Ecological Cities. Water City. WORKac & Ant Farm, 3.C.CITY: Climate, Convention, and Cruise, Chicago Architecture Biennale, 2015. Photo © Bruce Damonte. Devised as an amalgamation of Ant Farm's proposals in consultation with Chip Lord, 3.C.City is a research lab for communication with other species, a conference centre for global issues and a space for counterculture. Importantly, through this project WORKac filled in gaps in lost archives and the drawings of Ant Farm when the studio was destroyed by fire.

Figure 75.
Informal Cities. Space City. Onyx, Parsec City, 1968–1970, Signature Michaël B. Hinge, Photography © François Lauginie, Collection Frac Centre-Val de Loire. Parsec City is a large poster collection for the ONYX collective that, in a similar manner to Ant Farm, created free-form architectural visions without constraint, projecting visions dismembered from their present conditions.

Figure 76.
Hybrid Cities. Floating City. Clouds Architecture Office, Analemma Tower, Project Team: Ostap Rudakevych, Masayuki Sono, Kevin Huang, 2018. Analemma inverts the traditional diagram of an earth-based foundation, instead depending on a space-based supporting foundation from which the tower is suspended. By placing a large asteroid into orbit over earth, a high strength cable can be lowered towards the surface of earth from which a super-tall tower can be suspended. Since this new tower typology is suspended in the air, it can be constructed anywhere in the world and transported to its final location.

Figure 77.
Regulated Cities. Space City. Stefano Boeri Architetti. China, A Vertical Forest on Mars?, Shanghai Urban Space and Art Season 2017. This vision explores a 'New Shanghai' born from the rooting on Mars's surface of 'eco-systemic seeds', which would travel through an interplanetary space station, within which to create an atmosphere and a favourable climate for plants and human life.

Figure 78a.
Hybrid Cities. Cyber City. *Ghost in the Shell*. ARISE 6, p. 36. Ghost in the Shell. Stand Alone Complex, Chapter 1. Kodansha Ltd. 2018. Highly packed urban structures feature in this vision, with giant billboards and ubiquitous robots, implants and AI conscious. The cyborg protagonist Motoko surveys the city through physical ability to place herself at the highest vertex, but this is also used as a trope for the 'plug in' of connecting to a digitized world network through portals in the back of her neck.

Figure 78b.
Ghost in the Shell (2017). Directed by Rupert Sanders. Universal Pictures/Moviestore Collection Ltd.

Figure 79. (above)
Layered Cities. Water City. Shimizu Corporation, Green Float, 2014. © Image Courtesy of Shimizu Corporation, 2014. This vision for a Floating City on the equatorial Pacific uses a city-scale integrated ecosystem combining advanced environmental technologies to achieve a negative-carbon system. The structure is built at sea with a bonded honeycomb structure from magnesium alloy structural materials refined from sea water. The city is adaptable and expandable, growing like a lily floating on the water.

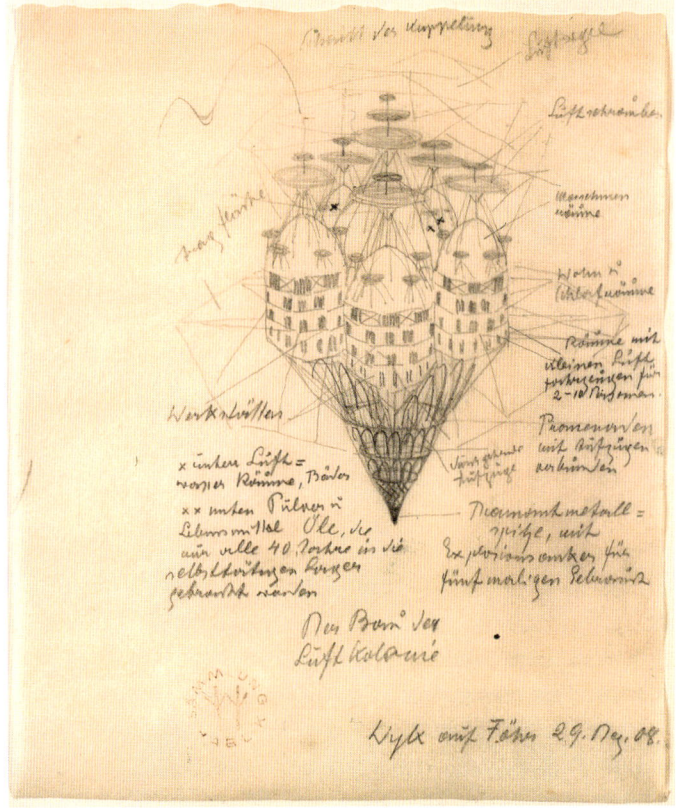

Figure 80.
Flexible Cities. Floating City. Wenzel Hablik, Der Bau der Luftkolonie (Structure of a Colony Floating in the Air), 1908, Pencil, 22.5 x 18.1 cm. © Wenzel-Hablik-Foundation, Itzehoe. Hablik, informed by geology, drew imaginative projections of Floating Cities similar to Laputa in Gulliver's Travels and later in the work of Hayao Miyazaki and Studio Ghibli.

Chapter 4

Technological Futures: Optimism, science fiction and infrastructural systems

Towards gleaming innovations

Technology plays a vital part of many predictions and ideas about the future. This chapter explores the role of technological speculation in future city scenarios and how it has shaped various perspectives and specific deterministic pathways. Although there is considerable diversity in how visions have portrayed technologically driven futures, they are typically characterized by their projected scale and comprehensive nature. These futures frequently depict the city as a series of systems, networks and processes rather than focusing on the lived experience of being in it. The visualization techniques employed favour aerial views, technical sections, axonometric drawings and perspectives that usually remove us from the street level condition and are rarely populated, focusing instead on the technological ingenuity and overall vision rather than how we might engage with it at a human level and interact with one another. Where we do encounter these environments in an experiential way is typically through science fiction as they have provided rich source material for speculation of collective life amidst technologically driven futures. A discussion of the dialogue between sci-fi future cities and their entanglement with reality, therefore, also forms part of this chapter.

The language used to describe technological futures is often quasi-scientific, deriving from developments in the military-industrial complex that incorporate terminology such as operation, management, systems, control, efficiency etc. Using technology as a critical lens has led to some of the most radical concepts for urban life we have had to date with particular emphasis on the period between the mid-1950s and late 1970s when optimism regarding the transformative powers of technology was arguably at its highest. As with many types of technological advancement and invention, some of these ideas have proved to be an inspiration for subsequent projects whilst others have been far more limited in both their reception and impact. Despite this uneven history we continue to be enthralled by what technology may provide solutions for (Montfort

2017). Given the developments in computation and digital technologies more widely, a new period of optimism in the ability of technology to shape the design of and reformulate our relationships with cities is apparent. The emergence of recent technologically driven concepts that seek to enhance urban life is therefore also discussed.

Cities are where many different elements come together including buildings, transportation, services, and, of course, people. The various interactions between these different parts of a city take on many alternative versions depending on multiple factors such as climate, geography, economics, politics and social values. The material facts of a city are directly connected to the technologies and tools used to produce them. From the highly dense Vertical Cities such as Shanghai to the horizontal sprawl of Los Angeles, or from the compact form of Amsterdam compared to the huge area covered by Lagos, how and why cities are built and evolve is underscored by technology. Architecture in this way can be viewed as the original situated technology, facilitating our various roles and relationships with each other and providing the support for different types of work, living and recreation. Many of our daily interactions in a city are shaped by technology, whether the fabric of the buildings we inhabit, the networks that enable transit, the services that provide power, heating and cooling etc.

Megastructures and endless cities

We have become accustomed to the idea of continuous networks wrapping around the planet for our communications technologies. Although these networks are provided by significant physical infrastructures and buildings to support them, they are typically hidden either as subterranean elements or as deliberately inobtrusive architecturally generic forms that rarely announce their presence, regardless of context. Yet the notion of a planetary urban network that offers a flexible infrastructure for urban life is far from new, as Yona Friedman's pioneering Ville Spatiale (Spatial City) (1958) demonstrates [figure 81]. Following the publication of his *Architecture Mobile* manifesto in 1958, Friedman continued his work on a new architecture for citizens whom he believed would be freed from existing work patterns via the increasing automation of production.

Friedman recognized that urban sprawl was highly undesirable, and so he applied his vision on existing cities to demonstrate how increasing the density of them through this elevated future city could form a methodical approach to urban growth. Within this framework, people would be free to construct their own homes with the guiding principle for the layout of each level being no more than 50 per cent coverage by dwellings to enable air and light to each residence and the context underneath. Not that the application of Ville Spatiale was limited to existing urban landscapes – it was also illustrated spanning across countrysides and bodies of water to present a continuous landscape to support all the connections, functions and interactions necessary for collective urban life. Flexibility and choice were integral to the proposal, but crucially these were to be delivered to inhabitants via technical Manuals (1973) that explained mechanisms in behaviour, economics and principles, whilst a computer programme, Flatwriter (1967), was conceived to enable self-planning of each apartment. In the same era, Eckhardt Schulze-Fielitz was developing innovative research into structural morphology in Germany. During the late 1950s, new structural configurations were derived from his experiments with the potential of mathematical and morphological principles for the organization and division of three-dimensional space. His vision for the future city, Raumstadt (1959), proposed a system for the occupation of space by structures capable of extending indefinitely in all directions [figure 82]. These flexible assemblages of trellises composed of tetrahedra and octahedra were conceived as a universal system able to be applied in any location.

The ongoing pursuit of modular, flexible systems able to provide an open framework for the future city led to the development of many projects known as 'megastructures'. The term has its origins in both

Figure 81.
Flexible Cities. Crossing City. Yona Friedman, Spatial City, project, Aerial perspective, 1958. New York, Museum of Modern Art (MoMA). Ink on tracing paper, 8 3/8 x 10 3/4' (21.3 x 27.3 cm). Gift of the Howard Gillman Foundation. Acc. n.: 1189.2000. © 2018. Digital image, The Museum of Modern Art, New York/Scala, Florence. Ville Spatiale proposed a new infrastructural framework of lightweight structures raised above the ground which could be deployed anywhere and was intended to be adaptable to any climate.

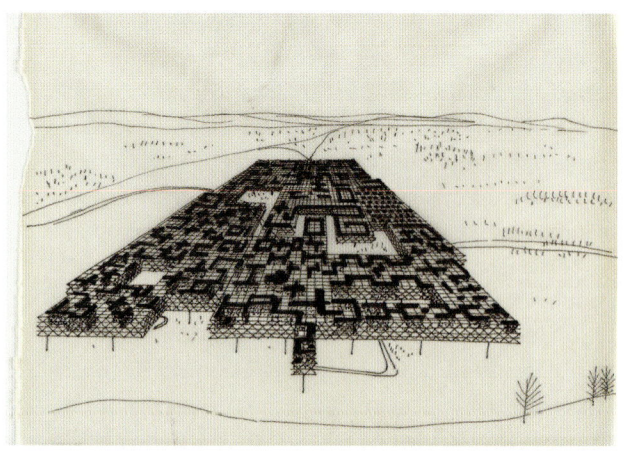

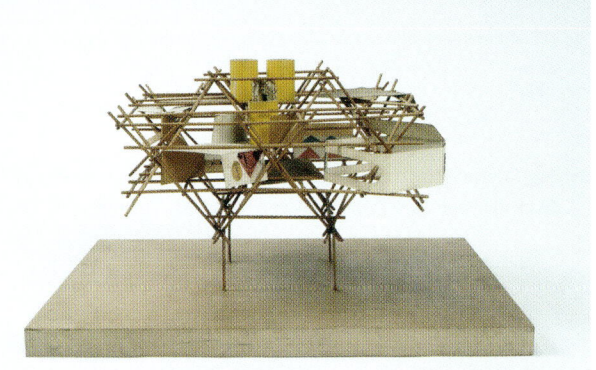

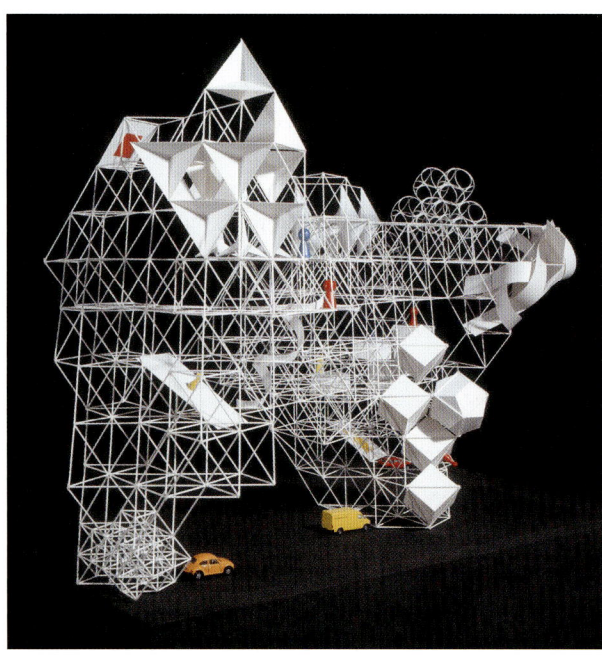

Figure 82.
Flexible Cities. Cluster City. Eckhardt Schulze-Fielitz, Raumstadt, 1959. Photography © Philippe Magnon, Collection Frac Centre-Val de Loire. This vision promoted an urbanized surface to the world, able to follow the form of existing landscape like a crystalline layer gliding over it. The three-dimensional trellis, combining the functionalism of right-angled construction with structural capacities of tetrahedral and octahedral ones, offers the future city as endlessly reconfigurable spatial structure resolute in its technical prowess and articulation.

Fumihiko Maki's *Investigations in Collective Form* (1964: 8), which defined a 'mega-structure' as 'a large frame in which all the functions of a city or part of a city are housed' and Ralph Wilcoxon's *A Short Bibliography on Megastructures* (1968: 2), which provided a four-part definition of 'megastructure':

> not only a structure of great size, but . . . also a structure which is frequently: constructed of modular units; capable of great or even 'unlimited' extension; a structural framework into which smaller units (for example, rooms, houses, or small buildings of other sorts) can be built – or even 'plugged-in' or 'clipped-on' after having been prefabricated elsewhere; a structural framework expected to have a useful life much longer than that of the smaller units which it might support.

Heralding this new era of technological optimism was Eilfried Huth and Günther Domenig's Stadt Ragnitz (1963 to 1969), originally conceived in 1963, that won the Urbanism and Architecture competition in Cannes in 1969 [figure 83]. Comprising an industrially prefabricated infrastructure which would accommodate clusters of housing units, the scheme sought to elevate the future city above existing terrain, a common feature of megastructural projects, to enable more space to be free for leisure and green spaces adjacent to the housing.

Meanwhile, over in Japan, the Metabolist Kiyonori Kikutake was experimenting with ways to address the country's shortage of land and housing. His Stratiform Structure Module (1972) proposed a vast A-frame into which detached houses could be plugged [figure 84]. During the next twenty years, Kikutake collaged Stratiforms running across various different locations within the Japanese archipelago: in dense cities, through countryside, over highways and in the shadow of Mount Fuji. The Ministry of International Trade and Industry, keen to find a potential solution for future cities constrained by Japan's geography and housing deficit, sponsored the construction of a 1:1 prototype. Though this was subjected to earthquake and fire tests, the scheme, despite its apparent adaptability to any context, was never built. Although imagined as hyper-flexible, it was frequently illustrated as being populated with two-storey houses and gardens. If future cities are about envisioning scenarios, then this is an unusual example as it is a scenario about scenarios that concretizes the limits of its seemingly infinite adaptability.

City as machine

Dreams of a highly functional and totally controllable city for the future began to manifest in the proposals of architects and planners seeking to address the increasing complexity of industrialized cities and their various, sometimes competing, infrastructures and forms of mobility. In 1914, in place of historical conventions and styles, Sant'Elia proposed a vision for a new city that resembled a gigantic machine [figure 85]. Central to his concept was the intense dynamism championed by his futurist contemporaries, which embraced notions of movement, industrial production and accelerating change. This was manifest in his drawings through the unfettered circulation of objects – people, cars, trains etc. – through what Reyner Banham (1960: 128) subsequently referred to as a 'knot'-like design, with each structure integrated within the overall composition via a 'network of multi-level circulation at their feet'. As powerful as this vision was, this obsession with circulation dominates all other aspects of the city as imagined. The critic Carlo Ragghianti has characterized this aspect of Sant'Elia's work as manifest 'vertically, horizontally and at times even obliquely and elliptically. Traffic channels penetrate everywhere, and are the only structures that have been determined . . . What else does the *Citta Nuova* do other than circulate?' (as quoted in da Costa Meyer 1995: 121). However, visions such as this have endured in the imagination of urban planners and architects who promote the efficient movement of people, goods and services around cities.

The growth in exploration of cities as machine-like has been a core theme of the modern architectural imagination, paralleled by the engineering innovations

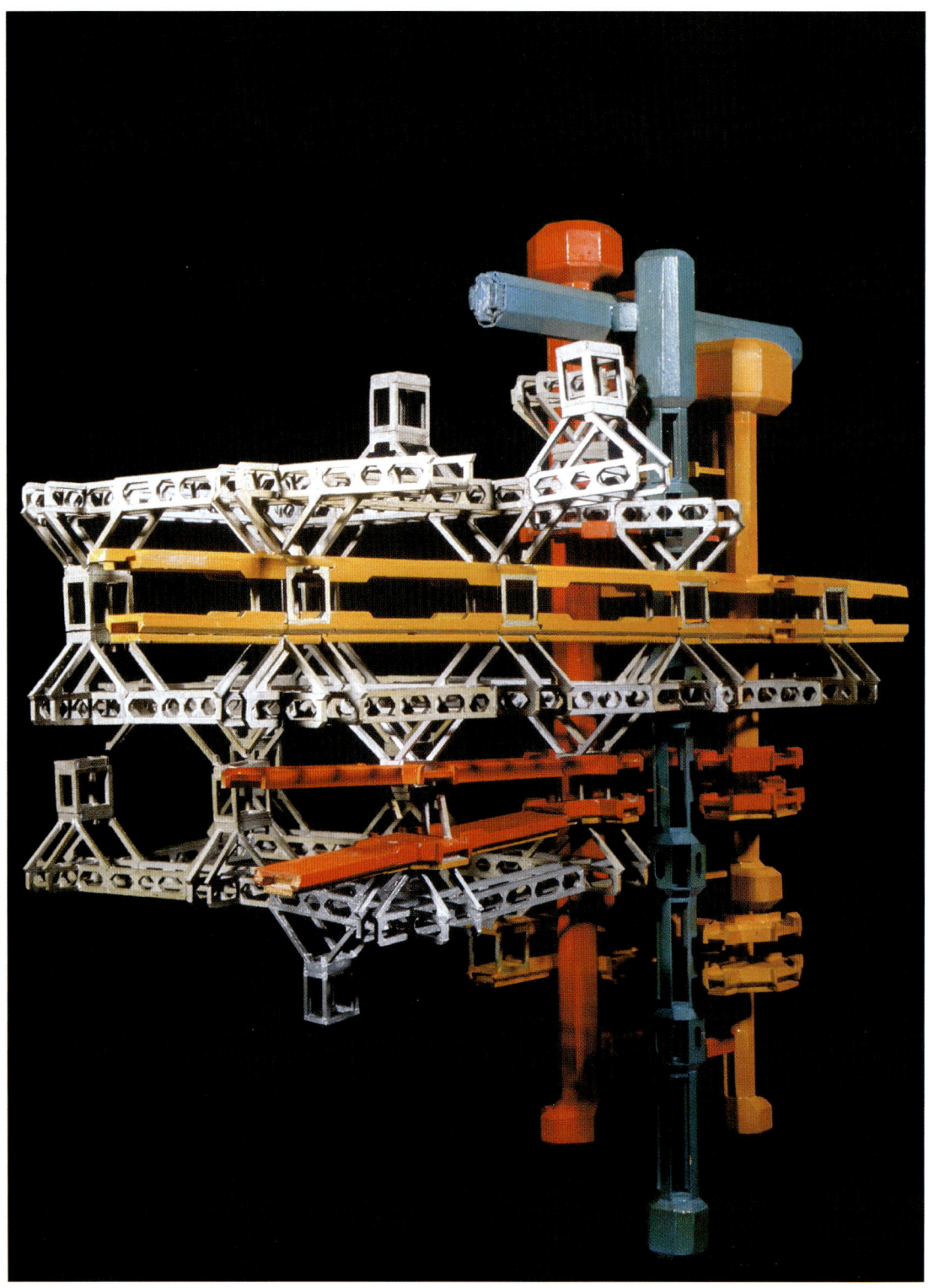

Figure 83. (facing page) Flexible Cities. Vertical City. Eilfried Huth and Günther Domenig's Stadt Ragnitz (1963–1969). © Philippe Magnon, Collection Frac Centre-Val de Loire. This 'industrialized urban habitat' was powerfully communicated by the model made to visualize it. The detail of the model, part of which is shown here, conveyed its authors' commitment to their concept of the future city as a series of infrastructural systems and led Reyner Banham (1976: 160) to consider it 'the richest, fullest, most complete academic megamodel ever built'.

Figure 84. Informal Cities. Connected City. Kiyonori Kikutake – Stratiform Structure Module, Takenaka, 1972. The objective was a low-budget approach to long-term issues of environmental sustainability; the idea was to make land without mass. The space frame provided a light and deployable infrastructure within which train tracks, highways and industry could all be buried underneath stepped platforms of greenery.

Figure 85. Layered Cities. Vertical City. Antonio Sant'Elia, The New City (La Citta Digital Nuova), buildings and steps with four street levels, 1914. Private Collection. Black ink on paper © 2018. DeAgostini Picture Library/Scala, Florence. The clean and bold lines of Sant'Elia's drawings for the scheme described machine-like structures, stepped skyscrapers interlaced with suspended walkways and highway overpasses, an aesthetic that has its echoes in many subsequent fictional future cities including *Metropolis* [see figure 22, Chapter 1] and *Blade Runner* [figures 95, 96 & 97].

of the period that enabled not only high structures above ground but also considerable downwards excavation to support modern urban life. In these visions, the future city was often a series of layers to support different urban functions and infrastructures. As the twentieth century progressed, numerous projects began to explore radical alternatives for the city and how they might encompass the globe. Raimund Abraham's Linear Cities series between 1963 and 1966, are notable for their commitment to the future city as an enclosure for urban life within seemingly inhospitable surroundings. These machines, for example Universal City (1966) [figure 86], move unhindered across barren landscapes, seemingly signalling the dawn of a new world (McQuaid 2002). Abraham's visions were intended to be complete in themselves as he asserted the autonomous, essential value of a drawing as a manifestation of architecture. From a representational point of view Abraham's carefully constructed compositions provide enough evidence to be understood, but throughout his career he maintained key distinctions in his methods of representation between drawings for imaginary projects and those which were to be realized (Groihofer 2011).

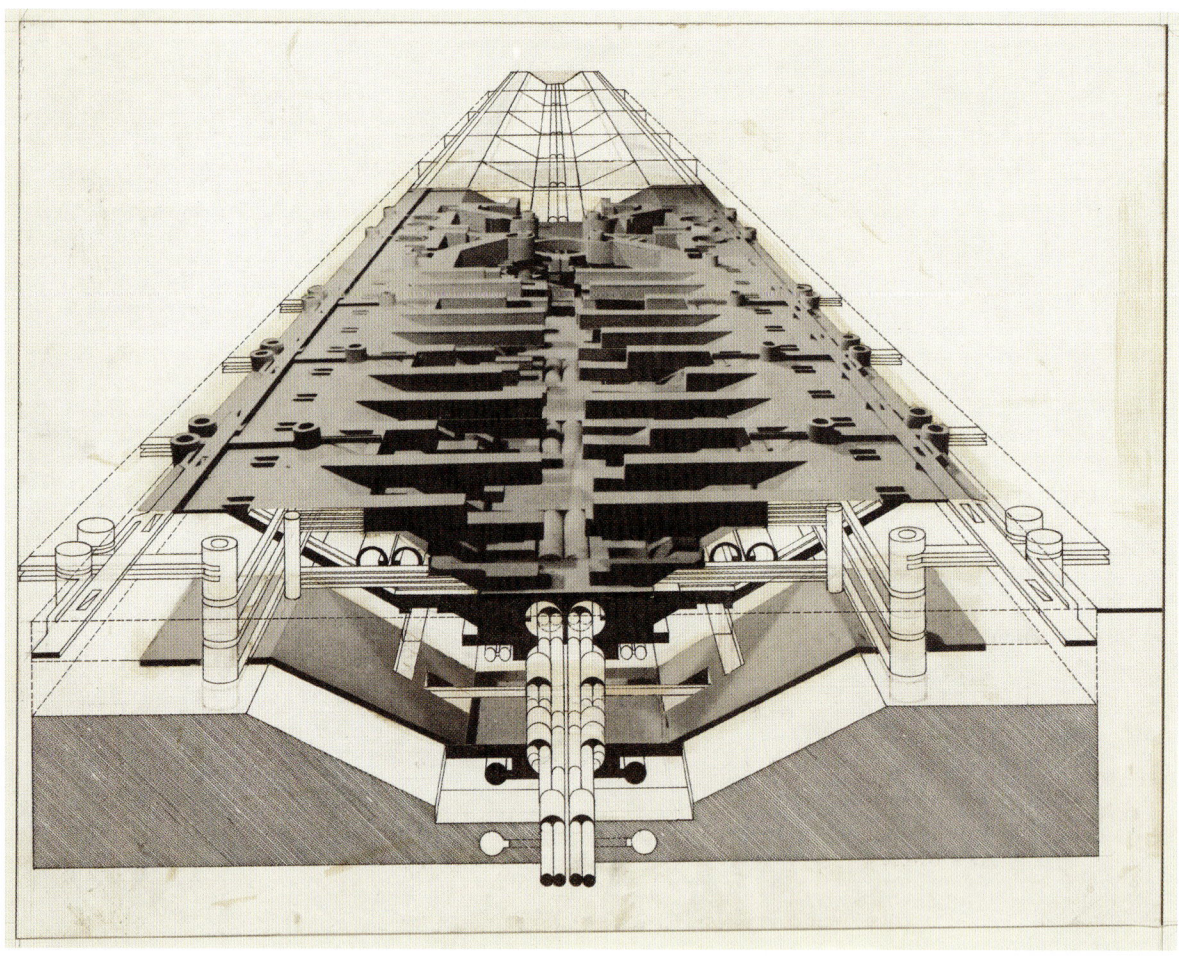

Figure 86.
Regulated Cities. Horizontal City. Raimund Abraham, Universal City, 1966. Gift of the architect. The Museum of Modern Art, New York/Scala, Florence. A project that formed part of his *Linear Cities* series, this proposal shows the future city as a machinic landscape capable of unrestricted expansion along its length.

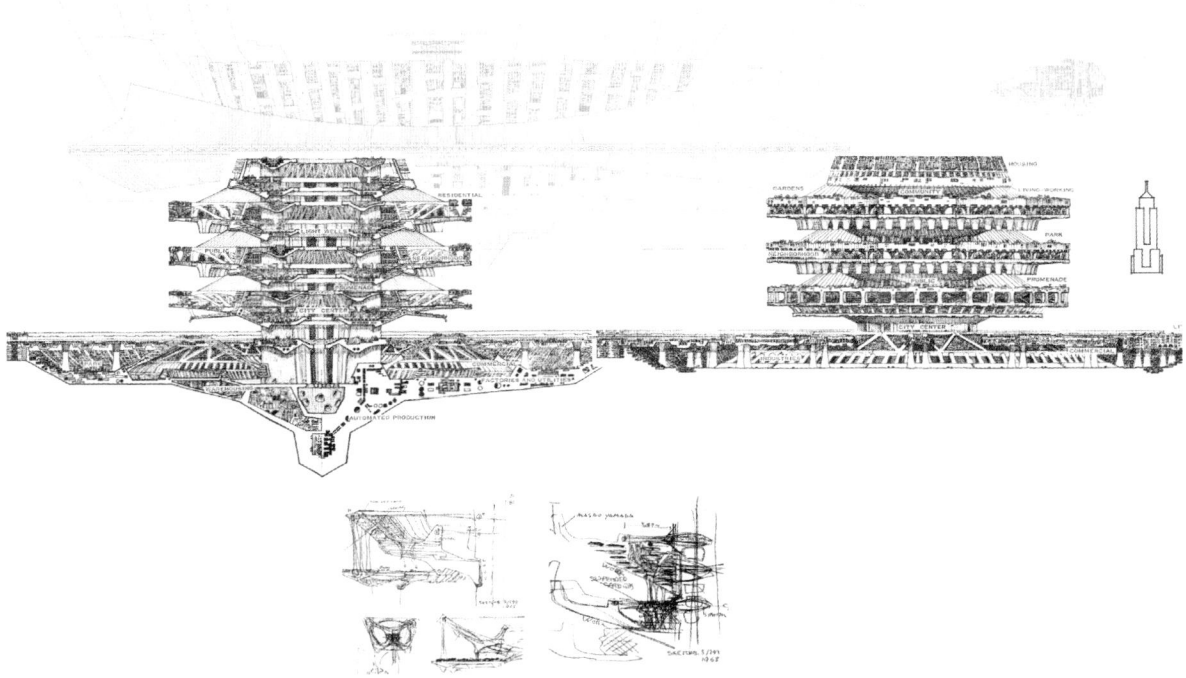

Figure 87.
Regulated Cities. Spectacle City. Paolo Soleri, Babel IIB, Arcology: City in the Image of Man, 1969. Soleri used his series of arcologies to examine different ways of compacting city structures in three dimensions to combat two-dimensional urban sprawl and economize on transportation and other energy uses. Integral to this approach was the exploration of reductions in resource consumption and duplication and land reclamation, whilst also proposing to eliminate most private transportation.

Considering this approach in a very different manner, the future city could be conceived as a self-contained machine or ark. The term 'arcology' – a portmanteau of 'architecture' and 'ecology' – was first coined and then popularized by Soleri, having since appeared in a number of science fiction works. Its key feature is to reduce the impact of human habitation on any particular ecosystem. Intrinsic to this concept, arcology designs typically apply conventional building and civil engineering techniques in huge projects in order to achieve pedestrian economies of scale that have proven, post-automobile, to be difficult to achieve in other ways. Soleri's BABEL IIB Arcology is designed for a population of 520,000, with a density of 662/hectare, at a height of 1,050 metres [figure 87]. Shafts carry a vertical transportation system. Anchored to the shafts are the platform-grounds of the city: at the periphery are residential spaces; in the medial belt, gardens and waste processing plants; towards the centre, civil facilities and work. The top platform-ground is for cultural institutions: schools, labs, studios, theatres and libraries. At the ground is a system of parks, gardens and playgrounds that altogether make up a hyper structure. Although described quite differently, the idea of a self-contained city has endured throughout the twenty-first century under the concept of eco- and zero-carbon cities.

Highways and skyways to the future

An important aspect of technology and how significantly it transforms how we live lies in the degree to which it is adopted. Throughout the twentieth century, an influential way through which people could experience technological developments and lifestyles for the future was through world expositions. These expos played an important part in providing people access to new types of architecture and construction alongside other technological drivers that were used to demonstrate what benefits may be brought with them. One of the most influential and enduring attempts to imagine how things might be was Futurama, a giant model of an urban future designed by Norman Bel Geddes in 1939 [figure 88]. It was exhibited in the General Motors pavilion and is a significant example of futures thinking and design being combined to illustrate how technology may benefit us. The model presented a preview of what the city would be in 1960; astounded visitors circulated the huge model via a conveyor belt, observing a networked landscape of skyscrapers, expressways and automated farms. The exhibit is widely understood to have first introduced the general American public to the concept of expressways connecting the nation. Bel Geddes's subsequent book *Magic Motorways* (1940) further promoted his ideas for transportation and infrastructure, as well as related concepts such as driver assist and autonomous driving. Describing the importance of this new automobile landscape, he explained

Figure 88.
Regulated Cities. Divided City. Viewing the World of Tomorrow, Futurama, New York World's Fair, Norman Bel Geddes, 1939. © Courtesy of the Harry Ransom Center. Participants at the General Motors Futurama exhibit orbited on motorized seating around a diorama of America in 1960. The onset of the automobile age enabled the promotion of a super-road infrastructure and landscape that was predicated for the car.

(1940: 4), 'Futurama is a large-scale model representing almost every type of terrain in America and illustrating how a motorway system may be laid down over the entire country – across mountains, over rivers and lakes, through cities and past towns – never deviating from a direct course and always adhering to the four basic principles of highway design: safety, comfort, speed and economy'. Importantly an example such as this reminds us that visible futures are branded, shaped as arguments – with different registers of information and as specific options are promoted, this may mean alternatives are concealed or even discredited.

The widespread destruction across Europe during the Second World War led to the possibility for numerous cities to reconsider how they might reconceive and thus reconstruct significant inner urban areas. The aftermath of the war led numerous inner-city areas, already ravaged by warfare, to become emptied out, as many abandoned dense urban districts in favour of better environments. As a consequence, these areas often suffered from ghettoization as only those with low socio-economic status remained with poor quality housing conditions, increasing crime rates and poverty. Meanwhile, a highly influential, concomitant set of forces was also beginning to reshape our relationship to place and the city – the rise of consumer culture. Initiating in the United States, the emergence of labour-saving devices, increase in leisure time, and lower cost of automobiles combined to offer new choices and lifestyle options for those who could afford them. This Western-derived set of values rooted in consumerism would dominate the development of many countries as it directly influenced the decisions people made about how and where they lived.

Earlier it was stated that when some ideas within futures are promoted, others become concealed. This is particularly true of those future cities in the twentieth century that promoted private automobile ownership and use at the cost of negating alternatives. Arthur Radebaugh featured Jellicoe's *Motopia* ideas in a syndicated comic strip 'Closer Than We Think' [figure 89]. Jellicoe proposed a separation of transport creating a Layered City of elevated streets for the suburbs of London. For a vision whose principal selling point was the freedom to not worry about getting hit by cars, it would have a rather strange name: *Motopia*. It was a bold – if somewhat impractical – plan for a city built from the ground up and all its inhabitants living in a grid-pattern of buildings with an expanse of rooftop motorways in the sky. There would be schools, shops, restaurants, churches and theaters all resting on a total footprint of about one thousand acres. The community was imagined as modern but tranquil; where accepting the bold new postwar future didn't mean giving up the more peaceful aspects of daily living. As such, the planners were quick to point out that a special kind of insulation would be used to block out any of the noise from all the cars roaring along an inhabitant's roof. The idea of the multi-leveled city of infrastructure repeats itself throughout the twentieth century.

The motor car was synonymous with the age of technological prowess, consumer culture and individual freedom that characterized the Western world in the mid-twentieth century. Its impact upon

Figure 89.
Layered Cities. Divided City. *Motopia*, Geoffrey Jellicoe, 1961. Illustrated in 1960 by Arthur Radebaugh for 'Closer Than We Think'. © TribuneContent Agency, LLC. All Rights Reserved. Reprinted with permission. This vision for a radically new kind of British urban centre promoted distinct layers of circulation, where the bubble-top cars of tomorrow moved freely on elevated streets, and the pedestrians circulated around quickly and safely on moving sidewalks.

Chapter 4 Technological Futures: Optimism, science fiction and infrastructural systems the design of cities was unprecedented as it rapidly became ubiquitous to movement across the urban landscape. In the short film *Crash!* (1971) inspired by the story 'Crash' from his novel *The Atrocity Exhibition* (1970), J. G. Ballard observed, 'I think the key image of the 20th century is the man in the motor car. It sums up everything: the elements of speed, drama, aggression, the junction of advertising and consumer goods with the technological landscape.' Indeed, the socio-material system of motor cars propelled many realized and unbuilt visions for cities, so endemic was it to the notion of progress and aspirational values. Visions for future cities from this period thus enthusiastically incorporated the motor car, illustrating the future as place that could be simply driven to. A prime example of this is an image produced as part of the vision for Cumbernauld New Town (1963) by Geoffrey Copcutt [figure 90]. The role of the motor car as integral to the future city was deeply enmeshed in the proposal for Cumbernauld, a 'colossal living vessel' (Wakeman 2016: 272). One of the few megastructures to be built, it moved architectural critic Wolf von Eckardt (1965: 93) to write, 'Leonardo da Vinci, nearly five hundred years ago, envisioned a city where all the vehicles move underground, leaving man to move freely in the sun. Leonardo might also have sketched Cumbernauld's town centre, a soaring citadel surrounded by meadow.'

Although it has remaining an enduring and powerful motif, this is not to suggest there have been a lack of alternatives to motor car travel. For example, in the 1950s and early 1960s numerous cities were fascinated with the possibility of helicopters for urban transport with the enormous advantage of accessing airspace directly above congested streets of great appeal. This led to various future city visions featuring heliports in an attempt to radically improve urban mobility – for example, R. Nicolas's City of Manchester Heliport (1956) [figure 91]. In their analysis of this striking image, Brook and Dodge (2012: 37) suggest, 'The modern, white clean surface of the heliport literally and metaphorically overlays – and almost seems to supersede – the train station, cathedral to technological progress in the nineteenth century city. The future has arrived not on the rails, but from the air above.' Whilst excitingly modern in its promise the actual premise of inner urban helicopters quickly vanished due to the economic realities and the spatial difficulties of accommodating the technology as part of a routine public transport system.

Figure 90.
Regulated Cities. Cluster City. Geoffrey Copcutt, Cumbernauld New Town, 1963. Bryan & Shear, courtesy of North Lanarkshire Archives. © North Lanarkshire Council / Culture NL Ltd. The image illustrates the approach to the first phase of Cumbernauld New Town. This vision was ready to embrace the motor car, the driver was going to be the first to arrive in the future! The image offers a perspective of the centre, a megastructure ready to accommodate its future inhabitants.

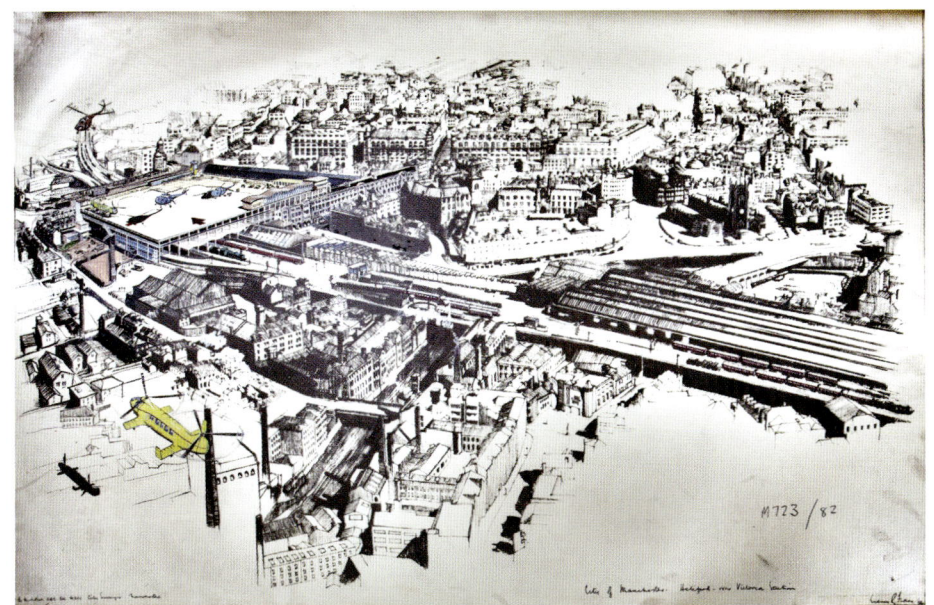

Figure 91.
Regulated Cities. Sky City. City of Manchester Heliport near Victoria Station, R. Nicholas, City Surveyor. Drawn by Sidney R. Fisher, 1956. Courtesy of Manchester Archives. This perspective drawing is taken from an elevated position, further reinforcing the new layer of mobility afforded by helicopters. Hand-drawn elements and colour bring vibrancy to the preexisting black and white city, illustrating the extensive technological change and new consumerism of the period.

Cities of moving parts

Although different forms of transportation have proved instrumental in shaping visions for future cities, another lineage concerns those cities whose constituent parts are able to move and be changed. Driven by the possibilities of mobile architecture in various guises, architects and urban designers have sought to exploit the adaptability of systems that enable the future city to be a kit of parts, versatile and amenable to recombination. One of the first post-war architects to propose a completely moveable town, Péré-Lahaille continued to purse the idea of mobility in architecture as a means of adapting to the technical and social transformations occurring in modern life [figure 92]. Along with Yona Friedman, Guy Rottier,

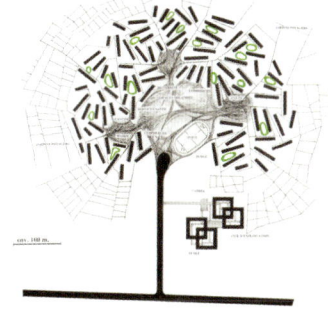

Figure 92.
Informal Cities. DIY City. Charles Péré-Lahaille – La Cité Mobile, 1953. Collection Frac Centre-Val de Loire. This early project by Péré-Lahaille utilized a series of rails to facilitate the buildings' movement. His commitment to the role of technology to provide housing that could be assembled by non-technical construction workers culminated in a version of his visionary Alternative Habitation project of 1500 housing units for Kuwait being built in France.

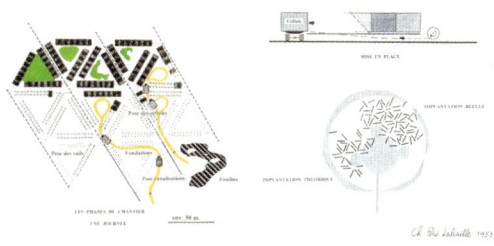

Chapter 4 Technological Futures: Optimism, science fiction and infrastructural systems

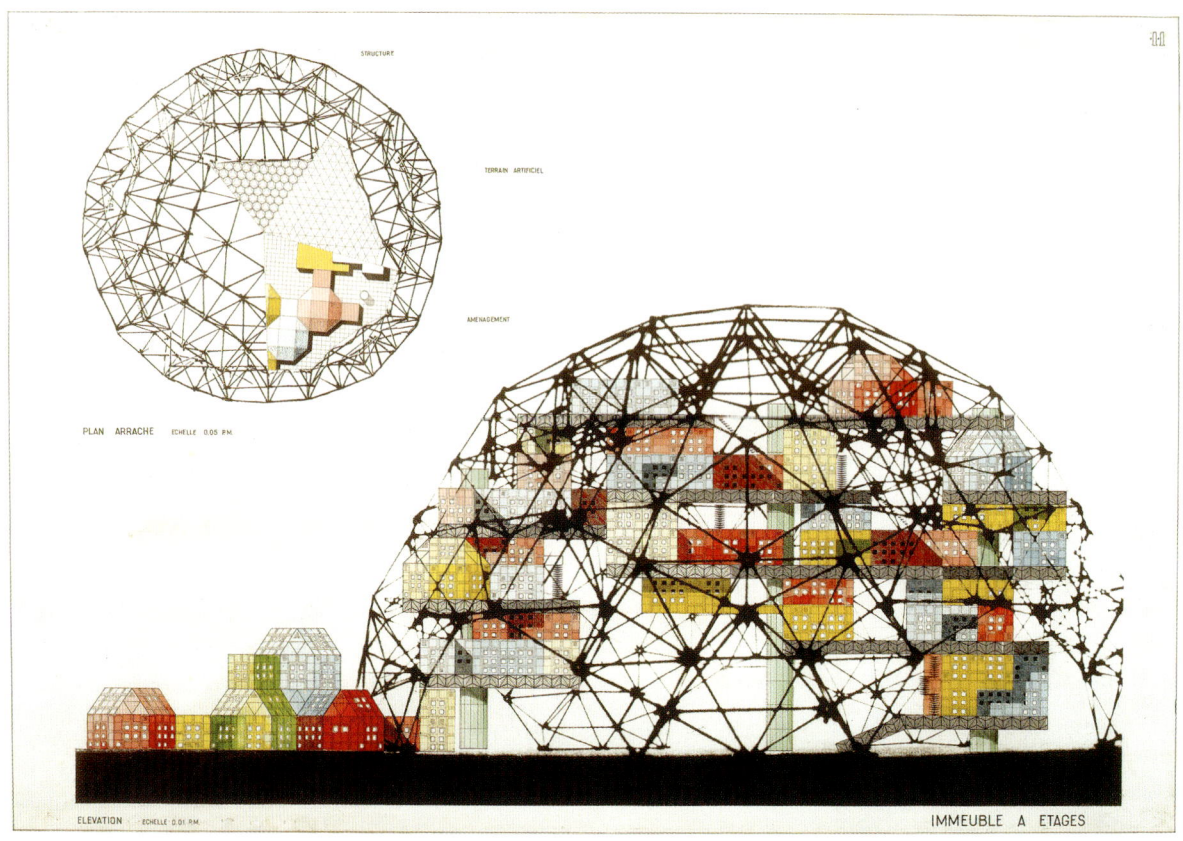

Figure 93.
Layered Cities. Cyber City. David George Emmerich, Agglomération (sous une coupole stéréométrique), 1958–1960. Collection Frac Centre-Val de Loire. Emmerich was a strong advocate of the wholesale adoption of modular building systems to create flexible architectural and urban structures, looking for inspiration in crystals, soap bubbles, and paper-folding techniques.

Georges Candilis and Jerzy Solten, he formed the GEAM (Mobile Architecture Study Group) which would have a significant influence in the 1960s.

Slightly less conventional at the time was the idea of a city as a self-organized community. The possibilities of three-dimensional tensile structures, initially developed by Konrad Wachsmann and Buckminster Fuller, were further explored by David George Emmerich for polyfunctional organic habitats [figure 93]. The potential of new material constructions offered inherent flexibility; here architecture was envisioned as a motive force for a future city of numerous, ever-changing dynamics in one place (Busbea 2007).

Post-war, the atomic age suggested new possibilities for clean energy production and power which, combined with the race for space that was gathering momentum between various nations although predominantly the USSR and United States, focus on where we might live and how our collective gaze had turned towards the stars. However, many ideas we have had presented to us are exactly that – they are stories broadcast *at* people, rather than being more open, suggestive and enabling, perhaps empowering, the viewer to respond and actively shape her or his own formulation. A key enabler in this regard was the widespread popularity of television throughout the 1950s and 1960s with a burgeoning number of households having a TV set in their home. Such technology was transformative in a way that previous objects such as wireless radios were not. Most significantly, in addition to being able to simultaneously broadcast into millions of homes, television was able to engage with its audiences visually. Images entered the collective imagination at an unprecedented rate, having previously been the preserve of cinema. This mass media facilitated the transmission and reception of many imagined future worlds involving spectacular technologies, time travel, roads and trains in the sky, robots, off-earth communities, and so on.

Inevitably, a new generation of architects was inspired by the possibilities of the atomic and space ages. A founding member of Archigram, Peter Cook was instrumental in fostering the British counterculture in the 1960s. The group promoted the view that the preceding modernist period's functionalist architecture was worn out. Taking multi-level infrastructure in a very different direction, Cook's Plug-In City (1964) is a network of configurable clusters and replaceable units supplementing the city [figure 94]. Pushing flexible architecture to an extreme, the project consisted of a megastructure of adaptable, diagrid space-frames that facilitated zoning whilst promoting endless reconfiguration via the cranes at the top of each structure. Communication pipes connected the different zones to one another, with a monorail system to connect existing cities and a hovercraft route way running parallel, complete with removable roads, railways, and public spaces and pneumatic roofs for bad weather. Some of these ideas of flexibility and functionality eventually manifest in the Pompidou Centre in Paris designed by Renzo Piano and Richard Rogers the following decade.

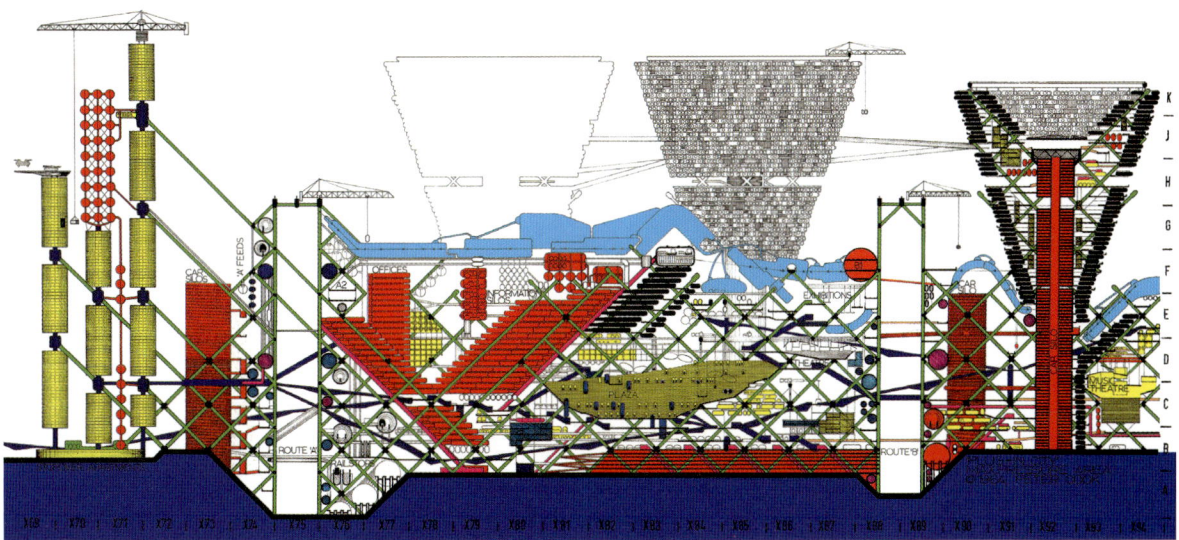

Figure 94.
Flexible Cities. DIY City. Archigram Plug-in City, Plug-in City Max Pressure Area, Peter Cook, 1964. A visionary urban megastructure intended to accommodate and encourage changes necessitated by obsolescence, on an as-needed basis, the building nodes (houses, offices, supermarkets, universities), each with a different lifespan, would plug into a main 'craneway', itself designed to last only forty years. The overall flexible and impermanent form would thus reflect the needs and collective will of the inhabitants.

Do architects dream of electric sheep?

In this book we are also interested in the complex ways in which fiction explores plausible near-future urban contexts that, in addition to speculations about the future, can also provide powerful commentaries on, and critiques of, the nature of contemporary social life. This relationship appears to be mutually beneficial as writers have also discussed how the boundaries between fiction and nonfiction are increasingly porous, enabling possible futures to be explored. The sci-fi writer Bruce Sterling (2005) defined this process as 'design fiction'. Architecture and urban design employ visionary aspects in their routine professional practices since both typically work with futurity as they project ideas about how our urban landscape might be. Viewed in this way, the interface between science fiction, architecture and urban design appears fluid and fertile (Abbott 2007, 2016; Clear 2009). Indeed, as Kitchin and Kneale (2002) have argued, this reciprocal relationship has led to contemporary urbanism informing science fiction, which in turn then influences visions for future cities as powerful imaginaries or translations into built reality.

The sci-fi theorist Darko Suvin (1972) defined the resultant process of taking viewers out of the everyday worlds into a world that appears strange and disjointed, but in a credible manner. as 'cognitive estrangement'. More recently, Steven Shaviro (2016: 9) directs us towards the powerful capabilities of the genre to transport our imagination elsewhere: 'By telling stories, science fiction asks questions about all sorts of things: consciousness and cognition, the future, extreme possibilities, nonhuman otherness, and especially the deep consequences – the powers and limitations – of both our ideologies and our technologies.' In a similar manner to science fiction, future city imaginaries create small worlds that help shape the materialities of contemporary cities. The prevalence of future cities across various media results in numerous encounters with them that may overshadow, or noticeably overlap with, our experiences of constructed reality, as Stephen Graham (2016a: 395) suggests, 'Contemporary portrayals of future cities are so hyper-mediated in films, fiction, video games, architecture and other media these days that science fiction, film and media, rather than reflecting the lived worlds of built cities, very often become a dominant initial experience which, in turn, powerfully shapes their production.' From the outset, the future cities of science fiction are obviously influenced by both their creator's experience of existing, built cities and prevailing concepts of futurism in culture and media, not least architecture. Cinema has been particular powerful in its rendering of future cities into our subconscious, adding further potency to the fluidity between fiction and reality (Neumann 1996). In the following sections a number of key themes are examined to elicit a better understanding of this interplay and how it has informed ideas for future cities as technological futures.

The ongoing development in high-rise building technologies throughout the twentieth and twenty-first century has led to a proliferation of skyscrapers and an increased emphasis on the vertical in a number of cities. Whilst some cities simply have a lot of high-rise buildings, others such as Hong Kong have devised new relationships with the ground due to geographical constraints, almost becoming 'cities without ground' (Frampton, Solomon and Wong 2012). The continuing spectacle of skyscrapers has led to their frequent inclusion in visions for future cities. A seminal example is the portrayal of Los Angeles in 2019, reimagined in the film *Blade Runner* (1982) as a high-density Vertical City akin to Hong Kong or areas of Tokyo [figures 95 & 96], although to complicate matters and illustrate how multifaceted

Figure 95. (facing page, top)
Layered Cities. Cyber City. *Blade Runner*, Ridley Scott, 1982, Warner Bros. Christophel / Photo Scala, Florence. The highly influential aesthetic of the future city depicted in this film recasts the Los Angeles of 2019 as high density, neon-lit landscape. The city backgrounds designed by Syd Mead included the flying cars, Spinners, which as well as being driven as ground-based vehicles can take off vertically, hover and cruise using jet propulsion.

Figure 96.
Layered Cities. Cyber City. *Blade Runner*, Ridley Scott, 1982, Warner Bros. Christophel / Photo Scala, Florence. The dark, brooding and claustrophobic atmosphere of the city would prove popular with those creating near-future scenarios and be replicated in many subsequent films including Batman (Dir. Burton, 1989) and Ghost in the Shell (Oshii 1996). Since its release, *Blade Runner* has established itself as a retro-futurist classic that invoked historic ideas about the future refracted through the tropes of Manhattan's history, further refracted through film noir L.A.

these interpretations can be, the film's director, Ridley Scott, has since explained that this future city owed as much to his childhood in the steel and chemical industrial landscapes of Tyneside and Teesside in the northeast of the UK. Adapted from Philip K. Dick's novel *Do Androids Dream of Electric Sheep?* (1968), the film presents a dark, dystopian future city run by global corporations where technological advancement is prioritized over human and environmental concerns. The aesthetic of L.A. in *Blade Runner* has proved highly influential and enduring, with many subsequent sci-fi films developing its blueprint of a noir, intense metropolis as a template. Meanwhile in urban theory Mike Davis (1990, 1998) has drawn on the film's bleak future for his incisive accounts of contemporary Los Angeles urbanism and the forces that have shaped it. Indeed, the ongoing impact of the original film has carried with it considerable weight of expectation for the genre, not least the recent sequel *Blade Runner 2049* (2017) [figure 97]. The original *Blade Runner* offered an immersive neo-noir dystopia of a rain-soaked and shadowy future city complete with animated neon billboards amidst a seemingly endless night. By contrast, the second film fuses both its past of the dark, eerie and overcrowded cityscape of future Los Angeles whilst also stretching out into a future of climate catastrophe with a suffocating planet of desolate wastelands, solar farms and the sand-swept future Las Vegas.

Woven into such future cities are the apparent results of globalization: dense if not cramped conditions, multi-ethnic populations, social inequalities etc. A dominant feature in many future cities is the depiction of new forms of personal transportation, in particular different variations of a flying car, a motif which has continued to capture our collective imagination (Gyger 2011). Whilst these add a new method of moving around the urban landscape, when coupled with the high-density cityscape they also describe the drama of the verticality of these cities as they reveal some of the complexities of navigating amongst the architecture and roofscapes. Such issues are dramatically brought to the fore in *The Fifth Element* (1997), which depicts Manhattan in 2259. Using a vibrant combination of physical and digital modelling techniques, the film immerses the viewer

Figure 97.
Layered Cities. Cyber City. *Blade Runner 2049*, Denis Villeneuve, 2017. Ryan Gosling. © Alcon entertainment / Scott free productions / Warner Bros. Christophel / Photo Scala, Florence. This cyberpunk vision remains in the sequel but is expanded by sequences in greyed-out countryside landscapes, a future San Diego reimagined as a vast wasteland, and the decrepit, crumbling future Las Vegas, all of which heighten the dark decadence of future Los Angeles against a wider backdrop of ecological degradation if not global climate disasters.

Figure 98.
Regulated Cities. Floating City. *The Fifth Element*, Luc Besson, 1997, © Columbia Pictures/Courtesy: Everett Collection. The striking retro-futurist verticalized style of this film, along with the 2005 to 2008 *Batman* trilogy and numerous others, has surprising and relevant links to the retro-futurist architecture and infrastructure mushrooming in contemporary cities such as Shanghai.

into the urban landscape, often through vertiginous drops between buildings during some of the chase sequences, which are both intimate in detail and expansive in scale. In this vision, some of the issues of personal transportation being able to hover and fly are explored in various scenarios as the cars wait at traffic signals, pursue one another, and travel both horizontally and also, crucially, vertically [figure 98].

Given all the problems we currently have with cars on our streets such as air pollution, accidents, traffic jams, parking issues etc., the effective implementation of similar vehicles that can also fly may be compelling but is fraught with complications. At a practical level, the recent popularity of drones has led to the development of specific legislation to ensure there are rules to protect built-up areas and other no-fly zones from their use, which suggests we are not ready for the ramifications of lots of personal vehicles in the skies of our cities (Cureton 2020). This has not slowed down the attempts of various corporations, start-ups and investors in developing flying personal transport, with several leading developments predicted to be in use from 2020. How these vehicles move around in future cities may change the relationships between the cityscape and its architecture as explored in *Minority Report* (2002), with its soaring, vertiginous ramps and high-speed driverless cars able to connect passengers to the future city's high-rise facades [figure 99]. The production designer, Alex McDowell, and his team created the entire city in considerable detail at the beginning of the film-making process, an unusual decision at the time, but by doing so its infrastructures and architecture directly influenced the film's plot. McDowell refers to his holistic design-led process of 'world-building' for ensuring the credibility of the many advanced technologies developed for the film. It is not alone in this regard, with various devices designed for science fiction becoming self-fulfilling prophecies by generating a desire for them through mass public audiences [see figure 136, Chapter 5]. The film has remained a high-water mark for the way in which ideas developed in science fiction have influenced the development of real world technologies.

Key to many visions of future cities is the aerial view, of which the emphasis on vertical urbanism often provides a crucial element not least in science fiction, as Hewitt and Graham (2015) have discussed. This technique of representation has been instrumental to the way modern architecture has been communicated, as both Morshed (2002) and Boyer (2003) have argued. The subsequent dominance of its purview across cartography, photography and planning has resulted in a significant impact on our perception of, and relation to, urban space. Likewise, Mark Dorrian has argued that the perspective of detachment and power enabled by the aerial view has been a key narrative in Western modernity. He suggests (2006: 20) that 'the departure from the terrestrial surface is conceptually linked to notions of transcendent subjectivity, futurity and abstraction that have the potential to license a violence directed towards the surface'.

Processes of urbanization and thus ideas about future cities are a global phenomenon. Whilst considerable attention has been paid to the Western tropes, there is abundant evidence of divergent attitudes towards futurity and cities. As Western science fiction abounds with high-rise future cities within barren, horizontal landscapes, there can be a strong sense of the uncanny and eerie (Fisher 2016) when these apparent futures appear manifest in the materialized cities of Abu Dhabi, Dubai and Saudi Arabia. Dubai in particular seems to be constructed from intermingled sci-fi stage sets as the very embodiment of technological progress being the primary driver for future city-making and seemingly unstoppable development [figure 100]. As the largest and most populous city in the United Arab Emirates, Dubai has experienced tremendous recent urban growth in its strategic pursuit of a global

Figure 99.
Regulated Cities. Cyber City. *Minority Report*, Dir. Steven Spielberg, 2002. TCD/Prod.DB / Alamy Stock Photo. The future city of Washington, DC, in 2054 provides the context for this science fiction replete with its wearable technologies, gestural interfaces and flexible displays. A key feature are the driverless cars which can move both horizontally and vertically up the facades of buildings, taking the soaring ramps of Jellicoe's *Motopia* [figure 89] to a radical conclusion.

Figure 100.
Regulated Cities. Vertical City. Bachir Moukarzel, Dubai, drone photography, 2016. Its quest to remain in the imagination is explicit with many iconic projects to assure its status as futuristic and luxurious, in particular the Burj Khalifa which has been the tallest structure and building in the world since completed in 2008.

image since 1990. The developed area grew from 149 square kilometres to 224 square kilometres in 2005, and it has since accelerated this process which – coupled with the terraforming that has resulted in over 300 km of new coastline – has produced an urban spectacle based on technological prowess over environmental conditions. The technological future of humanity's dominance over some of the most inhospitable terrain has rendered it a powerful global player amongst cities, which is reflected in its ambitions to host Expo 2020 and also make the city the happiest in the world by the same year. What is less clear is how its ambitions to be the smartest and most sustainable city can be balanced with the considerable degree of conspicuous consumption that drives the city's economy and image.

In China, the impact of *Blade Runner* and its retro-futurism, itself influenced by orientalist Western imaginations of Asian cities, has subsequently been very influential in the architecture and design of Vertical Cities (Graham 2016a). Given that the belief in progress towards prosperity via new technology and architecture has sustained in Chinese culture, cities such as Beijing, Guangzhou, Hong Kong, Shenzhen and especially Shanghai demonstrate urban futurity in the twenty-first century. To view this from a Western perspective would be to undermine and misunderstand the confidence and dynamism of China's ambitions and sense of progress which are enacted through the construction of such cities. As a result, it is entirely possible to experience glimpses of the future city in the present day [figure 101].

Figure 101. (facing page) Flexible Cities. Spectacle City. Paul Tsui, Macau, Southeast China. 2017. The building in the background is the Grand Lisboa hotel; with its unusual form and physical distance from the street in the foreground, it appears much lighter and almost computer generated. The resulting composition resonates with many future cities from science fiction, an apparent glitch in reality where real life appears stranger than fiction with the future seemingly already here.

The culture of technological desires

Several decades on from New York World's Fair, Expo 67 held in Montreal represented what we can now understand with hindsight as perhaps the zenith of technological optimism broadcast at a world exposition. With the future as its primary theme, Expo 1967 showcased architecture that suggested the future would be one of flexible, dynamic and universal living. The title of Expo 67, 'Man and His World' (Terre des Hommes), was taken from the name of a 1939 book by Antoine de Saint-Exupéry which contains a passage in which the author looks out from an aeroplane at night and becomes distinctly aware of the fragility of human existence on the earth below. This awakened global consciousness reflected a growing public awareness of science and ecology alongside recent space explorations that were very much in the forefront of the public imagination. From an architectural perspective, Expo 67 was an exciting departure from the sci-fi conceits of previous years, with technical prowess on display through a combined aesthetics seemingly derived from the filigree of radio transmitters, space-age facilities, factories, and other recent advances in materials and structures. Bearing in mind that at the time the world was well informed about countercultures, youth cultures, hallucinogenics and other drugs, artists, architects and designers sought to experiment with new sensory experiences as audio and visual technologies became more advanced and architecture itself withdrew behind mediated screens and membranes. Although the Expo 67 site contained a spectrum of architectural futures, one in particular has remained in the public imagination fifty years later. The US Pavilion, a huge geodesic dome, seventy-six metres in diameter and sixty-two metres high, translucent by day and glowing by night, provided a powerful and enigmatic symbol of optimism in the future [figure 102]. With its vast yet delicate frame, the pavilion appeared to contain the full potential of humankind within a bubble of minimal technology. Such a metaphor was not lost on its creator, Richard Buckminster Fuller, who ensured that everyone knew his structures were essentially based on the building units of nature and in this particular example that its literal shape was an explicit visual metaphor for the planet. He profoundly believed in technology as the key to developing a better world for all, dedicating considerable time to education and expounding a new way of looking at the world which was highly optimistic, as he stated that 'utopia is possible now, for the first time in history' (Hays and Miller 2008: 209).

It is in moments of great optimism or great crisis that architects and urbanists have returned to the more visionary side of architecture. Following the peak oil crisis and the collapse of various countercultures or their absorption into the mainstream, there was an identifiable dearth of technologically driven futures for the best part of two decades. However, boosted by pre-Millennial optimism and alloyed to the rapid advancements in various technologies as the twentieth century moved towards its close, an increased interest and growth in visions for future cities began to reestablish itself. Parallel to this development within the built environment professions was the continuing interest in visions that were, and still are, deeply enmeshed in culture and the various ways in which society's perceptions of future cities are shaped by their articulation in popular artefacts. In SimCity [figure 103], the objective is to design and build a city without specific goals. There are two aspects to the game that are of considerable interest here. Firstly, the huge success of the game reinforced the idea of a city

Figure 102.
Layered Cities. Spectacle City. Richard Buckminster Fuller with a model of the United States Pavilion for the Expo 67. Comprising an enclosed structure of steel and acrylic cells, the vast dome also featured a complex system of responsive shading. The latter was intended to echo biological processes that regulate the human body's temperature and was very much in tune with the burgeoning interest in cybernetics of the period.

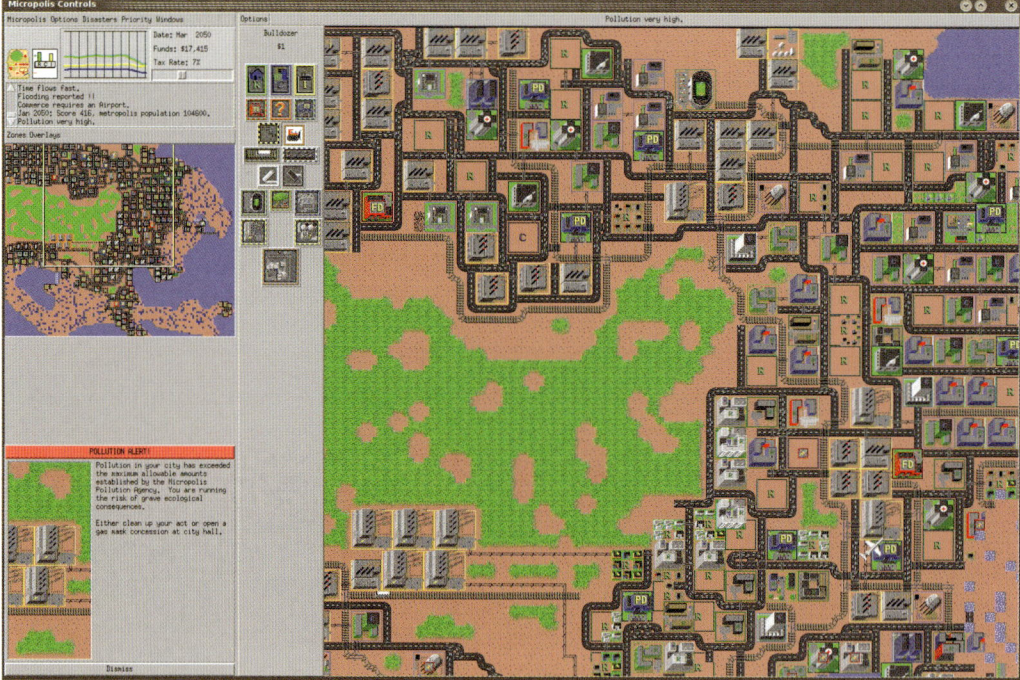

Figure 103.
Hybrid Cities. Smart City. Will Wright, Don Hopkins, SimCity, Micropolis, 1985, Maxis. © (1989–2007) Electronic Arts Inc (Open Source). The game enables the design of imaginary cities or the reconfiguration of real life cities such as Rio de Janeiro or Tokyo. The player is empowered to demarcate functional zones in the city, add buildings, change the tax, and build a power grid and transportation systems amongst many other actions.

Figure 104.
Hybrid Cities. Smart City. Cities of the future, extract from *How Cities Work* by James Gulliver Hancock, 1st ed. With permission from Lonely Planet © 2016, Lonely Planet pp. 24–5. This example from a recent children's book is interesting in its depiction of future cities since in this vision they are anticipated to be technological futures where features such as domes, drones, self-driving cars and vertical farming support future urban life.

being organized and viewed from above in a detached manner to millions of people who played it. Secondly, the vision of a future city that is a complete entity, controlled and managed by a software platform, has found its legacy in development of Smart City engines and dashboards. In a different way, visions for future cities as illustrated in children's books [figure 104] are significant for how they inform how people begin to think about future cities from an early age. Games and books such as these contribute to or arguably, and perhaps unintentionally, limit the future options we have for collective life.

Is there an art to being 'smart'?

In both *Le Droit à la Ville* (1968) and *La Révolution urbaine* (1970), Henri Lefebvre put forward the radical hypothesis of the complete urbanization of society. This condition, from his perspective, required a fundamental shift from the analysis of urban form to the investigation of urbanization processes. Lefebvre also projected the trajectory of urbanization evident in his era into the science fiction imaginary of Isaac Asimov's *Foundation* (1951) saga – i.e. not simply that cities would expand, or a new urban reality be formed, but a phenomenon far more significant: planetary urbanization. Asimov's fictional planet Trantor provides an arresting allegory of contemporary and near-future earth. Its forty billion inhabitants for whom green landscape is a distant memory all live within a single, world-scale city that has spread across the entire surface of the globe. Underneath millions of steel domes that rise into the sky, the majority of the population can be found living in machinic warrens with much of the planet's social life buried into these deep, climate-controlled architectures. From this standpoint, it is clear that Lefebvre's notion contains some rich elements amidst a rapidly urbanizing world and a growing recognition of the urban as a specific category of space.

As a sociologist, Lefebvre was specifically concerned with the implications of liberating social powers that could potentially enable new forms of human experience, albeit within an expansive frame that sought to better understand the entanglements of philosophical, political and ecological inquiries with his own discipline. However, it is also possible to detect some synergies with technology that would facilitate the urban supplanting the city since it is a spatiality predicated on both its universality and its capacity to expand, connect, unify and homogenize. Indeed, the restless nature of technological developments has proved fruitful inspiration for many architects and urbanists. It is possible to go even further and emphasize the importance of technology as politically motivated transformative power whose scope could both delve into the most intimate facets of everyday life and, at the same time, operate at a planetary scale. This was explicitly behind a number of ideologies from the late eighteenth century onwards whose work influenced major infrastructural and spatial projects across the nineteenth century and beyond, in essence laying the foundations for what subsequently we have come to recognize as an anonymous, global project that has extended to the present day.

Technology usually promotes efficiency amongst other benefits. A key development over the last twenty years has been the emergence of 'Smart Cities' (Crang and Graham 2007; Hollands 2008). The premise of most Smart Cities is that we can use real-time, connected data to track and trace communication, signals and transactions. Integral to how many of these hi-tech futures are presented are the aesthetics of greenness and neatness. Outside of the dim and somewhat dismal environment of *Blade Runner* aesthetics, a considerable number of speculations for future cities seek to demonstrate a world that is free from grime, pollution and debris. These seemingly frictionless, clean futures are utopian wherein technology is often portrayed as providing the capability towards such seamlessness and cleanliness. Yet the future is likely to be grubby and, for most places, piecemeal in its development where the majority of cities are concerned. These complications are not evident in the projections made for Smart Cities such as the proposal for Paris 2050 by Vincent Callebaut Architectures [figure 105]. Commissioned in the wake of the Climate Energy Plan of Paris, this Smart City aims to significantly reduce greenhouse gas emissions by 2050. In order to address the urban heat-island phenomenon by increasing in the same time the density of the city in the long term, the proposal uses towers to repatriate the nature in the heart of the city and integrate from their design the rules of bioclimatism and the renewable and recyclable energies in short loop through innovative systems. The environments shown in examples such as this illustrate a gleaming, shimmering world of transparent surfaces

Figure 105.
Hybrid Cities. Horizontal City. Paris 2050: A Smart City, Vincent Callebaut Architectures, 2015. This proposal for multiple high-rise buildings with positive energy output (BEPOS) comprises eight multi-use structures inhabiting various locations within Paris; the plan strives to address major sustainability problems affecting each district while providing key functions for the city.

and greenery. Although often visually enticing, many of this type of city vision forgo the reality of cities and thus remove the challenges and obstacles of clean energy production, let alone those of maintaining them free of detritus. Such complete sterilization of complete cities seems unlikely, especially those which already exist in some form, due to the complexities of integrating new systems for energy, transport, and new architectural envelopes within existing conditions which have often been built up in layers, sometimes over many years.

Amongst all the hype, experimentation, idealism, policymaking, research, play and commercialization, several large corporations are making an extended effort to visualize Smart Cities. Indeed, the term 'smarter city' was trademarked by IBM in 2011. As mentioned earlier in this chapter, it matters a great deal to these corporations not only that certain stories are told about Smart Cities (Söderström et al. 2014) but also that they are visualized in particular ways. One of the most well-known developments is the Masdar development in Abu Dhabi by Foster + Partners [figure 106]. The urban future depicted here is intended to be the first modern community in the world to operate without fossil-fuelled vehicles at street level. As such, a number of its design principles are based on street-level urbanism, ensuring that the city encourages walking via shaded streets and courtyards along with a maximum distance of 200 metres to the nearest rapid transport links and amenities. Similar schemes, such as Arup's Dongtan Eco-City, Chongming Island, Shanghai (2005 onwards), also reflect the combined approach of a walking-based, sustainable living strategy, with ambitions to harness renewable energies and have zero waste. Despite the seductive instantaneous nature of the many digital technologies employed in the Smart City rhetoric, the long design and construction timescales typical of these projects reflect the complexity of such an undertaking.

The burgeoning initiatives for Smart Cities that appear almost ubiquitous in many different countries around the world are perhaps symptomatic of the

Figure 106.
Hybrid Cities. Smart City. Masdar Development, Abu Dhabi, United Arab Emirates, Foster + Partners, 2007 onwards. This project seeks to combine state-of-the-art technologies with the planning principles of traditional Arab settlements to create a desert community that aims to be carbon neutral with zero waste.

many challenges in addressing the complexity of cities: their organization and management, coupled with the relative ambiguity and fluidity with which 'smart' is defined and interpreted in different contexts. Smart Cities' prominence as part of a city's future vision is evident in the significant growth of urban developments that incorporate Smart City ambitions within a wider set of objectives – for example, the Seed Capital Area Masterplan, Amaravathi [figure 107]. In 2015, India's Union Ministry of Urban Development launched their 100 Smart Cities Mission for one hundred existing cities to be transformed. The challenge for cities competing to be chosen for the list partly lay in the difficulty of defining what 'smartness' is, a term which continues to have multiple and diverse meanings and interpretations in the context of urban development. Whilst not officially recognized as one of these, the Seed Capital Area project has important and admirable goals in the transition towards a resourceful, safe and healthy city, as found in many similar projects around the globe.

What is particularly striking about so many of the visualizations for these developments is how similar they are becoming. This appears to be borne of several primary factors. Firstly, the elasticity of the Smart City concept has enabled it to envelop other possible directions for future cities within its wide and

Figure 107.
Hybrid Cities. Smart City. Seed Capital Area Masterplan, Amaravathi, 2015. © Government of Singapore. This development for Amaravathi, capital of Andrhra Pradesh in India, is envisaged to be smart, green, and sustainable and is reflective of future city ambitions more broadly with its commitment to pedestrianization, blue and green infrastructures, and resource recoveries.

ill-defined remit. Secondly, the interconnected and pervasive qualities of digital technologies, not least modes of representation, have supported the production of visualizations for future cities to operate within a relatively narrow bandwidth in terms of how they are stylized. Thirdly, processes of globalization have ensured that visions being communicated with credibility on a world stage have led to content of repetitive motifs and recurrent themes being employed within the images, and thus there has been a flattening of difference, nuance and diversity of vision. The quest for totality through knowledge, control and management of urban systems in visions for Smart Cities is often founded on the potential benefits of such an approach, especially in terms of environmental and social sustainability as illustrated by SHAU's proposal for Jakarta Jaya – The Green Manhattan (2012 onwards) [figure 108]. This future city is envisaged to address current problems and be able to anticipate future issues through a sustainable framework for living in a compact, diverse area inspired by the Manhattan grid. Technology will play a fundamental role in delivering the city's aims to meet its ambitious objectives of 50 per cent green and blue open spaces, zero net CO_2 emissions, 50 per cent of food self-grown and produced, 80 per cent of water self-provided, 150 per cent of green energy produced, 150 per cent of garbage recycled, 90 per cent car-free zone with automated public and private transport, 1 public white solar car for every 10 inhabitants, 20 per cent of people using boats to commute, 200-metre maximum distance between public transportation stops, and 1:1 people to bicycle ratio.

Figure 108. (facing page) Hybrid Cities. Smart City. SHAU Architects, Jakarta Jaya – The Green Manhattan, 2012 onwards. Designed for 1.9 million inhabitants, this green masterplan proposal at the Jakarta Bay is a 58 km², multi-grid design that seeks to integrate ecological and social projects through its comprehensive Smart City strategy.

Whether we will reach the kind of technological singularity needed for Smart Cities to be able to operate as designed is questionable. Perhaps of greater concern is whether such interconnection is even desirable. As the capability of artificial intelligence appears to increase exponentially, there has been considerable unease that we might soon witness the invention of artificial superintelligence that will rapidly produce runaway technological growth with unknown consequences to human civilization. Such powerful and networked intelligence is emerging through greater integration of the physical world with computer-based systems as evident in the Internet of Things. At this point in time, the majority of visions focus on personal gadgets and new forms of interaction in daily life rather than any significant departure from architectural typologies or vehicle design. Many of these imaginary futures are facilitated through various screens for either collective or individual communication. The key difference in such visions is that they tend to dispense with the hardware we are familiar with. For example, the floating interfaces in *Minority Report* are engaged using gestures rather than tactile interaction behaviour, a form of interaction which has now become much more common. The rollout of technology to implement mass surveillance networks such as the example of China's Social Credit System, anticipated to be fully operational by 2020, points to one possible way future cities may manage their citizens. Rather than simply monitoring the nation's nearly 1.4 billion people, it is also designed to coerce and control them within a gigantic social engineering experiment that has been referred to as the 'gamification of trust' (Ramadan 2018). This mandatory system for all China's citizens scores them on their behaviours, with rewards for those citizens it believes to be trustworthy, and limits, even prohibits, the activities of those it recognizes as discredited. Different societies, their governance and cultural values represent a complicated heterogeneous landscape of great contrast, diversity and plurality. However, it remains to be seen over time whether technological futures such as this create socially responsible and just urban communities or if further extrapolation of algorithms and computational power take us into potentially bleaker territory under the guise of efficiency as depicted in *Logan's Run* [figure 109]. Despite being free to enjoy a hedonistic lifestyle, in this future city the population levels are managed by ritual execution when citizens reach the age of thirty. As a contribution to the science fiction genre the film has had mixed reactions but as a potential warning about decadence, overpopulation and allowing technology to control our lives, it perhaps resonates more strongly now. In the next chapter the role of technology as the dominant force in shaping future cities is questioned as we examine those visions for urban life that place greater emphasis on people, their relationships and interactions – what we term to be social futures.

Figure 109.
Regulated Cities. Spectacle City. *Logan's Run*, Michael Anderson, 1976. M.G.M. © 2018. Album/Scala, Florence. Based on a novel by William F. Nolan and George Clayton Johnson, 1967. Set in 2274 the film depicts a utopian city enclosed in a series of geodesic domes which is run by a computer that takes care of all aspects of the inhabitants' lives.

Chapter 5

Social Futures: Experiments, ephemerality and experiences

What is the city but the people?

In the last chapter, we encountered the compelling visions for technological futures that strive to project a total replacement of, or revision to, the city. By contrast here we explore social futures where alternative lifestyles are promoted and future cities are less formalized or top-down in their formulation. That is not to suggest they are any less radical in their reimagining of an urban society. Key to many of these approaches is the subjective nature of urban life and how qualitative methods for understanding cities have informed their future design alongside bottom-up and emergent processes of urban development. In addition, a regularly occurring feature of this type of vision is the human-scale approach to the future. Rather than viewing the city as technocratic object, social futures orientate us towards visions that consider the city as lived experience, i.e. how we live, what we do, where we eat, how we interact etc. This necessarily brings us towards alternative, sometimes radical approaches to

future cities where the emphasis is on countercultural forms of expression and challenging accepted conventions which lead to a particularly strong focus on both Flexible Cities and Informal Cities.

The continuous city for a new society

The quest for a radical, emancipatory form of urbanism was a fundamental pursuit for a number of key figures in the post-war period. Driven by an urgent need to question the status quo and propose alternative models for society, these future cities embraced totalizing concepts for urban life not as technocratic logical conclusions but as a means of redefining the relationship between the city and its inhabitants. A core feature of these schemes was their sheer scale as many of them envisioned a seemingly endless urban condition, relentless in its capacity to span around the globe. Henri Lefebvre's (1968) book *Le Droit à la ville (The Right to the City)* proposed to reclaim the city as a co-created space in direct response to the increasing effects of capitalism and commodification. In its place he (1996: 172–3) suggested that

> To the extent that its contours of the future city can be outlined, it could be defined by imagining the reversal of the current situation, by pushing to the limit this inverted image of the world upside-down . . . The ideal city would involve the obsolescence of space: an accelerated change of abode, emplacements, prepared spaces. It would be the *ephemeral* city, the perpetual *oeuvre* of the inhabitants, themselves mobile and mobilized for and by this *oeuvre*.

The important point here is that the conditions of the present were to be transformed by the radical reformulation of everyday life. Constant Nieuwenhuys along with the Lettrist movement sought to explore the circumstances of everyday life by examining the actions and routines of citizens for their potential to affect change and renew society. Core to this approach was the evolution of 'unitary urbanism' as a critique of the existing state of urbanism, by bringing arts and technologies together coherently in the interest of promoting new values of life. Through his New Babylon (1956 to 1974) project, Constant proposed 'the worldwide city of the future' (Constant 1974), a vast network of gigantic multi-level interior spaces spreading to ultimately wrap around the planet (de Zegher 1999: 3). These interconnected sectors float above the ground on tall columns, while road traffic rushes underneath and air traffic lands on the roof. The inhabitants, *homo ludens*, were free to perpetually reconfigure and reconstruct their environment as social life is reframed as collective creativity on a huge scale. Here the social future was central to the future city vision rather than a secondary element of a technological one (van Schaik and Mácel 2005). Although Constant had been developing three-dimensional work and collaborating with architects since his rejection of painting in 1953, his commitment to this radical vision for the future city aligned directly with his role as a founding member of the Situationist International in 1957. Constant contributed significantly to the group's early ideas and projects until he resigned three years later. Envisaged neither as determined urbanist plan nor as utopian project, New Babylon was considered by Constant as an experimental city [figures 110a&b].

A significant multimedia project spanning a decade and a half for its creator, New Babylon comprised many drawings, models, paintings, films, manifestos, books and newsletters. It was initially presented as a set of large architectural models, each dedicated to a different 'sector' of the future city of a seemingly infinite playground for a new society freed from labour due to underground automated machines. Alongside many drawings were maps to appropriate existing cities and illustrate the new urbanism atop of them. These were compelling, literally redefining plans and their boundaries towards a unitary condition. As Mark Wigley (2001: 52) has observed, 'While he devoted himself to a single project for an unprecedented amount of time and exposed it with an unprecedented diversity of representational techniques, the point was to never reveal what New Babylon looks like yet provoke desire for it.' This apparent mirage of the future city provides enough information to stimulate viewers' imaginations of the liberating image of the global nomad amidst a network of multi-levelled interior spaces wrapping around the planet. In this manner, the various modes of representation used to articulate the project create both a new city and new politics for assembling it through the very interface between these artefacts and their viewer.

If the future city visualized by Constant through his vast multimedia project was one of interplay and imagination, somehow always shifting kaleidoscopically through the different modes of representation, then the consistency and precision of Superstudio's oeuvre in terms of how it was communicated provide a useful contrast. As part of a significant wave of avant-garde Italian architecture groups in the 1960s and 1970s, Superstudio brought radical ideas combined with a uniform visualization technique that produced startling effects. Unlike many of their contemporaries, they were unusual in their view of 1960s technological advancement as a malevolent rather than a progressive

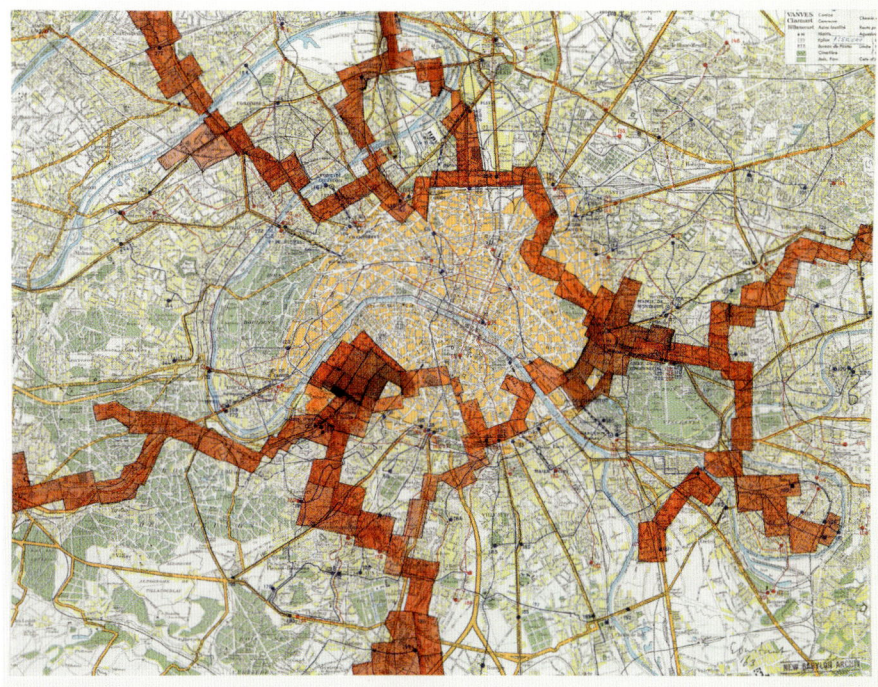

Figure 110a.
Flexible Cities. Crossing City. Constant Nieuwenhuys, New Babylon/Paris, 1963. Collection of the Gemeentemuseum Den Haag. Constant was keen to demonstrate that networked, continuous unitary urbanism was possible. Here the new future city extends across Paris, resolute in its apparent systemic logic to form part of a global condition. Similar drawing/map hybrids were produced for numerous Dutch cities and larger areas including the Ruhr region.

Figure 110b.
Constant Nieuwenhuys, New Babylon, 1963. Photography François Lauginie, Collection Frac Centre-Val de Loire. This sketch is typical of the many produced as part of the project with its suggestion of structure, frames and platforms but no inhabitation. Reading these representations as incomplete or imprecise would be erroneous since Constant worked carefully to ensure they had an openness, enabling the viewer to project into its spaces and imagine their qualities.

force, yet they also opposed conservation favouring a polemical stance that sought to question the very nature of architecture from all angles.

The Continuous Monument: An Architectural Model for Total Urbanization (1969) illustrated the group's conviction that a single architecture could 'realize cosmic order on earth' with a series of collages featuring a white, typically gridded, monolithic structure that spanned the natural landscape and asserted rational order upon it [figure 111]. Superstudio viewed this singular unifying act, unlike many modern utopian schemes, as nurturing rather than obliterating the natural world. Containing some of the group's most evocative images produced by a series of carefully layered collage and airbrushed perspectives, the project extends its glacially translucent grid structures around the world, enveloping buildings and cities, across various landscapes, to propose a monument to end all monuments. The provocative and sublime nature of the images ensured their impact on the international architecture scene and a wider public audience. The method of representation – i.e. slick photo-collages similar to those found in the consumer literature of the day – provided a commentary on the standardization and globalization that were changing the world alongside a critique of the increasingly generic international modern architecture of the period. However, such visions were harder to reconcile with the group's ambitions for an egalitarian society which appeared at odds with such monumentality (Lang and Menking 2003).

Understood in these terms, The Continuous Monument is an architecture than does not portray architecture but instead works as a vehicle of critical meaning to question values. Its vast scale and extreme formal reduction drew from diverse sources including industrial forms of architecture combined with references to ancient monuments such as the Great Wall of China. Perhaps understandably such a proposal was not without its critics and detractors. Kenneth Frampton (2007: 288) came the closest to recognizing the groups' intentions: 'it is significant that Superstudio chose to represent such a non-repressive world in terms of an architecture that is virtually invisible, or, where visible, totally useless and by design auto-destructive'.

In 1969 Manfredo Tafuri published his seminal essay, 'Toward a Critique of Architectural Ideology', in the Marxist journal *Contropiano*, which would provide the foundation for his polemical pamphlet, *Architecture and Utopia* (1973). Across the essay, Tafuri outlined a critical genealogy of modern architecture, not least what he viewed as its problematic relationship within the capitalist system. A generation of young architects viewed this critique as the catalyst for a radical revision of the role of the architect. Amongst the Italian avant-garde group which included Superstudio, Gruppo 9999, and UFO, it was Archizoom that most fully embraced the challenge of translating Tafuri's position into architectural design.

Figure 111.
Flexible Cities. Continuous City. Superstudio, Manifesto New New York (in nero e azzuro), 1969. Photography François Lauginie, Collection Frac Centre-Val de Loire. The Continuous Monument, 1969. In this image the uniform megastructure glides across the Atlantic, enveloping part of Manhattan as it extends across the planet.

If the gleaming vision for the future city of Superstudio's The Continuous Monument was total in its stance against the forces of consumer culture, there were others than took such drivers *ad nauseum* to explore their effects. Archizoom's No- Stop City (1969) proposed the ultimate accelerated consumer landscape as an instrument of emancipation via its continuous field of anonymity, inviting inhabitants to be anyone, anywhere, anytime (Branzi 2006). No-Stop City thus envisioned the future city without architecture, devoid of any tangible expression as it comprised the vital infrastructural elements needed to cover the world's surface with a landscape of production and consumption [figure 112]. A model for global urbanization, this future city was originally published in *Casabella* magazine in 1970 under the title 'City, assembly line of social issues, ideology and theory of the metropolis'. The endless city visualized an organization of repetitive patterns made from neutral infrastructural components, echoing the basic language of the factory or supermarket and thereby embodying the disappearance of architecture. An early drawing of the scheme created using a typewriter depicts No-Stop City as a grid layout of structural columns and lifts, deliberately free from any architectural forms.

The intense politicization of the work of both Archizoom and Superstudio was their strength but also contributed significantly to their downfall. In *Architecture and Utopia*, Tafuri accused groups such as these as simply regurgitating avant-garde tropes, a criticism which as Aureli (2013) has noted led both groups to be omitted from accounts of Italian architecture for two decades, only to be recognized in the late 1990s.

Key to understanding these visions is the cultural context within which they were produced. The peak of counterculture in the late 1960s represented the coalescence of different strands of art, design, film, music, performance, theatre etc. across which architecture played an essential role in its projection of new visions for a new society. As such, multimedia presentations and exhibitions featuring improvised elements and 'happenings' sought to destabilize previous boundaries between creative disciplines and provide a platform for alternative futures to mainstream culture to be acted out. The formation of

Figure 112.
Flexible Cities. Continuous City. Archizoom, No-Stop City, 1969. Archizoom Associati. Photography François Lauginie, Collection Frac Centre-Val de Loire. The open and continuous vision portrayed here in the seemingly infinite model of urbanism was envisaged as an immaterial city dedicated to flows, markets, networks and services. The antithesis of many projects that sought to define the future city as a place, No-Stop City framed it as a condition.

Figure 113.
Informal Cities. Media City. Günther Feuerstein – Salzburg Superpolis, 1965–1967. Photography François Lauginie, Collection Frac Centre-Val de Loire. Despite the enormous city-machine aesthetic, the formal treatment of the scheme reveals Feuerstein's particular interest in archaic forms.

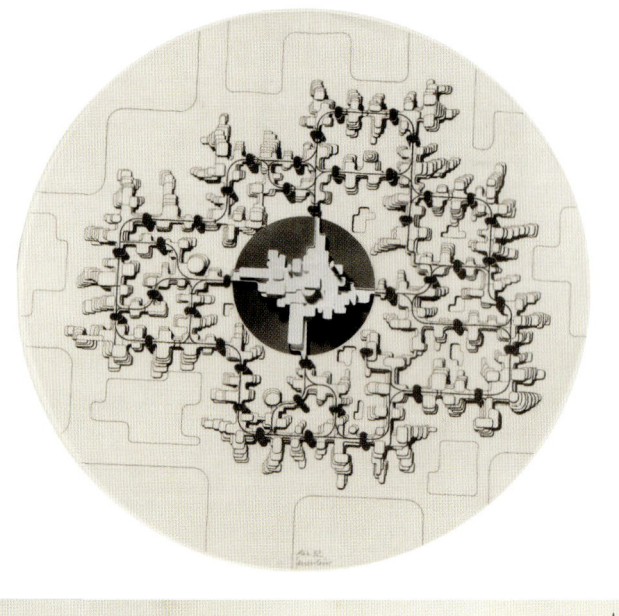

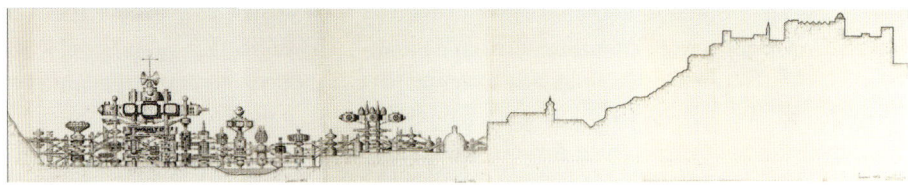

loose collectives and formalized groups gave significant momentum to their ideologies, whether these were utopias as instruments of change or reflective on emerging cultural conditions such as flexibility and mobility [figure 113]. The work of Austrian architect Günther Feuerstein, for example, helped promote the experiments of a young generation engaged in a social and spiritual reshaping of architecture. He curated the exhibition Urban Fiction, 1966 to 1967, which brought together works by Hans Hollein, Walter Pichler, future members of Haus-Rucker-Co, and other influential figures from Vienna and Graz, with its opening taking the form of a happening. Feuerstein screened a film and random images, depicting 'naïve' and popular forms of architecture and pop environments, with a soundtrack consisting of children's nursery rhymes. The models, for their part, also stemmed from performance: one was edible, and another flew with the help of helium balloons. As an architect, Feuerstein contributed to that visionary research which incorporated questions of the day about collective dwelling and communication. His project Salzburg-Superpolis proposed a futuristic extension to Salzburg city with vertical densification to keep existing relationships between the old city and surrounding countryside intact. Within the vision of automated and electrified rapid transport are the repeated light panels across the city displaying the word 'wählt' ('vote'; 'choose'), emphasizing the founding principle of flexibility in response to the inhabitants.

Architecture and its dissolution

These radical proposals were deliberately provocative and encapsulated different approaches to the core question of how urban life might evolve outside of the business-as-usual scenarios that dominated the contemporary planning processes in the mid-twentieth century. That they were never built, and perhaps are even unbuildable, has only served to reinforce their enigmatic qualities and enable their ideologies and intentions to be interpreted in a variety of ways from the vantage point of different eras and contexts. Though extreme future cities such as these did not materialize, interrelated issues concerning the experience and interactions between ourselves and the built environment were examined through a number of architectural projects. Essential to these bold visions were post-war reimaginings of how architecture could go beyond building envelopes to create something more adaptive, fluid, temporal and responsive.

A seminal figure in these innovations was the British architect Cedric Price, whose work explored ways in which architecture might promote social change and enhance human life. Price's projects were ground-breaking in their redefinition of what architecture could be, a point not lost on Alvin Toffler who wrote about two of the former's projects in *Future Shock* (1970), citing them as important examples of a new architecture that sought to embody fluidity, mobility and transience. One of these projects was the Fun Palace (1961 to 1967), a collaboration with theatre producer Joan Littlewood that integrated concepts of social participation and improvisation with technological interchangeability as an alternative vision for education and entertainment. The Fun Palace questioned the very nature of architecture because it wasn't a building in the conventional sense but a virtual architecture melding art and technology to provide a highly responsive environment [figure 114]. The filigree of structure and variety of elements often evident in the project's drawings have a clarity and precision, even if they represented mere moments in the scheme's endless mutations. This echoed Price's

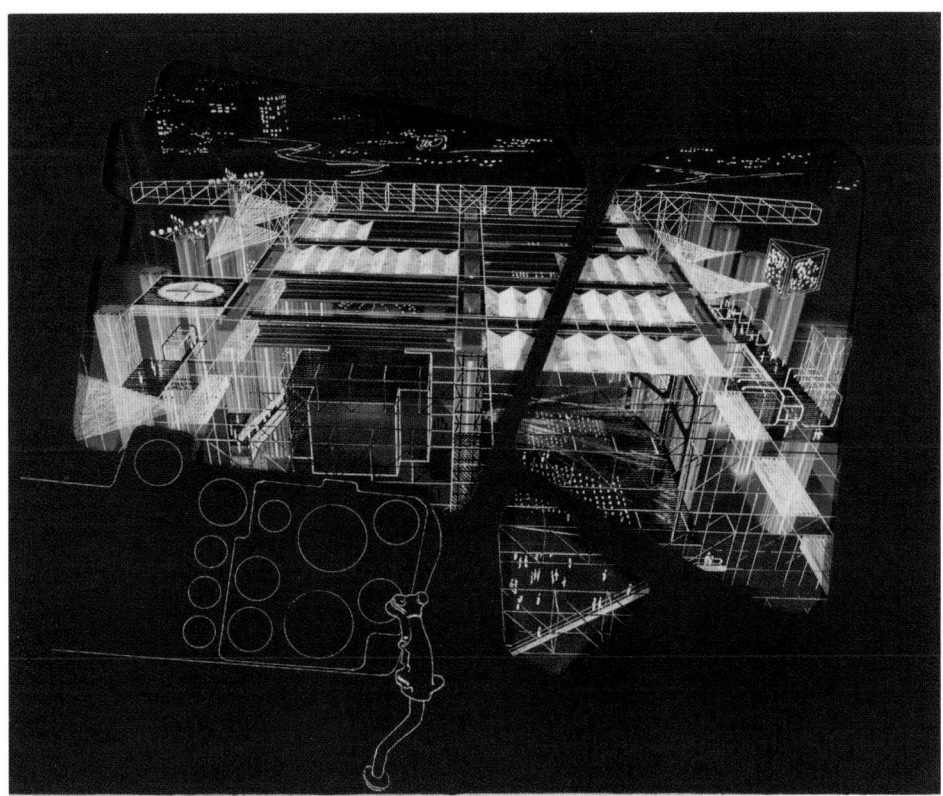

Figure 114. Informal Cities. Sky City. Cedric Price, Fun Palace for Joan Littlewood, Stratford East, London. Project (unbuilt) 1959–1965. The Museum of Modern Art (MoMA) New York/Scala, Florence. Aerial perspective from cockpit. This visualization is typical of the many drawings and sketches Price produced to convey the 'laboratory of fun'. With no doors or solid roof, the Fun Palace eschewed traditional architectural components, leading it to be referred to as an 'anti-building'.

vision that architecture should reflect and support the social transformations within wider society, enabling possibility rather than determining human behaviour. In this way, the Fun Palace examined similar concepts to Constant's New Babylon as they both sought to provide flexible, indeterminate environments for play and appropriation depending on the inhabitants' needs and desires. The principal difference lay in the motivations of the two projects since although New Babylon formed a mesmerizing vision for a new global urban society, both its strengths and weaknesses were intrinsic to its very intangibility. By contrast, the Fun Palace was designed from the outset as a genuine and realistic proposal. The significance of the project was recognized by various key figures, including Buckminster Fuller, who understood it as a huge social experiment in new ways of building, thinking, and being. For Price, the city was not structure that generates meaning but an unstable system undergoing continuous change that reorganized and rearranged itself constantly by contracting and expanding.

The Fun Palace aimed to provide a reconfigurable architecture that responded to constantly shifting programmatic requirements of its users. The challenge of producing an architecture whose behaviour was unknowable and responsive whilst simultaneously providing the infrastructure necessary to anticipate and respond to patterns of use led Price to the fields of cybernetics and game theory. In addition to the eminent cybernetician Gordon Pask, the vision for this proposal of architecture for a new society was considered so profound that it brought with it teams of scientists, psychologists, politicians, sociologists and others keen to contribute and collaborate. Despite this groundswell of support there were many obstacles that delayed the project's development and ultimately prevented its realization. Stanley Mathews (2007: 175) has suggested that the revolutionary potential of the scheme was a key factor towards its unbuilt status: 'The Fun Palace might indeed have empowered citizens to redefine the parameters of their lives, and they may have begun to question the definition of their own realities. However desirable this sort of coming-to-consciousness may have been to some people, it was threatening to those

charged with maintenance of an orderly society.' Though the Fun Palace was never constructed, many of its ideas regarding architecture as a frame for free space and interaction were admired and influential for realized projects, most notably the Centre Georges Pompidou in Paris by Richard Rogers and Renzo Piano, 1976. Its unbuilt status appeared to be a moot point for it represented wider societal transformations as Toffler observed (1970: 57): 'whether or not precisely these visions become reality, the fact is that society is moving in this direction'.

This dematerialization of architecture and optimism for social futures was also shared by Archigram, the radical British group who were contemporaries of Price. Deriving their name from a portmanteau of 'architecture' and 'telegram' to reflect the new, instantaneous nature of their work and its reflection of wider societal transformations and technological progression, Archigram were fascinated with many diverse influences, not least the space age and consumer culture. As Simon Sadler (2005: 134) writes, 'Archigram saw beauty in the unheroic, partially hidden technologies of the late twentieth century – air-conditioning, refineries, engines, portable televisions, camping equipment, things made of plastic and nylon, cellophane bags, gaskets, connectors, cables, networks.' Such sources were crucial to Archigram's ideologies and aesthetics which were underpinned by their modes of representation. Embracing different types of printed media including comic strips, fanzines, poetry and radical statements, the group produced experimental visualizations that frequently integrated collages, drawings and text within unconventional layouts and compositions to convey their ideas. Their visualizations echoed their influences, comprising components from a diverse range of styles and sources, cut and pasted to create fluid and evocative images. Archigram's visions for future architecture and cities resonated deeply with the public's excitement about the future as they were vibrant, playful and balanced radical ideas with everyday objects and situations, literally rendering them accessible.

Archigram's vision for the future city was clearly articulated by one of its members, Warren Chalk (1963), in Archigram 3: 'Cities should generate, reflect, and activate life, their environment organized to precipitate life and movement. Situation, the happenings within spaces in the city, the transient throw-away objects, the passing presence of cars and people are as important, possibly more important, than the built demarcation of space.' Central to this vision was a coordination-as-design approach, bringing diverse components together to instigate change. The mobile, instant future that appeared possible to Archigram was developed through a series of projects that explored what kind of impact pop-up, temporary interventions could have on existing environments to transform lifestyles. This thematic inquiry recurred through schemes such as Peter Cook's Blow-Out Village (1966) which proposed habitable and movable units and Ron Herron's Tuned Suburb (1968) which sought to revitalize the homogeneity and drabness of British suburban streets. It perhaps reached its zenith in Peter Cook's Instant City (1968) [figure 115], the intention of which was for some elements to remain as cultural, social and technological residue whilst the rest of the intervention travelled on to its next destination.

Instant City was an informal, travelling metropolis that consisted of mobile objects including airships, tents etc., alongside technology such as cranes, robots, refineries etc., that permeates a community temporarily to create a dynamic and stimulating environment. Architecture disappears in favour of education, entertainment, an information network and facilities for a mobile population. In this manner, the project encapsulates the group's vision for the future city via a package that travels to the community only to then move on. The visualizations

Figure 115.
Informal Cities. Cluster City. Instant City, Archigram, 1968. Photography François Lauginie, Collection Frac Centre-Val de Loire. A mobile technological event that sought to dematerialize and, to some extent, deterritorialize urban life. Using provisional structures and air balloons, it brought stimulation to underdeveloped towns through mass culture and advertising aesthetics through a sequential process.

for the scheme are typical of Archigram's output, depicting colourful and vibrant scenes of vague perspectives and ambiguous forms. In addition, there is a comic book–style sequence explaining the process of how Instant City infiltrates an existing context to create a new architectural situation. Archigram's radical ideas and forms of representation were symbolic of the time, as Martin Pawley recalled in 1975 (1975: 431): 'they did their best work at one of those times when visionaries believed that what they had drawn and described had really happened'. Issues concerning the representation of an increasingly diverse population were broadly overlooked by the group, which despite their sharp awareness of culture seemed naïve if not highly problematic given the wider shifts in equality across society. The very 'now' of the instant future was seemingly reliant on the hip, young generation to bring it forth, as Simon Sadler (2005: 183) has observed when reviewing their visual output: 'Mostly absent was anyone working, elderly, ordinary.' These aesthetics, coupled with their manifestos, initially propelled Archigram to the very forefront of the architectural avant-garde, but the same imagery and its omissions when combined with the group's neutral political stance also contributed to their demise as they came under attack from various quarters, including newer radical architecture groups who demonstrated their commitment to change through gestures rather than projects.

The exploding plastic urban inevitable

During the period of the mid-1960s to late 1970s, a number of groups emerged with visions for how the future city could be influenced by active citizenship. One such group were Haus-Rucker-Co formed by Laurids Ortner, Günther Zamp Kelp and Klaus Pinter in Vienna in 1967 and later joined by Manfred Ortner. Their work commitment to utopian architectural ideas was explored through interactive events during which people became participants rather than passive onlookers. By engaging people directly in the performative potential of architecture, Haus-Rucker-Co 'understood the city as their field of activity, the fertile ground of which allowed their projects to germinate better than in any laboratory and bring future urban situations to light' (Blomberg 2015: 14). Their projects often involved prosthetic devices, for example Environment Transformers (1968), or inflatable structures, such as Oase No. 7 (1972), to temporarily transform the perception of the city or intervene directly within its spaces. Connecting their various artefacts, happenings and installations was the desire to experiment with the nature of utopian cities through technically mediated environments. Pneumacosm, their founding project of 1967, embodied their manifesto as a bold vision for pneumatic-cell expansion of New York conceived as a way to continuously expand the city by providing a new electric beating heart for it [figures 116a&b]. Using a transparent skin to extend the mass of architecture into the city, the project proposed a series of parasitic interventions that would plug into existing building facades. In their project description, Haus-Rucker-Co explained, 'Pneumacosm is your very own living planet, made of plastic and functioning like an electric light bulb. Plug it into the sockets of existing urban frameworks and appreciate life in three dimensions, immersed in the surrounding environment. Thousands and thousands of Pneumacosms are shaping a new urban landscape.'

Though Pneumacosm remained unrealized, the group did temporarily intervene in New York through their Giant Billiard (1970) project which provided a gigantic pneumatic environment designed for one hundred people installed on 53rd Street in Manhattan. Haus-Rucker-Co's critique of the idea of technological progress, industrialization and its consequences for the environment became increasingly urgent in the early 1970s as they sought to respond with counter-visions of a better future following the Limits to Growth report by the Club of Rome of 1972 and the first oil crisis in 1973. The realization of humankind's impact on the planet would provide much fertile ground for new ecologically orientated visions for future cities. Before this, however, there were extreme future scenarios that took existing consumer patterns to outrageous conclusions. One

Figure 116a.
Informal Cities. Media City. Haus-Rucker-Co, Pneumacosmic Formation, 1971. Photography François Lauginie, Collection Frac Centre-Val de Loire. One of a series of collage images that enabled the possible future atop Manhattan's dirty urban backdrop to be explored: whether as fresh air reserves over the Broadway Bridge, artificial seasons to be experienced in the Four Seasons Hotel, or numerous bubbles to escape the stifling conditions below.

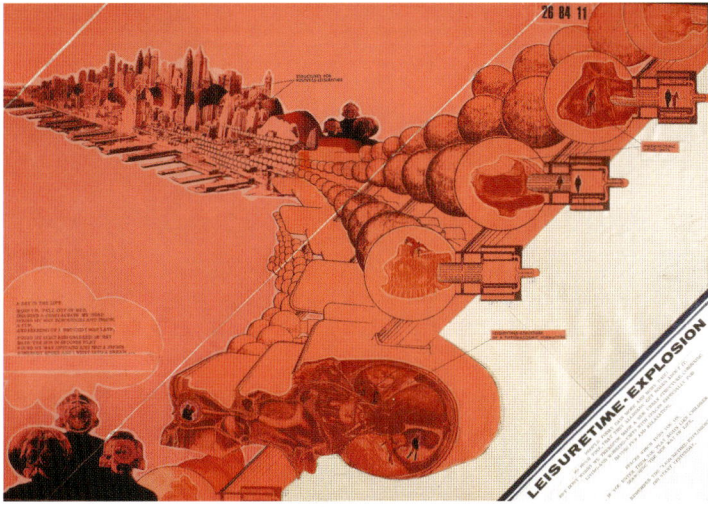

Figure 116b.
Haus-Rucker-Co, Pneumacosm – Leisuretime Explosion, 1967–1968. Photography François Lauginie, Collection Frac Centre-Val de Loire. In this photomontage the units are anchored within a megastructure to form an endless landscape, providing escape from the 'oppressive' existing metropolis beyond. As communal residential capsules, they were intended to be large enough to house numerous interacting inhabitants and their private domains.

such provocative example was by another Viennese experimental architecture group, Zünd-Up. With their name derived from 'burn up', their programme was to 'set fire' to conservative society and their vision for the future city was to transform it into an experimental and spectacular amusement park. Their Auto-Expander (1969) project questioned the prevailing fascination with cars and consumer culture by proposing an enormous pinball machine–like flipper in the centre of Vienna that would flip the cars around the urban landscape [figure 117]. For the same project, they designed a racing car intended to fly over two tubes which were twenty metres in height and then land in a parachute. The final act was for the car to be destroyed in a shredder and become a little package that the driver could take home.

Over in the United States, the work of Archigram and other European groups had not gone unnoticed. Ant Farm was formed within the countercultural movements of San Francisco in 1968 by Chip Lord and Doug Michels, with Curtis Schreier joining later. Their work conceived a future beyond consumerism and mass media but used these as primary sources to comment on environmental degradation and industrialization. Utopian in their approach, Ant Farm dealt with the intersection of architecture, design and media art to promote alternative visions for collective life that reflected the emerging nomadic, communal lifestyles and rejected the rampant consumerism of their era. Preoccupied by social and spatial networks, their projects have turned out to be prescient in

Figure 117.
Informal Cities. DIY City. Zünd-Up, Auto-Expander, 1969. Photography François Lauginie, Collection Frac Centre-Val de Loire. The proposal describes the future city as gigantic amusement attraction, enabling visitors to do mechanics, customize a car body or experience new multimedia interfaces. This visualization shows the entrance to a garage imagined as the gateway to a vast pinball machine ready to flip cars as if pinballs.

their exploration of various media and its effects. Their *Inflatocookbook* (1971) provided a manual for do-it-yourself pneumatic structures, an informal and participatory architecture that enabled users to create their own environment. This reaction to the fixed heaviness of traditional architecture, especially the Brutalist movement, was significant in its potential to express new forms of inhabitation for a new society. In doing so, it carried with it a powerful political message, as Marc Dessauce (1999: 14) has stated: 'beyond the fun and play, the inflatable ethos possessed a subversive constitution which recommended it to avant-garde practice, and to the discourses of alienation and ecology – two discourses which were the same but often irreconcilable, each caring for its own sanctuary of disobedience, in the wild or in the city'.

Ant Farm absorbed prevailing cultural trends and combined them with a keen interest in the communicative potential of new media technologies to propose visionary projects that would energize the future city such as Convention City (1972), Freedomland (1973), and Dolphin Embassy (1974 to 1978). The third is of particular interest here given its research into communication between human beings and dolphins, signalling the ambitious hopes for media technology to enable such an interface. The architectural scale of the proposal belies a greater vision to collect essential knowledge about our planet and oceans so that in the future we can evolve towards a harmonious coevolution of these two living worlds [figure 118]. Ant Farm gained substantial funding in Australia to develop the project and conduct extensive research, but it became clear that it would not be enough to implement it effectively. Perhaps one of the most fantastical-seeming ideas, it belied the considerable rigorous research and serious conceptual inquiry that were essential to Ant Farm's

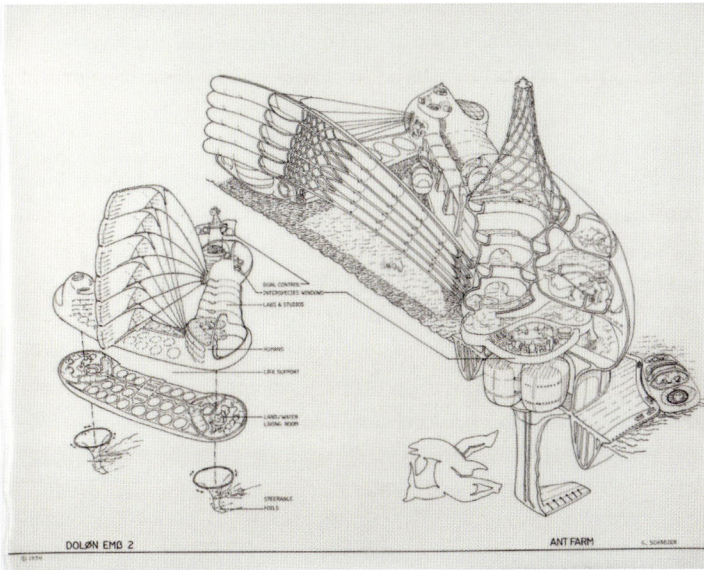

Figure 118.
Informal Cities. Cyber City. Ant Farm, Dolphin Embassy, 1974. Photography François Lauginie, Collection Frac Centre-Val de Loire. Emblematic of the social and spatial interrelationships across their work, Dolphin Embassy took the notion of exchange of information to a whole new level through its exploration of interspecies communication. It was intended to be mobile, constructed from asbestos cement and capable of motion via a solar panel and motor.

Chapter 5 Social Futures: Experiments, ephemerality and experiences vision as Michael Sorkin (2004: 10) has commented: 'the Dolphin Embassy was both a completely realizable scheme and a recapitulation of the ideology of the moveable feast, here at the service of an encounter with the most priapic of beasts'. The idea did not disappear. Following the disbanding of Ant Farm in 1977 until his unexpected death in 2003, Doug Michels continued to pursue the concept. By 1987, it was retitled Bluestar, a joint dolphin-human-compatible space colony with a 250-foot diameter sphere of water 'ultrasonically stabilized' within a wall of space-made glass.

New forms and organizations

The expression of new technologies and their implications for how lifestyles might evolve and the new types of cities that could support them led to various explorations of form and organization. Many projects of this era rejected functionalism in favour of alternative models for urban planning and form concerned with social values. This approach was embedded in Walter Jonas's Intrapolis (1958 to 1967) which sought to develop a more human urban form. The concept for this future city lay in a series of funnel towns consisting of terraced, inwardly arranged apartments to form communities away from the road traffic below [figure 119]. Jonas believed that such a funnel structure would promote the interconnectedness of the residents and would better integrate the older generation into the community. A funnel should ideally have a diameter of 150 to 230 metres and a height of about 100 metres. With a funnel opening of around 90 degrees, according to Jonas's calculations, around 700 apartments, each with three rooms, would be accommodated in one unit, and thus a cone would be able to hold around 2,000 residents.

Inherent to many of these visions was an attempt to physically represent the freedom and opportunity presented by consumer culture and media technologies. Yet such liberation came with a price as awareness of the environmental impacts of air pollution, energy production and consumer waste increased. This led to the proposal of radical alternatives for the future such as Athlestan Spilhaus's Minnesota Experimental City (MXC) (1966 to 1973), which sought to address these issues along with the negative aspects of urban life through a bold vision for an entirely new city [figures 120a&b]. The MXC was a response to the growing population of the United States, projected to be 400 million by the twenty-first century which translated into the equivalent of building twelve new cities of 250,000 people each year to accommodate this increase. Although the future city was underpinned by many technological features, its ambition to form a new social vision and type of urban community through a 'total systems experiment' was a core principle of the scheme (Vivrett 1971). This desire to be free from the constraints and compromises of past cities would manifest itself in reusable building components and innovative urban management systems for traffic and waste. Spilhaus sought to remove the internal combustion engine from the city centre, connecting people with a people-mover and large central pedestrian zone. An integral part of his social vision was the idea that there would be no schools but the city itself would foster lifelong learning. Intended for 250,000 people, the city would dedicate 80 per cent of its public space to parks, wilderness and farms, and would be at the forefront of air-pollution removal and recycling. His vision for a socially vibrant and environmentally innovative future city was a direct response to America's growing population and the by-products of its consumer-driven lifestyles.

From an architectural perspective, the temporary and reconfigurable qualities of these visions for future cities typically sprang from prefabricated elements and lightweight structures housed within a megastructure such as the Radio City (Hill City) (1970) project by Justus Dahinden [figure 121]. Dahinden was a contemporary of Archigram and the Metabolists, and his projects summarized the futurological dream of the period, drawing on the most advanced technologies for the service of communications and well-being of the future city's people. His 'hill city' and 'leisure city' proposals sought to provide an alternative

Figure 119.
Layered Cities. Crossing City. Walter Jonas, Intrapolis, 1958. © Stiftung Walter and Rosa Maria Jonas.
A response to the perception of turbulent urban development, this scheme inverted the city by placing homes and living spaces up in the cones and placing services beneath.

Figure 120a.
Regulated Cities. Media City. Athelstan Spilhaus, 'Our New Age', 1957–1973. Northwest Architectural Archive, University of Minnesota. Viewing science as the solution to the world's problems, Spilhaus became a public figure presenting his utopian ideas for everyday life to a mass audience through his weekly comic strip, 'Our New Age', which was widely syndicated in US newspapers.

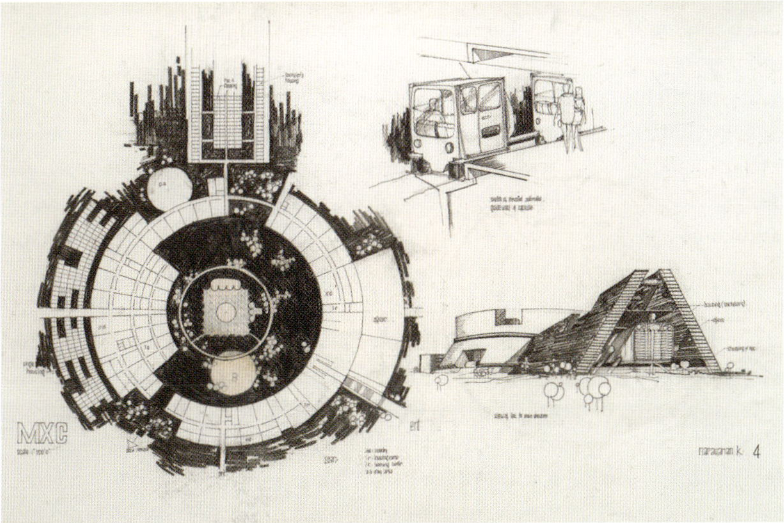

Figure 120b.
Athelstan Spilhaus, Minnesota Experimental City (MXC), geodesic dome covering city centre, 1966–1973. Northwest Architectural Archive, University of Minnesota. Envisioning the future city as a public-private partnership able to prototype experimental approaches to urban living, the MXC was to implement a new waste management system that would reprocess any waste as useable elements within the city.

Figure 121.
Informal Cities. Media City. Justus Dahinden, Radio City (Hill City), 1970. Photography François Lauginie, Collection Frac Centre-Val de Loire. The public place was organized like an 'open and available' structure, dedicated to the organization of cultural and festive events. The lightweight structures of oriental nomadism here overlapped with Western pop imagery, and autonomous dwelling cells, completely prefabricated, were added to the macrostructure using a crane.

to traditional urban planning by conceiving them as wholly dedicated to the ideal future city, its vision led by the mobility of its inhabitants. Dahinden resolutely believed that new media technologies and the emergent forms of sociality that coevolved with them would be intrinsic to the future city. He explored new conceptions of public and private space to speculate on more flexible and vivid alternatives to the fixed and uninspiring contemporary urban landscape. His book *Urban Structures for the Future* (1972) was the first volume to examine the subject of megastructures among various future-orientated projects of the time and in doing so brought together a generation of architects as the new avant-garde.

Amidst the pursuit of a new architectural language to represent these technological impacts on everyday life, as they were envisaged, was a repeated emphasis on organic and natural forms. This fascination has transcended national boundaries, being evident in the Hungarian Antti Lovag's 'bubble houses', Englishman Arthur Quarmby's Corn on the Cob and the cellular pod formations of Frenchman Jean-Louise Chanéac. Chanéac's pursuit of free and open architecture was evident in his early studies for Crater cities (villes cratères) (1963), in which he proposed artificial topography to enable green space to be limitless and enable the future city to coexist with the benefits of a 'natural' landscape. Chanéac's collaboration with Claude and Pascal Häusermann for the competition to design the Centre Beaubourg (1971 to 1974), is a bold attempt to bring the visual and spatial complexity of organic forms into a large urban context [figure 122]. This vision proposed to occupy the entire site and utilize a structural arch to provide

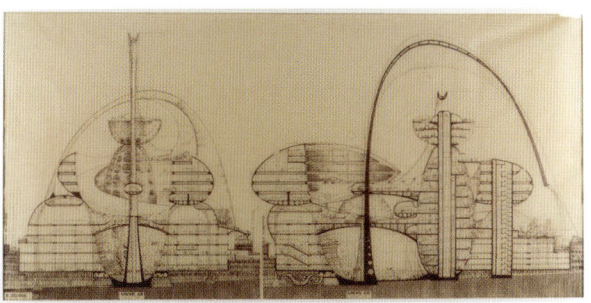

Figure 122.
Informal Cities. Vertical City. Jean-Louis Chanéac and Claude & Pascal Häusermann, Centre Beaubourg Competition Paris, France. 1971–1974. Photography François Lauginie, Collection Frac Centre-Val de Loire. The upper image is typical of the many freehand, colourful and playful drawings produced for the scheme. The lower image of a section drawing shows the design in its later stages, exploring how to accommodate the various functions of the centre within its organic forms.

rigidity to the remaining volumes as an organizational strategy for the different programmes of the centre. These new forms appear fluid and in motion due to their amorphous geometries and seemingly random organization, proposing a new architecture for what they believed to be a new relationship between an urban environment and its people.

Questioning the status quo and prevailing approaches to cities is a vital role for experimental architecture and urban design. Many designers found expression for their more radical ideas in theoretical projects where they could explore without the limitations of the real-world built environment and its stakeholders. One such figure is Léon Krier whose various visions for future cities, including Labyrinth City (1971), were a conscious departure from the prevailing modernism and contemporary technological approaches [figure 123]. This series were an escape from the formal and social principles that drove his realized works of the same era. Krier applied fictional motifs to explore novel compositions and continue his pursuit of an architecture that rejected both modernism and contemporary technology. In doing so, he lay the political foundation for New Urbanism, a movement that reclaimed pedestrian-orientated urbanism from the increasingly car-led urban society.

As debates between inner urban living and the suburbs continued in the latter decades of the twentieth century, the potential conflict between personal freedom and choice versus large-scale developments' apparent anonymity and lack of social cohesion continued apace. Finding alternatives to traditional housing design in the city was at the heart of these issues. Highrise of Homes (1981) by SITE (Sculpture In The Environment) aimed to achieve just that. Its radical vision for urban living proposed a multi-storey matrix of private houses stacked to form a vertical community [figure 124]. By prioritizing the psychological and sociological needs of the inhabitant over the aesthetic sensibilities of the architect, the proposal merges city and suburb as the solution. Its creator, James Wines (McQuaid 2002: 220), explains

Figure 123.
Regulated Cities. Haptic City. Léon Krier, Labyrinth City, 1971. The Museum of Modern Art, New York/Scala, Florence. One of numerous visionary projects produced by Krier between 1967 and 1974, Labyrinth City is typical of the series in its speculation of forms in remote locations, combining Krier's interests in architecture, architectural theory and urban planning.

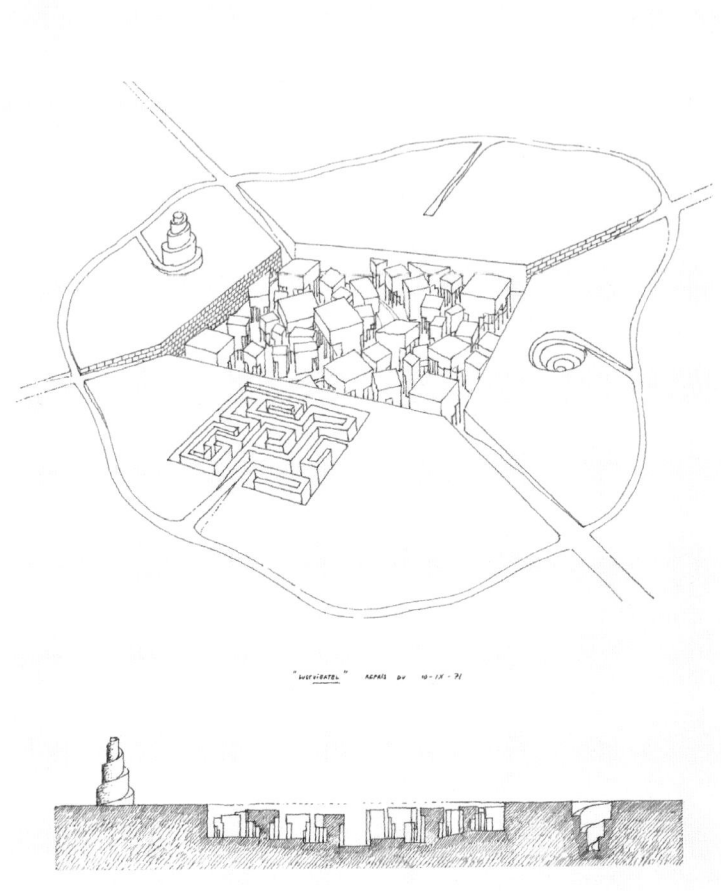

the concept to 'accommodate people's conflicting desires to enjoy the cultural advantages of an urban centre, without sacrificing the private home identity and garden space associated with suburbia'. The project, intended for urban locations in the United States, offers its inhabitants the unique advantages of personalized architectural identity and a garden within a large framework containing many such varied units. Just a few years later, the very modes of representation used to produce visions were about to be revolutionized.

The introduction of visualization techniques comes laden with the possibilities of new ways of speculating on how the future city may be envisaged through novel formal expression. The development of CAD and increasing sophistication of rendering packages throughout the 1980s and 1990s coupled with the advances in computational power quickly placed digital workstations and architects in the same office. Rather than simply enabling annual tasks to be replicated, CAD software has evolved to a stage where the imagination of the user may generate and express designs that would be difficult to achieve with traditional methods of representation. The proliferation of computers and advanced modelling software has fuelled architects

Figure 124.
Layered Cities. Vertical City. SITE (James Wines) – Highrise of Homes, 1981. Photography François Lauginie, Collection Frac Centre-Val de Loire. The wide variety of house styles, gardens, hedges, and fences described in this intricate rendering provides a sense of the personal identity and human connection that are generally erased by the austere and repetitive elements of architectural formalism.

and urban designers to experiment with data, as the newfound opportunities of data visualization, generative design and complex biological properties are accessible to them (Dunn 2012).

As the descriptions of Smart Cities in the previous chapter remind us, data is ubiquitous and enables a city that is controllable and knowable in many different ways, some of which are novel. But what would a city entirely made of data look like, and what would be the definitions of its parameters? Metacity/Datatown (1999) by MVRDV proposed the future city would be one described by information alone, with no prescribed ideology or given topography [figure 125]. Pushing the limits of a contextless, purely data-driven urbanism, the project defines the size of the city in a traditional sense, based on one hour of travelling. However, given that a bullet train can travel at 400 kilometres per hour, this new city is defined as 400 by 400 i.e. 160 billion square metres. It is conceived as the densest city on earth with 241 million people as a means of exploring the proportions. Through their projects and books such as *FARMAX* (1998), MVRDV were key in the pioneering of 'datascapes' as a means of exploring statistical spatial data to

Chapter 5 Social Futures: Experiments, ephemerality and experiences

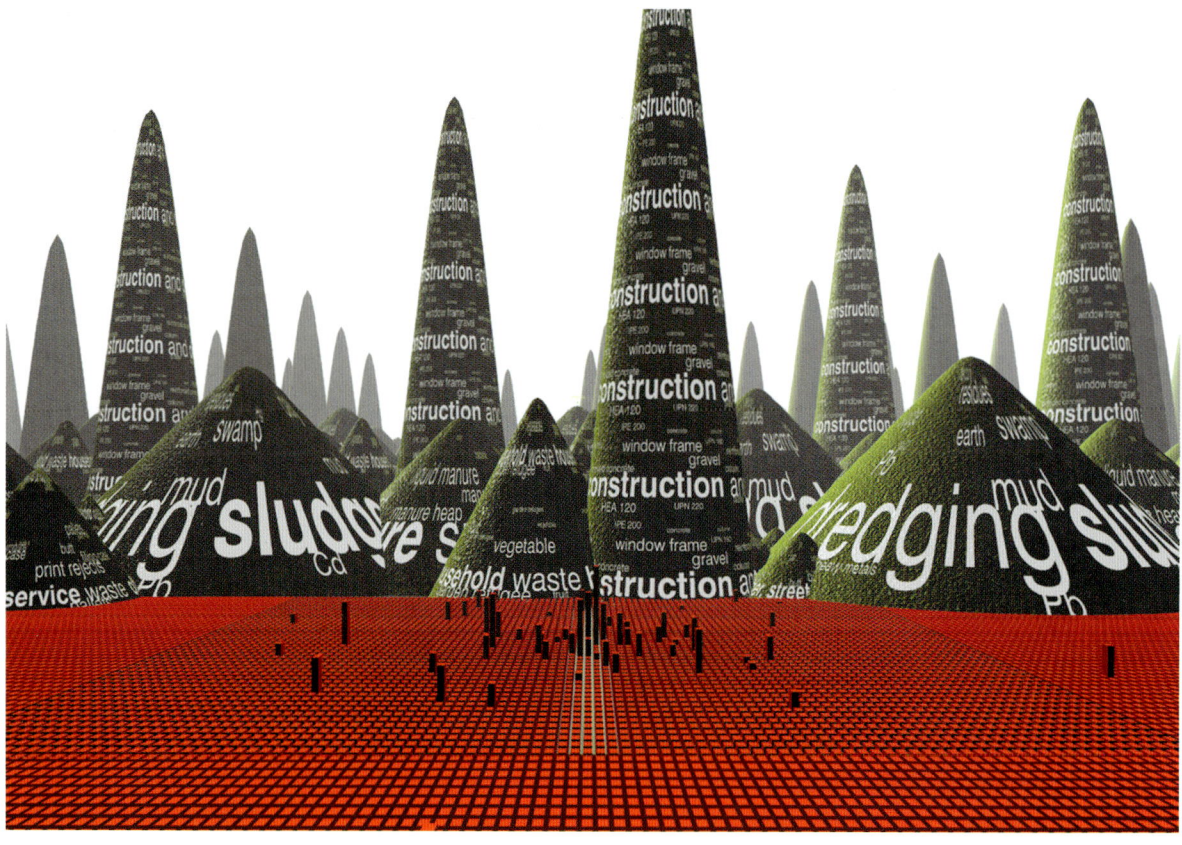

Figure 125.
Hybrid Cities. Cyber City. MVRDV, Waste Sector, Metacity/Datatown, 1999. In this project, the hypothesis of using all the world's available territories for urban development is followed as a means of imagining the most extreme state of urban conditions. Extrapolated from data collected from the Netherlands, Datatown is constructed as a series of sectors relative to percentages of existing users.

better understand context and constraints in order to question current perspectives, values and behaviour. Metacity/Datatown is symbolic of this method, used to reveal latent urban information and its relationships to speculate on the nature of the future city and develop large-scale urban visions.

The possibility of the data-driven future city that is able to fully exploit the complex morphology and spatial gymnastics afforded by computational design has continued to inspire architects and urban designers. These visualization techniques when combined with a vision for urban life have produced some seminal works. Zaha Hadid Architects' One North Masterplan for Singapore (2001 to 2021) was the first of a series of radical masterplans by the practice that led to the concept of parametric urbanism and then to the general concept of 'parametricism' (Schumacher 2009). It was developed using parametric software, which enables the designers to construct 'deep relationality' between the various elements of the scheme and across different scales, such as streets, blocks, buildings etc., to produce a combinative, dynamic overall masterplan [figure 126]. The adoption and innovation using parametric software by Zaha Hadid's practice is interesting, as it appears to provide a logical extension beyond her earlier, seemingly weightless, Suprematist-style paintings.

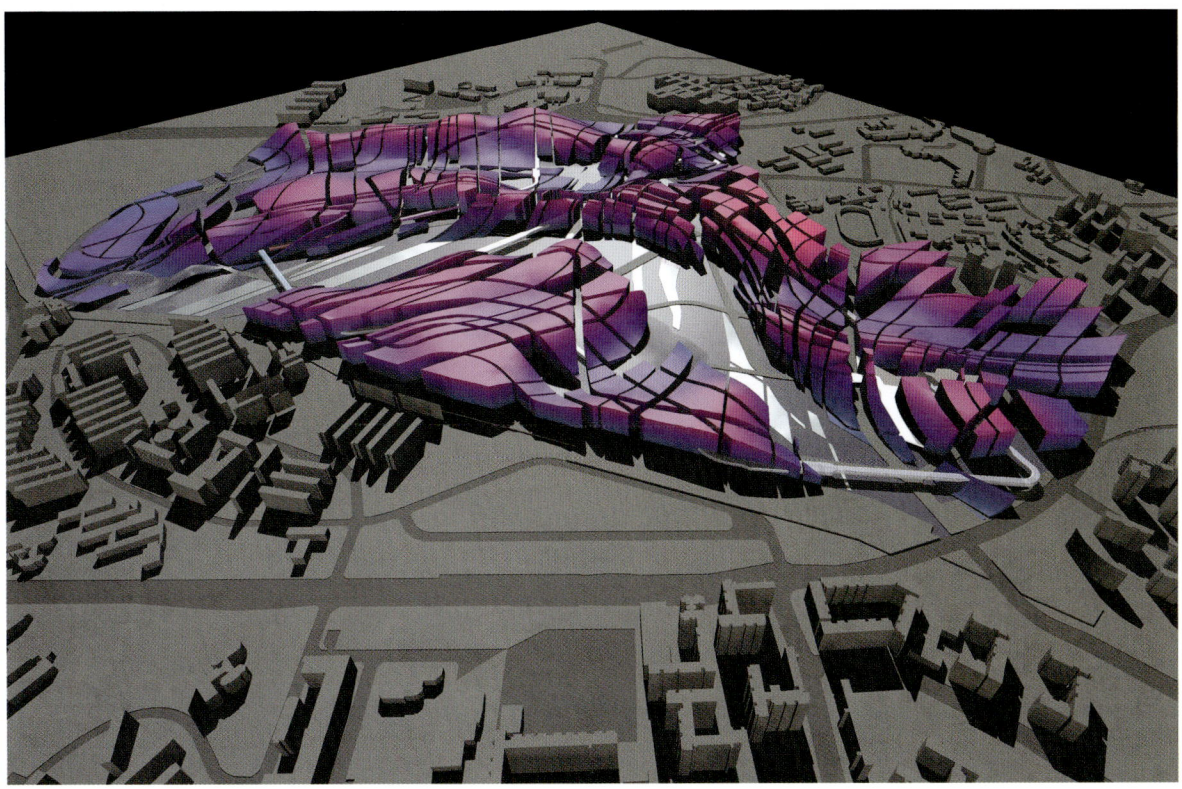

Figure 126.
Hybrid Cities. Cyber City. Zaha Hadid Architects, One North Masterplan, Singapore, 2001–2021. Courtesy of Zaha Hadid Architects. The free-flowing dynamics illustrated in this image project a future city vision of adaption, flexibility and motion, largely unconcerned with the physics of urban space.

Recent formulations for futures

As the complexity of cities has continued to increase, accompanied by a series of technologically driven responses to address this, there has also been a notable resurgence in visions that express less deterministic alternatives. These more socially orientated proposals for cities are united by their exploration of viable ways for future urban development to be people-focused and coexist with ecological objectives and technological innovations. In articulating these characteristics there are attempts to illustrate democratic, equitable, vernacular and courteous scenarios that support social sustainability and resilience as a priority. For Heathrow City (2014) by Hawkins\Brown, the vision is one where London's largest airport and one of the busiest in the world is relocated and a new borough is created [figure 127]. The proposal offers a speculative platform to investigate possibilities for a number of key London issues including housing, goods distribution, land productivity and the governance of digital structures. Amidst the drones, 'factory for homes' and airships is a clear statement for future communities to prosper.

Earlier in this chapter we encountered a number of radical, utopian projects that sought to establish a vision for the future city as a means of proposing a new society. The political agendas and policy mechanisms that often drive or impede cities' futures are often latent in visions

Figure 127.
Hybrid Cities. Cyber City. Hawkins\Brown, Heathrow City, CGI artist: Factory Fifteen, 2014. This masterplan proposes the redevelopment of an airport site with a social future where people flourish alongside technological innovation. Core features include the UK's first airship port to continue freight transportation, new models of housing development through mass customization and an iconic London park built on the footprint of the old runways.

Figure 128.
Hybrid Cities. Horizontal City. 5th Studio, Stour City, 2016. View of a city for 60,000, built along the existing railway line from the North Sea port of Harwich to Manningtree, 2016. This vision explores the capacity of an 'enabling state' to establish an innovative city specific to its context that addresses the lack of affordable homes by rejecting the monocultures that the market forms through risk aversion.

rather than explicitly manifest. A foreseeable shift towards more open frameworks that enable decision makers, people and communities to inform adaptable, resilient and sociable urban development seems likely in some contexts (Campbell 2011) whilst also very remote in others. In 5th Studio's Stour City, The Enabling State (2016), the proposal initially speculated on how to address the UK's housing crisis but quickly concluded that a major challenge was a crisis in imagination for articulating how a society lives together [figure 128]. Created as a response to the dismantling of the UK state's strategic planning and building coupled with the sale of public utilities, the scheme seeks to provide an ethical horizon by promoting social justice and creating a cohesive identity through shared public space.

The 'enabling state' establishes an innovative city to draw investment for partnerships to develop the future city through process, catalysing a mix between top-down and bottom-up, between formal and informal economies. Conceived at the scale of a 'parish', the city can organize, through a programme of green quantitative easing, strategies for environmental and social benefit that are impossible in an atomized society. By contrast, the vision for Sidewalk Toronto (2017) by Sidewalk Labs is predicated on the application of technology to improve the quality of life for residents [figure 129]. The scheme seeks to address social inequality, commute times, and high housing costs and to reduce the environmental impact of urban living through mass-produced modular homes, flexible architecture to enable mixed uses, and walkable neighbourhoods. The visualizations depict a friendly, convivial atmosphere with flexible architecture and walkability being primary features. This vision draws on Jane Jacobs's (1961) assertions regarding the importance of people being the energy on the street, and the public realm is central to this vision deploying self-driving cars and data-driven management tools to enable communities to reclaim streets as social space. However, this vision of future city management has had privacy advocates concerned about the potential for monetizing citizen data alongside supposedly more intelligent and agile urban governance. Key to the proposal is public input into the future of their city which is commendable if perhaps suspect given the parent company's track record on data privacy.

Through engaging diverse interests, knowledges, types of expertise, creativity, and practice to envisage and contest what positive future might be, it is evident we need a range of methods for exploring what 'good' or 'better' might entail. One way to do this is through gameplay as examined in You + Pea's Peep Pop City (2018). This project invites members of the public to

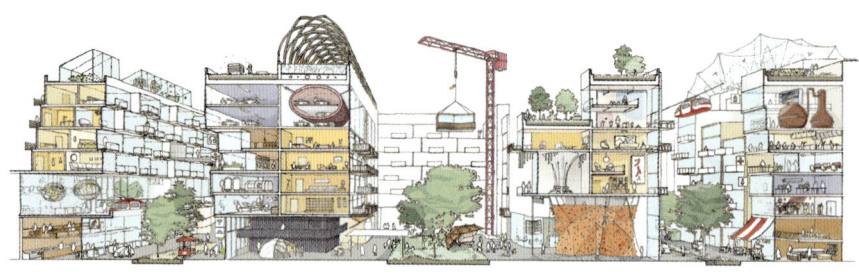

Figure 129.
Hybrid Cities. Smart City. Sidewalk Labs, Sidewalk Toronto, 2017. This proposal aims to fully integrate people-centred urban design and cutting-edge technology to achieve ambitious goals in affordability, economic opportunity, mobility and sustainability. The vision features a range of street types to promote pedestrian activity alongside self-driving buses and 'taxibots'. It shares many features with Price's Fun Palace albeit with less radical aspirations.

explore their ideas for the future city by participating in a multi-player city-building game [figure 130]. Peep Pop City consists of more than five hundred 3D-printed game pieces sourced from the past, present and future of London's urban morphology. Taking inspiration from Archizoom's No-Stop City [figure 112], the game engages audiences with the logics of city planning within a mirrored environment, enabling the future city to be infinite. Player 1 acts as the Administrator, drawing cards at random to reveal objectives for the city and peeping into the cabinet to instruct Player 2 who acts as the Architect to follow these instructions using city fragments in different configurations.

A common thread connecting these recent projects for envisioning the future city is the emphasis on people and their interactions. Historically, this was enabled by active street life and pedestrianization. In the next section we look at a number of projects that have their basis in the experience of the city through walking and the innovative ways different projects have sought to challenge tradition.

Figure 130.
Informal Cities. Haptic City. You + Pea, Peep Pop City, 2018. This project encourages users to explore ideas for the future city through an endless multi-player city-building game contained within a mirrored cabinet. The qualities of gameplay through the interaction between the players and physical objects introduce the future city as a social construct.

Futures afoot: new experiences of the city

Resistance to visions of the ideal city of the future, as suggested by rational proposals that abstracted urban life and its intrinsic patterns and behaviours, was to find an important voice through the work of the Situationists. 'It is known that initially the Situationists wanted at the very least to build cities, the environment suitable to the unlimited deployment of new passions. But of course this was not easy and so we found ourselves forced to do much more', wrote Guy Debord (1974), the irrepressible leader of the Situationist International (SI) which existed between 1957 to 1972 in various forms. Key to their modus operandi was a searing critique of the capitalist forces that they believed were driving urbanism and the future of the city away from the lived experience of people. This fervour for the social ecology of the city and an apparent solidarity with the urban lower classes led to emphasis on extant living patterns as being the seeds of a new city for all. In 1956 and 1957, Debord and Asger Jorn cut up street maps of Paris to provide a psychogeographic guide, The Naked City, as a visual critique of the processes of redevelopment in the city centre that were then underway [figure 131]. By retaining those parts that were still worth visiting and removing all those tainted by bureaucracy and capitalism, the maps gave an impression of a city almost disappearing. These maps were produced by their makers 'drifting' around the city, finding stimulating elements and experiences. The actual poetics of the practice and their use as a means of detecting the future city were quasi-methodical and somewhat questionable in its results, 'as if the special, unreal conditions of the drift might occlude a more profound insight into the city' (Sadler 1998: 80). With The Naked City, the Situationists sought to evoke the future city by describing an urban navigational system completely independent of Paris's existing circulation patterns to offer a new way of experiencing the city in a direct and specific manner. Throughout a substantial and diverse body of work the group committed their vision for the future city as being achievable through the 'revolution of everyday life' (Vaneigem 1967). Vaneigem (1961) was keen to assert the implications for the cities yet to come: 'The new cities will wipe out the traces of the battles between traditional cities and the people they sought to oppress. To root out of everyone's memory the truth that each everyday life has its history and, in the myth of participation, to

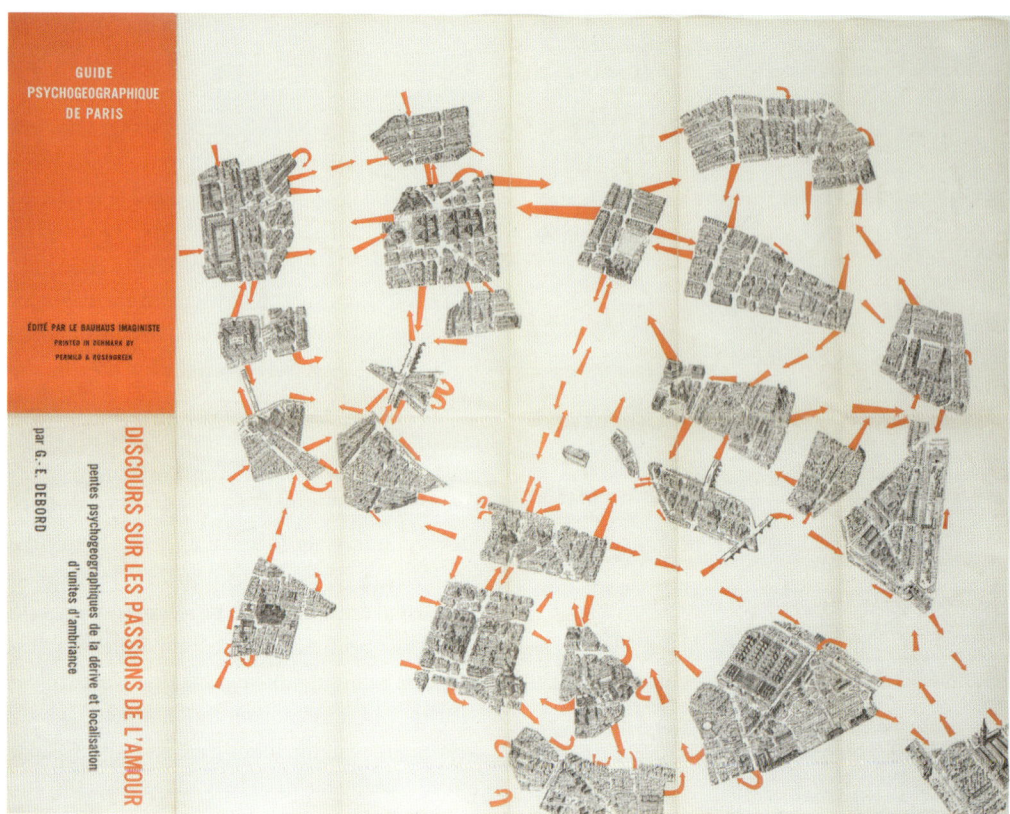

Figure 131.
Informal Cities. Haptic City. Guy Debord, Guide psychogéographique de Paris. Discours sur les passions de l'amour, 1957. Photography Philippe Magnon, Collection Frac Centre-Val de Loire. One of the most famous images to emerge from the Situationists, its literal remapping of Paris made explicit their dissatisfaction with the existing conditions of Paris whilst pointing towards the possibilities of the future city.

contest the irreducible character of lived experience – these are the terms in which urbanists would express the goals they pursue, if they deigned to suspend for a moment the air of seriousness that obstructs their thinking.' Even though the SI disbanded amidst acrimonious circumstances, their ideas and influence continue to reverberate through the work of many different practices and projects seeking to provide an alternative to the commodification of urban space.

The SI were fully aware of the power of their maps and rhetoric concerning the lived experience and connection to the streets rather than a distanced, abstract view of the city. In a very different manner but no less enduring or influential, the work of Kevin Lynch, in particular *The Image of the City* (1960), brought with it considerable attention to the relationship between the body and the urban environment. Lynch was interested in examining how people made sense of their city and constructed mental maps based on the information they took in which he categorized within five elements: landmarks, paths, nodes, edges and districts. The use of cognitive maps lays open the idea that cities are personal and lived experiences, and by exploring how people make sense of their urban surroundings, the clues to how to design the future city might be disclosed [figure 132].

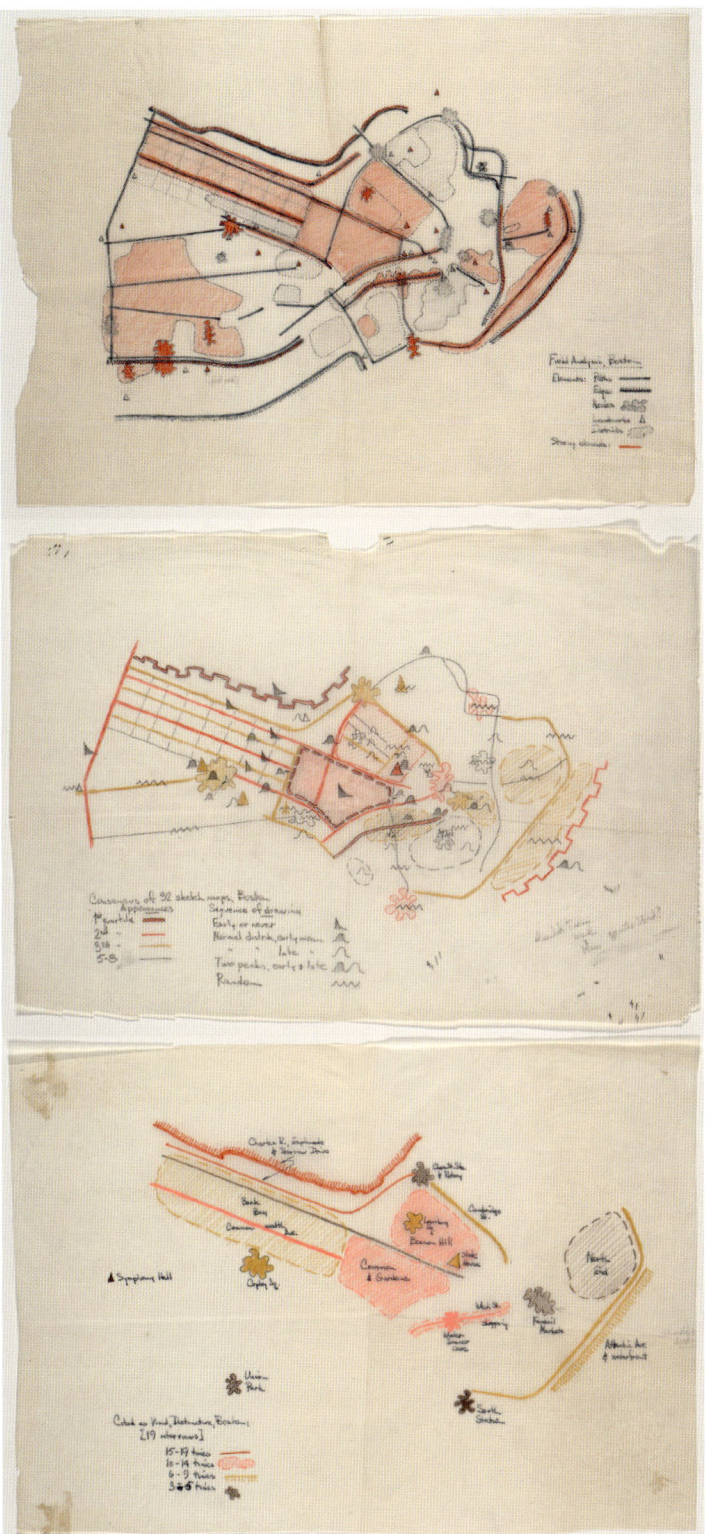

Figure 132.
Informal Cities. Haptic City. Kevin Lynch, Extract from The Perceptual Form of the City, Boston, Massachusetts, 1954–1959. MIT Archives. Lynch considered the visual information collected by city inhabitants and the mental maps formed. Using this information, a representation of the city can be formed. This approach has proved highly influential, re-emerging through novel mapping techniques using both analogue and digital methods.

Understanding the context of the city required new visually led fieldwork to be conducted. Another prime example of this is Lawrence Halprin's (1963) approach which developed perceptions of the city as participants recorded their experience through set walks [figure 133]. These perceptions were then collected in order to find commonality of urban experience. Halprin's work contributed greatly to the development of community planning in America, which would later become mandatory as part of the planning process. In Halprin's movement notation score participants are asked to describe and record their impressions of plazas and parks with specific tasks and time durations. The results are then compared and evaluated for similarity and experience of the city. This method sets and references a social practice, a performance in which the participant defines his or her relationship with place. Further work by figures such as Lucius Burckhardt (Fezer and Schmitz 2012), Philip Thiel (1997) and Randolph Hester (1982) amongst others also developed examples of approaches to decoding city space. Given the time of their development, the methods employed were analogue in nature and sought to elicit an understanding of the extant city whilst tapping into the latent relationships and energies that would indicate how future cities might work.

Figure 133.
Informal Cities. Haptic City. Lawrence Halprin, Fort Worth City Walk Map, 1974. © Lawrence Halprin Collection, The Architectural Archives, University of Pennsylvania. These signs and complex symbols represent the code of the space, a code that is recoded in paper form and compared. These comparisons allowed the study of the iterations and similarities of the participants, a sort of participatory urban rhythm.

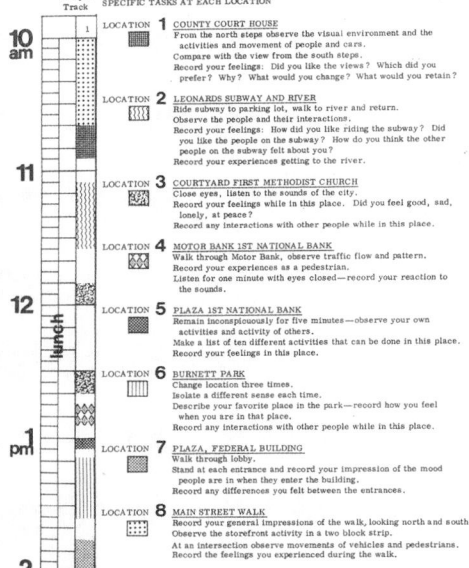

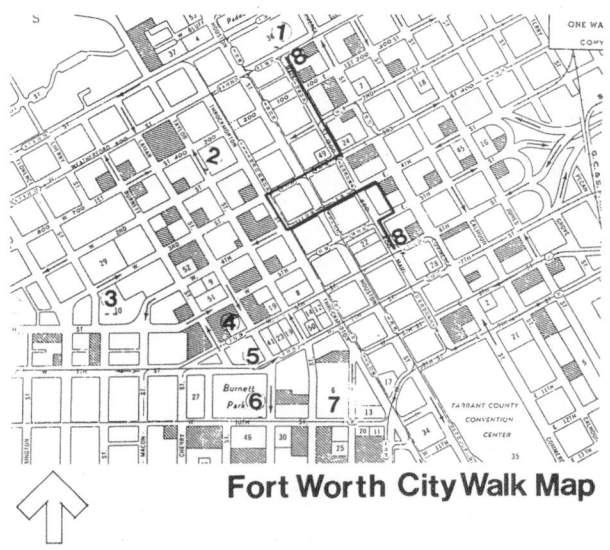

138   FUTURE CITIES: A VISUAL GUIDE

Disruption, hybridity and augmentation

The complexity of urban space has been a profound source of inspiration for many architects and urban designers keen to explore the ambiances, atmospheres and sensory experiences of how the future city might be. The close relationship between the development of cinema and its reciprocal relationship with architecture is relevant in this context in two important ways. Firstly, as described in previous chapters, the representation of future cities in film has had an enduring influence on the constructed materialities of cities. Secondly, and perhaps less obviously, the elements of cinematography that have a kinship with architecture and urban space such as framing, narrative, movement etc., have also provided useful devices for reconceptions of cities. An important figure in this latter category is Bernard Tschumi, whose prioritization of the idea of movement and event over architectural form underpinned the vision for the Parc de la Villette (1982 to 1998) and its new strategy for urban organization [figure 134]. This vision proposes urbanism as an expanded and distributed field within which cultural exchanges flow and merge. A key participant in architectural theory since the 1970s, Tschumi has drawn from a diverse field of influences including Russian Constructivism, Georges Bataille, Jacques Derrida, Roland Barthes and cinema. In this scheme the notion of

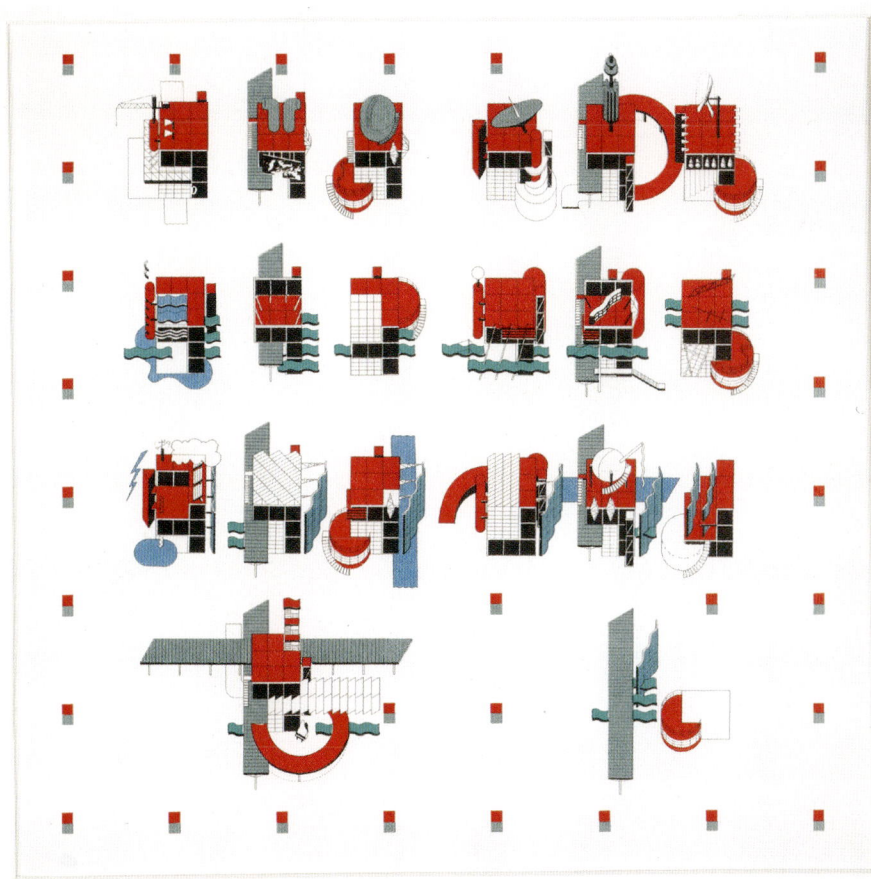

Figure 134.
Flexible Cities. Media City. Bernard Tschumi, Parc de la Villette, Paris, 1983. Photography Olivier Martin-Gambier, Collection Frac Centre-Val de Loire. Tschumi's competition-winning approach for the Parc de la Villette was to distribute the requirements of the programme across the entire fifty-five-hectare site as a series of follies rather than construct additional buildings.

architectural unity is supplanted by heterogeneity and fragmentation as fixed and hierarchical forms yield to the dynamic and, finally, synthesis is replaced by disjunction. The project embodies Tschumi's view of 'event' and 'movement' being vital to architecture and cities, continuing his exploration of notation of space and action, between the stage and the script, evolved through his earlier theoretical work, The Manhattan Transcripts 1976–1981 (1995).

These ideas of dynamic, hybrid and heterogeneous aspects to the city found new representation through the work of Atelier Bow-Wow in their Made in Tokyo (2001) project [figure 135]. Their research focuses on mapping the micro environments of city spaces and their evolution over time. These novel hybrid typologies provide speculation on the social future of cities as Kaijima et al. (2001: 251) propose: 'it is not people who creates space, but social spaces that use people to bring themselves into being'.

The development of cyberspace led to new, potentially emancipatory possibilities of personal freedoms and 'spaces' for sub-altern groups and communities. At the very crux of the interface with each other as mediated by technology, human relationships are foundational to this approach. How we might interact with the virtual world has been vividly projected in numerous sci-fi films, in particular *The Matrix* (1999), which due to advances in computer-generated imagery (CGI) enabled the visual effects to be mesmerizing in their blurring between reality and not.

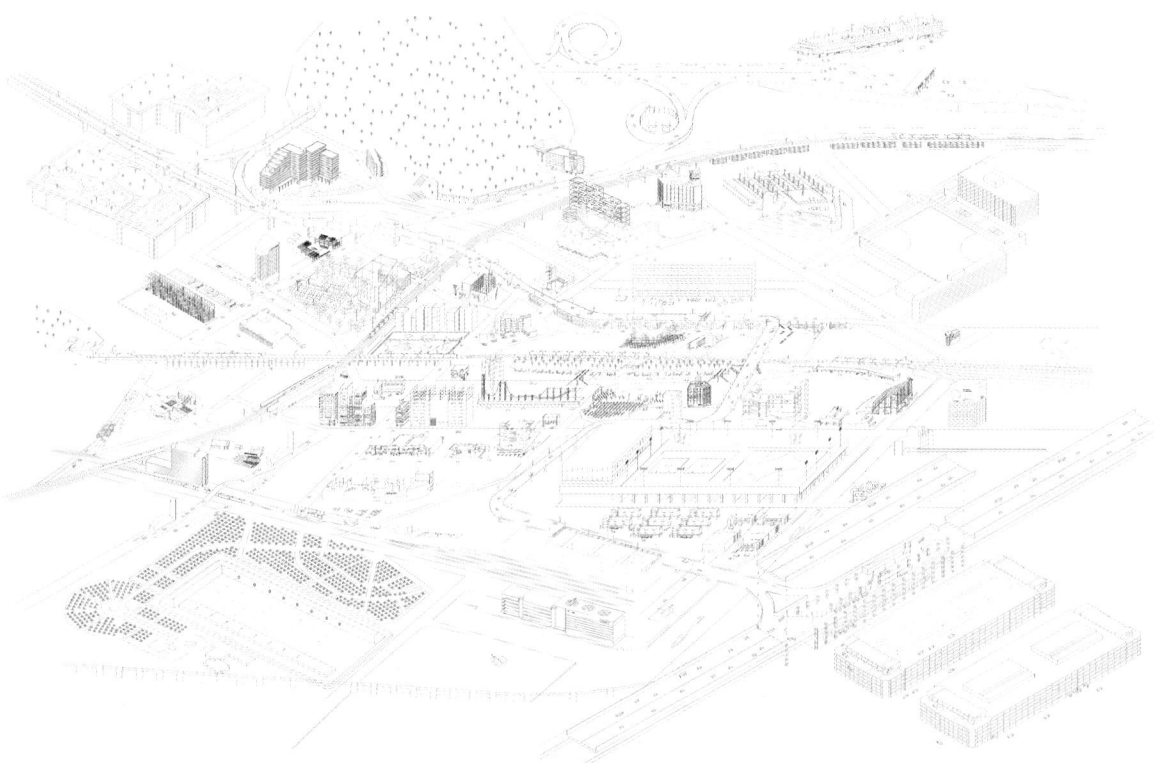

Figure 135.
Informal Cities. Collage City. Atelier Bow-Wow, Generations of Tokyo Architecture, Made in Tokyo Guidebook, 2001. The project documents novel juxtapositions of programme as a means of utilizing small, awkward urban spaces and creating social interactions. This examination of unusual functional-hybrid architectures and urban spaces provides valuable speculation on how the future city might evolve through the discovery of radical typologies.

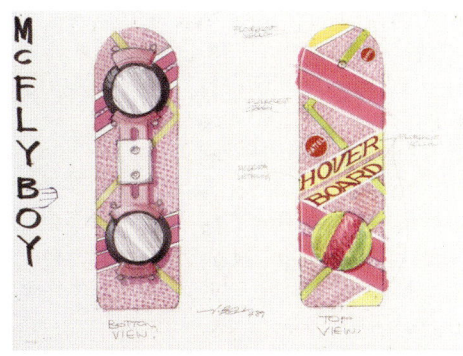

Figure 136.
Hybrid Cities. Moving City. *Back to the Future: Part II*, Hoverboard, conceptual sketch, 1989. © JohnBell Studio © Universal Pictures, Amblin Entertainment, U-Drive Productions. There have been various attempts to bring versions of the hoverboard into reality, but the complexities of small flying transport in built environments coupled with the technical difficulties of powering a floating device for sufficient time and load remain highly challenging.

The current developments in virtual reality appear to be catching up to the promise it heralded in the 1980s, but to date it remains a very different experience than being out in the built environment. At this juncture, more likely is the entanglement between augmented reality and our experience of cities to provide enhanced experiences. Going forwards, a return to more practical and essential types of interaction through street-level urbanism, walking, cycling etc. rather than hermetically sealed, capsular civilization of motor cars etc. is being celebrated and proposed for the multiple benefits such approaches provide in terms of health, environment, sustainability, quality of life etc. That the future city might be one of heightened experiences has not been lost on architects, designers, filmmakers and writers. For example, the fictional hoverboard featured in *Back to the Future: Part II* (1989) has transcended the screen even if it has not appeared quite as frictionless or versatile in reality [figure 136]. Originally described by author M. K. Joseph in 1967, this fictional levitating form of personal transportation was brought to a mass audience in the *Back to the Future* film franchise. It was one of many speculative objects devised for the 'future 2015' which also featured video goggles, flying cars and wearable technologies. The personal freedom of mobility and urban experience that the hoverboard signifies is less likely to manifest in physical form and much more likely to be brought about through augmented reality, yet its power to capture the collective imagination remains strong.

Whereas the future city has been previously envisioned as a place where technology is built into the architecture to enable all urban life to flourish, for example in Hans Kollhoff's Atlanpole (1988), we have now arrived at a point where technology is so ubiquitous and pervasive that it may simply overlay all facets of our urban lives. This augmented reality may reshape existing urban conditions to become future city experiences. Although nascent, the possibility of such an urban future is imaginatively explored in

Figure 137.
Hybrid Cities. Cognitive City. Keiichi Matsuda, Still from *HYPER-REALITY*, 2016. This short movie depicts a futuristic scenario where digital media and the physical world have merged to create a kaleidoscopic 'hyper reality'. Conceived as the glue between every interaction and experience, offering amazing possibilities while also controlling the way we understand the world, the project explores this exciting but dangerous trajectory.

Keiichi Matsuda's *HYPER-REALITY* (2016) [figure 137]. In this project, augmented reality is taken to an extreme with an urban environment entirely smothered by virtual interfaces. The short film features a protagonist bored and disillusioned with her current life in Medellín, Colombia, and so she embraces the games, services and other pop-up functions that complement her daily routines via augmented reality. The pop-up displays also give her the option to 'reset' her digital identity and accumulate points as she goes about her daily activities, while pop-up avatars act as personal advisors and a help line for the augmented reality system she is plugged into. Technologies such as virtual reality, augmented reality, wearables, and the Internet of Things are pointing to a world where technology will envelop every aspect of our lives. Heady visions for a social future such as this are both stimulating and serve as a cautionary reminder of the considerable resources that support, and indeed could augment, urban life. In the next chapter, the importance of considering the environmental impact of future cities and how they may adapt, resist or perish due to the effects of climate change is examined in what we consider to be global futures.

Chapter 6

Global Futures: Challenges and opportunities for collective life

Planetary problems and us

The question of how we address the many global challenges that now face us in the twenty-first century is substantial. With the major disruptions of increasingly frequent extreme weather events coupled with overall shifts around the planet due to climate change, how we create effective, resilient and sustainable cities for collective life now and for the generations that will follow is ever-pressing. The recent report of the Intergovernmental Panel on Climate Change (IPCC 2013) indicates that by 2100, global temperatures will have risen by over two degrees Celsius above pre-industrial records, and sea levels will rise by up to a metre and be considerably more acidic with greater risk of flooding due to increased atmospheric turbulence. A more recent special report by the IPCC (2018) makes clear the potential impacts associated with long-lasting or irreversible changes, including the loss of some ecosystems, the further consequences of which are not fully known. One of the major obstacles in thinking about climate change is that the challenges appear so multifarious and complex that it can be overwhelming and very difficult to imagine the possible futures it may lead us towards (Yusoff and Gabrys 2011). This has not prevented various creative attempts at examining the potential impact of climate change or speculating on ways to mitigate its effects from being produced. In *The Age of Stupid* (2009) a future archivist living alone in the devastated world of 2055 looks back on footage from the mid- to late 2000s, trying to discern where it all went wrong. The film is a drama-documentary-animation hybrid which enables the catastrophic effects of climate change upon cities including London, Las Vegas and Sydney as well as the Amazon rainforest and other regions to be powerfully conveyed. It is one of many different visions for future cities and the planet that do not flinch from the apocalyptic scenarios likely to come our way. By contrast, Jonathon Porritt's *The World We Made* (2013) adopts a similar approach, employing the narrative of a teacher looking back from 2050, but although there are descriptions of major shocks to the system of urban life due to accelerated climate change, these serve to add significant momentum to the need for the radical changes that are explained as to how we avoid outright global catastrophe and reach a better place in the future.

Our rate of consumption and the lifestyles that have enabled many of us to thrive so far are highly likely to undergo change. There is a paradox concerning future cities and the planet. On the one hand, cities are capable of being highly efficient in terms of density, energy, housing, and transport let alone civic life, blue and green infrastructures, education, workplaces, security etc. Viewed in this way, they may form viable pathways to enable the human species to continue to flourish. However, the flipside to this situation is that there are currently many cities around the world that are contributing to environmental degradation through pollution, waste, extraction of resources, consumption patterns and behaviours thus directly exacerbating climate change.

It is reasonable to assume that, at least in the current business-as-usual scenario, the global population will continue to migrate towards cities as indicated by the UN DESA Population Division (2018) indicating that more than two-thirds of us will be urban by 2050. Clearly, the many benefits of collective life – cultural, economic, environmental, political, social etc. – point towards an urgent need to explore how global urban futures might work. Indeed, this may require us to think of radical alternatives to cities as we currently imagine them and explore other possible domains that will enable their development. Further, we may have to make some difficult decisions about what can be sustained and what cannot, including critical questions such as where cities can be located and where they cannot; what arrangements of density and settlement size are viable; which materials will protect us and not contribute further to environmental degeneration; and how might we travel and why? Such questions are vitally important and urgent since the role of cities as part of a coordinated response to address the challenges of climate change is currently weighted towards mitigating its effects rather than adapting to them (Bulkeley 2013).

How we formulate a response to these complex issues to ensure our existence on the planet is set to become a defining feature of the decades ahead. It will require considerable imagination and vision to redirect us from existing path dependencies and towards viable alternatives. To achieve this, it will be necessary to embrace radical ideas that fundamentally question accepted norms of how we envisage future cities. Therefore, in this chapter we examine those visions that have sought to provide a global future for urban life, whether through superlative provocations, through inhabitation of new territories, or as responses to catastrophic ecological events. As part of this journey, we encounter new visions proposed as a response to the extreme impacts of these events, such as fantastical off-earth communities, floating cities, desert cities, drowned cities etc. In addition, we look at a number of projects that are seeking to rebalance relationships between cities and the natural world as useful signposts for how we might work with the many cities that already exist to secure their future. These visions are also reflective of an increasing global consciousness that underpins how and why we urbanize the planet, along with the impacts such processes have.

Ecological infrastructures and regional responses

There have been numerous proposals that seek to find a balance between urbanization and the natural world. Bold visions, symbolic of the supposed mastery of humankind to overcome the obstacles of the natural environment such as Mike Mitchell and Alan Boutwell's Comprehensive (Continuous) City (1969), made the delineation between urban and not extremely sharp [figure 138]. It proposed a gigantic, continuous linear city for one billion inhabitants that spanned from San Francisco to New York via Chicago and Detroit. The city was intended to be completely self-containing for all urban life, leaving the rest of the United States to be untouched by human beings. Using one-hundred-metre-high pillars, it ran across the American continent, gliding across considerably varied terrain whilst a complex traffic system differentiated by speed, distances and transportation enabled connection to all aspects of city life. Boutwell and Mitchell (1969: 4) described their project with

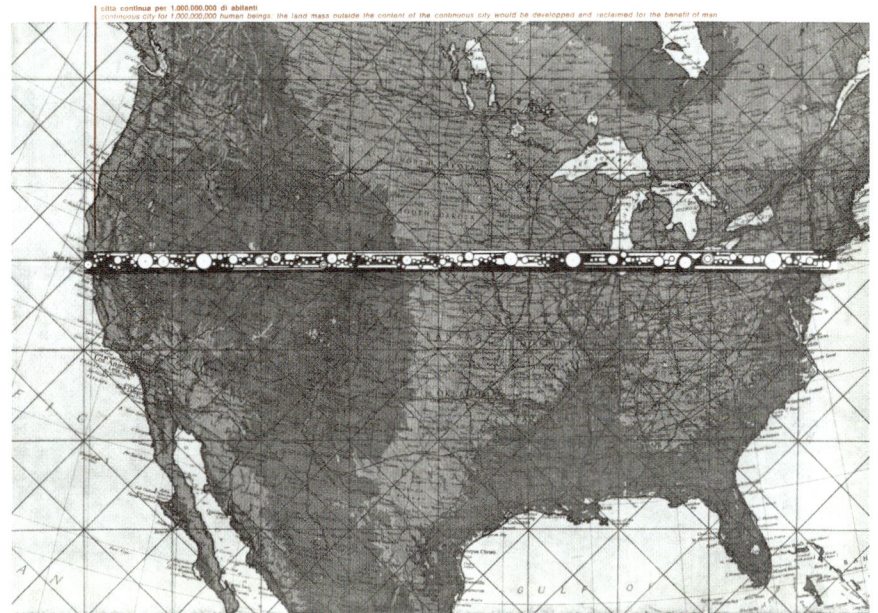

Figure 138.
Regulated Cities. Crossing City. Alan Boutwell and Mike Mitchell, Comprehensive City, Domus 470, 1969. This montage sets out the bold extent of the future city, though in essence the scheme describes an enormous transcontinental superhighway. Provocative at the time, the proposal echoed the heroic age of Modernism and embodied the functionalist urbanism objected to by Constant [figures 110a&b].

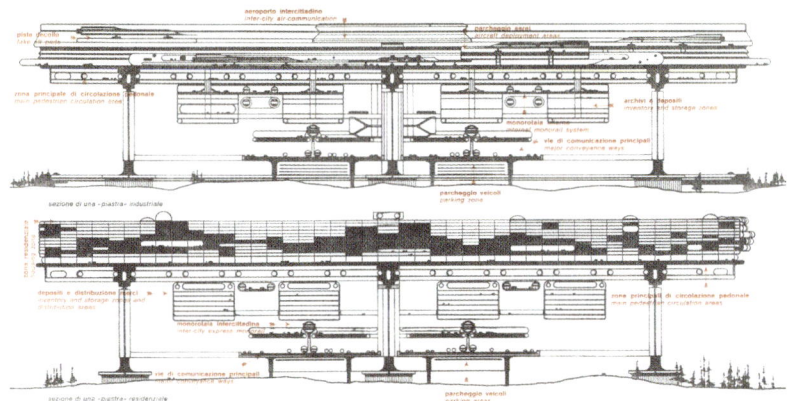

the assertive tone of their era: 'This is our city. We have not sensationalized. All that we have described is feasible today. We are not saying this is the city of the future, but rather one of the possibilities deserving of serious consideration.' Yet as Reyner Banham was to observe (1976: 198), Comprehensive City makes no concessions to the existing landscape: 'the scheme as drawn treats the map of North America as exactly the same kind of ideal surface as Le Corbusier had employed for this ideal *Ville contemporaine*, whose topographical accidents have no effect on the design'. Despite this, it was taken seriously enough to provoke debate as the project resonated with the times amidst various hypothetical proposals that questioned the very purpose of cities. It also predated the increased environmental awareness that was to come in the early 1970s, and its arcology-style approach resonated with the work of Soleri [see figure 87, Chapter 4].

Figure 139.
Layered Cities. Underground City. Luigi Pellegrin, Vector habitat at geographic scale – Research on linear infrastructural components. 1970. Drawing Cyanotype, collage, pastel, papier, 156 x 116 cm. Photography François Lauginie, Collection Frac Centre-Val de Loire. Investigating a way for the natural world and built environment to coexist effectively, nature regains its space as the artificial environment is limited to a few dense clusters that support the planetary loop of the future city.

Rather than viewing nature as an obstacle to urban progress, concerns regarding the need for harmony between the built environment and the natural environment became increasingly urgent as the effects of human societies on the planet entered into collective knowledge and awareness. Luigi Pellegrin, a member of the Association for Organic Architecture created by Bruno Zevi in 1945, was driven by a quest for an eco-urbanism that redefined the boundaries between artificial and natural environment. Fuelled by an organicist approach inspired by Frank Lloyd Wright and a strong predilection for science fiction, his vision for the future city was an intervention on a planetary level, relocating the world's population to an overhead ring running along the equator. Pellegrin argued that this temperate zone was the most appropriate place on earth to live in harmony with natural conditions and that by displacing us from its surface, there would be the required space for all other species, vegetation and important ecosystems to flourish uninterrupted. This vision was most powerfully rendered in his Vector Habitat (1970) in which his research on how the artificial should relate with the planet is articulated as a vast infrastructural ring that is able to navigate its way around the globe. The scheme forms a complete loop around the planet, stretching across oceans and penetrating through mountains to form a community for humanity that would have minimal ecological impact [figure 139]. By zooming out to such a considerable scale of thinking, Pellegrin chimed with the approaches of Buckminster Fuller and Soleri by suggesting a different way to consider sustainability through complex technological structures within primitive architectural forms.

If containing the entire urbanized population within an infrastructural ring that wraps around the planet appears unrealizable, the idea of better connections between urban centres to maximize resource efficiency and minimize environmental impact has been a compelling and recurrent idea. Buckminster Fuller's Dymaxion Map (1943) developed a flat map on the entire surface of the earth that revealed the planet as one island in the ocean, reinforcing the connectivity of the global population and land mass beyond city or national boundaries. Rather than traditional maps that have typically distorted relative shapes and sizes of countries, this representation demonstrated the inherent associations between people and planet. Taking its cue from this thinking, OMA/AMO's Eneropa Eurogrid (2010) gave a vision of a connected future city through a Europe-wide energy grid to reduce carbon emissions in Europe by 80 per cent by 2050 [figure 140]. The proposal taps into the various regions' different renewable energy capabilities and redraws

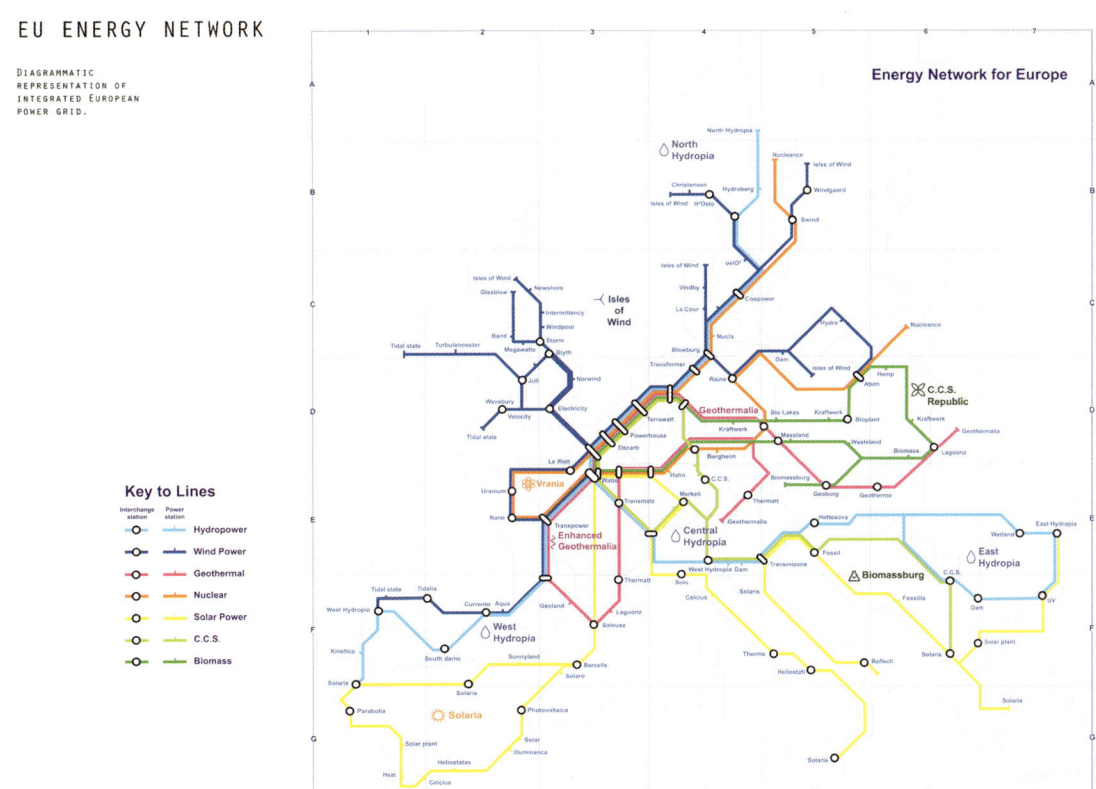

Figure 140.
Regulated Cities. Connected City. OMA/AMO, Eneropa, EuroGrid, Extract from Roadmap 2050: A practical guide to a prosperous, low-carbon Europe, 2010. © Image courtesy of the Office for Metropolitan Architecture (OMA). This map uses the familiar visual language of metropolitan transport maps to illustrate how the different power sources within an integrated European power grid would connect, reconceptualizing territories and renaming cities to reflect their contribution.

national boundaries based on these leading to the formation of new territories including Geothermalia, Biomassburg, Tidal States, Solaria and four Hydrophias. This radical reimagining of the relationships between cities formed part of a wider initiative of the European Climate Foundation, Roadmap 2050: A Practical Guide to a Prosperous, Low-Carbon Europe. Of the three volumes of work undertaken, one was entirely dedicated to the graphic narrative of the project which emphasizes the importance of how alternative futures are communicated effectively as provocations.

Developing strategic responses to enable urban life to be sustainable and resilient has fostered a variety of approaches for how we rethink our relationship with and responsibility to the city we live in. Various initiatives have sought to promote the social dimension to addressing the effects of climate change by combining innovative design with new models for active environmental stewardship. Key to a number of these visions is strategic thinking for the city-region to unlock wider capacities for sustainability and resilience. Representative of this approach is BIG's Loop City (2010 onwards), a master plan for the suburbs of Copenhagen, Denmark, that proposes to create an extensive new light rail system, the 'loop', as a catalyst to enable surrounding communities to flourish as well as for people to move around the city's region [figure 141]. Envisaged as a sustainable spine, Loop City incorporates strategies for electric car infrastructure, energy efficiency, waste management and water treatment. Threading together ten urban communities across twenty development zones, the loop aims to stimulate development for the cross-border region, fostering new and diverse programmes to emerge around the new stations.

In a similar vein but different context, Hassell and MVRDV's collaboration, Resilient by Design, South San Francisco (2017), draws on the history of the region's communities and their responses to both the devastating earthquake of 1906 and more recent wildfires that ravaged Northern California. The project proposes a series of waterfront communities with a dual function, acting as both public places and significant hubs for disaster response and environmental innovation [figure 142]. The scheme resonates with the

Figure 141. (facing page, top) Ecological Cities. Smart City. BIG, Loop City, 2010 onwards. This future vision forms a green and vibrant cluster of cities as a plan for urban growth in and around Copenhagen. By rethinking how municipal borders are defined, ten urban communities are brought closer together and the scheme aims to make them more prosperous and healthy through shared, integrated sustainable technologies.

Figure 142. (facing page, bottom) Ecological Cities. Water City. Hassell / MVRDV. Resilient by Design, South San Francisco, USA, Masterplan, 2017. 800 kilometres of shoreline for Resilient By Design – Stage 1 (Collaborative Research Stage). © MVRDV and HASSELL+. This scheme envisions a network of green spaces, creeks and high streets that facilitates rapid response to environmental disasters. Together, they aim to make the Bay Area more physically and socially resilient.

Chapter 6 Global Futures: Challenges and opportunities for collective life   149

increasing need for Ecological Cities that integrate with their inhabitants by promoting the appeal to 'engage' with communities at risk to the current common practice to 'protect', 'adapt', and even 'retreat' from areas endangered due to climate change.

The diversity of geographic contexts and circumstances necessarily raises different challenges for cities in relation to climate change. This has led to the city-scale being the focus for some visions. Foster + Partners' Dharavi Masterplan (2008) proposes a strategy that seeks to tackle primary issues of sanitation and provide resilience against flooding in one of the world's largest slums, with more than half a million people per square kilometre [figure 143]. By providing a framework for humane, sustainable and prosperous development, this Ecological City is indicative of those projects that seek to support a good quality of life for inhabitants balanced with minimizing its ecological impact on the planet. By contrast, Hydro-Net (2008) by IwamotoScott promotes a new aquaculture zone with

Figure 143.
Ecological Cities. Waste City. Dharavi Masterplan, Mumbai, India, 2008, © Foster + Partners.
In contrast to existing low-rise-built fabric and poor public realm and circulation, the proposal supplements the dense, impermeable city layout with new public transport connections and dedicated pedestrian routes. A diagonal street pattern allows the prevailing winds to spread through the urban fabric and aid cooling of buildings and public spaces.

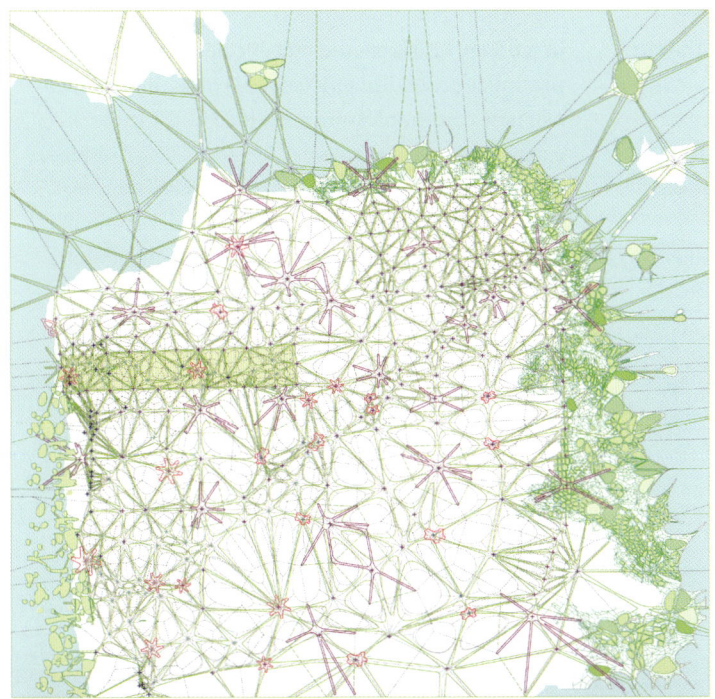

Figure 144.
Ecological Cities. Waste City. Iwamoto Scott, Hydro-Net, 2008. Envisioning 2108 San Francisco, this project promotes resilience through an underground arterial traffic network for hydrogen-fuelled hover-cars, and simultaneously collects, distributes, and stores water and power tapped from aquifers and geothermal energy housed within the earth below. Algae is grown as raw material for producing hydrogen fuel that is stored and distributed within Hydro-Net's nanotube tunnel walls.

forests of high-rise towers to reoccupy the lowlands of future San Francisco due to the rising seas of global warming [figure 144]. This vision for the future city of 2108 proposes an underground network for hydrogen-fuelled transport alongside innovative energy and water infrastructures to ensure resilience against the further effects of climate change and projected population growth.

The difficulty of formulating a practical response to global challenges is evident in the slow progress, and even total inertia, demonstrated by various governments, corporations and communities. Part of the explanation for this appears to be the intractable and interrelated problems that climate change poses which make even knowing where to start a tricky question. The crucial role that visions for future cities play in this process is in their ability to convey prospective pathways towards futures at a scale, the city, that is immediately recognizable and relatable to many people's way of life as it is now. Central to this capacity for enabling positive futures for collective life is the power of visualizations to communicate alternatives to the fundamental tenets and accepted, if rarely questioned, norms of cities, their development and principles. WORKac's Nature-City (2012) provides a visionary design for the American suburb by exploring the potential of a symbiotic relationship between housing and sustainable infrastructures [figure 145].

This future city promotes a close relationship to nature in tandem with dense, affordable neighbourhoods that maximize ecological efficiencies. Extending the idea of a new community, the prototype housing blocks expand suburban typologies by integrating one piece of vital new sustainable infrastructural services for the community as a whole, from the production of renewable energy to the natural processing of waste to the creation of water pressure to the collection of methane gas from compost. Proposed for suburban Keizer, Oregon, the scheme incorporates ecological infrastructure, sky gardens, urban farms and large

Figure 145.
Ecological Cities. Smart City. WORKac, Nature-City, 2012. Photo © James Ewing. This vision proposes a sustainable alternative to the American suburb. Commissioned by the Museum of Modern Art for the Foreclosed: Rehousing the American Dream exhibition, this speculative future city is founded upon ecological urbanism principles and explores ways to live sustainably and close to nature.

Figure 146.
Ecological Cities. Desert City. EYRC Architects + Tom Wiscombe Architecture, Blockchains City, Sparks, Nevada, 2018. Envisioned to have decentralized blockchain underlying all infrastructure coupled with artificial intelligence, 3D printing and nanotechnology, this future city aims to be fully regenerative and sustainable. Energy is to be provided by renewable sources including next-generation solar and wind, whilst water will be recycled and reclaimed.

swathes of natural habitats including oak savanna, wetlands and fir forest.

The optimism in technology as a means to provide solutions for the many challenges that face humanity continues to endure despite the impact of the Anthropocene and the various technological progresses we have made within it that have led to huge environmental degradation and mass extinction of other species. This has not deterred the ongoing fascination and hope for advanced technologies and how they might guide us through an uncertain planetary future. Speculating on how innovative technologies may support sustainability and social cohesion is Blockchain City (2018) by EYRC Architects + Tom Wiscombe Architecture [figure 146]. This vision for the future city in the Nevada desert aims to integrate business development, residential living and commerce using blockchain technology that will transform the way inhabitants interact on a daily basis. The city is proposed to be human-centric, prioritizing walkability and community, with all vehicles being autonomous and electric. Given the advanced technologies that underpin the design, the blockchain offers an innovative approach to future cities and their social and sustainability objectives by providing transparent, fair and democratic systems.

Envisioning climate change for rethinking future cities

The question of resilience in dealing with the effects of climate change is complicated. One of the difficulties in understanding the significant changes that may occur as a result of climate change is the complex, even overwhelming nature of the myriad issues it raises. Despite the increasingly frequent images of environmental destruction caused by its effects, for many people climate change appears as phenomena that impact on other faraway places, and so the serious threats also feel distant. A powerful way to challenge this misconception is through visions of future cities that describe the aftermath of major changes to our urban lifestyles. Robert Graves and Didier Madoc-Jones's Postcards From the Future (2010) series present iconic views of London that have been disrupted due to the effects of climate change [figure 147]. Across six distinct themes the artists present Flooded London, Hot London, Frozen London, Self Sufficient London, Living in London, and Powering London, providing compelling imaginaries for how the future of the global city may be transformed. As an accessible form of communication, postcards perpetuate myths of identity and place. Through their provocative use here, the clarity and definition of future London overwhelmed by the visual language of climate change make the effects of such changes relatable as indicated by the significant public and global media interest the project generated.

In a less apocalyptic but equally potent manner, the Villes éteintes (Darkened Cities) (2012) series by photographer Thierry Cohen form a vision of global cities without electricity [figure 148]. By combining photographs of global cities with one taken at a less populated location at the same latitude with greater atmospheric clarity, Cohen's arresting images encourage us to reflect on our reliance upon manmade infrastructures and perhaps point towards future cities where we reconnect with darkness through more responsible and less environmentally impactful ways of collective living. The need to rethink our relationship with darkness and develop more effective strategies for urban illumination to reduce the severe detrimental effects of excessive artificial lighting upon our health and that of other species and the environment, let alone the waste of valuable energy resources, is a global challenge that requires urgent attention (Dunn 2016; Edensor 2017). Whilst not explicitly created as visions for future cities, images such of these are an important reminder of the agency of visual materials and their power in contributing towards new imaginaries for futures.

Where future cities are imagined as responses to the effects such as global warming, rising sea levels, and extreme weather events, they are often envisioned as places to protect and sustain our ways of living or depicted as apocalyptic scenarios. Perhaps the manner in which some cities will evolve in the future lies between these two contrasting situations. Studio Lindfors's Aqualta (2009) – itself a play on the Acqua Alta, the increasing high tides flooding Venice – visually explores what a coastal metropolis might feel like in the future as a result of rising sea levels [figure 149]. The project illustrates two major international cities – New York and Tokyo – adapting to, rather than resisting, the rising waters. Rather than focusing on technological innovation, the series of visualizations form a vision for future global cities that rely on social ingenuity, illustrating everyday life as people navigate Manhattan

Figure 147.
Ecological Cities. Water City. Robert Graves and Didier Madoc-Jones, Flooded London, Postcards From the Future, 2010. In this series, the possible effects of climate change on London's famed landmarks are interpreted, illustrating how the future city might be. Startling visions of iconic places are here shown as drastically altered urban conditions as a result of imagined environmental change.

Figure 148.
Ecological Cities. Spectacle City. Thierry Cohen, Villes éteintes (Darkened Cities), Hong Kong, 2012. This series of highly evocative images seek to remind city dwellers of the importance of other realities, especially our connection to, and understanding of, nature. With light and air pollution having huge impacts on human health, these composite images are a powerful vision for the world beyond urban landscapes.

Figure 149.
Ecological Cities. Water City. Studio Lindfors (Clouds AO), Aqualta, New York, 2009. The project predicts that communities will adapt to the changes by building piers and navigable canals to replace flooded transport networks. Here, the future city is partially submerged by melting glacier water, and in response, riverside plants climb towards neon signs, aquaculture flourishes underneath bridges, and gondolas are used as a form of travel.

using gondolas or fish from newly formed river banks in the middle of Tokyo. In contrast to the empty future cities of Alan Weisman's *The World Without Us* (2007), here the post-apocalyptic scenarios are more akin to J. G. Ballard's *The Drowned World* (1962), as the urban landscapes are populated with people farming, fishing, foraging and travelling on boats as airships and high-tech people-movers trail across the sky. The importance of such work lies in provoking us to think beyond what we know a city to be.

The sky isn't the limit

The development of construction technology continues to enhance the possibilities of how we inhabit space in cities, but this has been furthered by the actual building of urban imaginaries into territory that was previously the stuff of theoretical projects. This quest to inhabit a series of vertical strata formerly out of reach, whether significantly above or dramatically below what we typically would consider the city, has led to radical proposals and constructions as Stephen Graham (2016b) has demonstrated. Following the advancements in design and engineering that enabled skyscrapers, the ongoing search for how we live in the air has endured in the imagination of many architects, designers, filmmakers and writers. How we achieve this whilst not contributing further to the congestion found at street level has led to numerous proposals that seek to claim the sky and beyond for cities. An early example is El Lissitzky's Cloud Iron (1928) which comprised eight horizontal skyscrapers in response to Moscow's problems of overcrowding and public transport deficiencies by connecting directly between living and office space on the upper floors with new tram and metro stations below. This desirable fluidity between spaces above and below the busy street level has been the goal of many different visions for future cities though it essentially rests on the acceptance of existing urban conditions and finding ways to overcome them rather than speculating on alternatives.

The Metabolists' vision was underpinned by the belief that architecture should be able to meet the rapidly changing requirements of the contemporary city as well as reflect the human dynamic reality of life. Broadly speaking this was construed to propose buildings that were mechanized in a manner analogous to biological processes that occur in the human body to ensure the former could be adapted in the future. Arata Isozaki's proposal for a city in the air was emblematic of how the group of forward-thinking Japanese architects approached the sprawling urbanism of their country following the post-war period. Clusters in the Air (Cluster City), Shibuya (1960 to 1962), envisioned a new type of housing to be built above the existing city of Tokyo [figure 150]. These spectacular tree-like formations feature cantilevered housing units from their 'branches' which are metaphorically intended to represent the leaves. The proposal was conceived to be able to grow and extend organically according the evolving requirements of the future city. A key concern for Isozaki was the issue of whether urban design could give identity to a city after urbanization had left the city streets and city area uncontrollable. At the time of his scheme height restrictions limited buildings to less than thirty-one metres. Isozaki's vision raised the urban structure into mid-air on cores driven into the ground, leaving existing buildings untouched. Isozaki's project was the most futuristic of several schemes that would be developed by the group based on the idea of megastructures and the potential of industrialized capsules for lowering housing costs. This iteration was one of several proposed for different districts in Tokyo, with the others focusing on office space rather than housing.

Super-tall skyscrapers such as the Ultima Tower (1991) designed by Eugene Tsui and envisioned to accommodate one million people in San Francisco or Sky City (2012) proposed by Broad Sustainable Building for the Chinese city of Changsha and due to reach a height of 666 metres and be constructed in only 210 days, have either remained unbuilt or been beset with complications. Vertical urbanism as a means to enable the future city to evolve from an existing urban landscape is increasingly common as architects and urban designers examine the potential of subterranean and skyward development.

Figure 150.
Layered Cities. Layered City. Arata Isozaki, Clusters in the Air (Cluster City), Shibuya, 1960–1962. Deutsches Architekturmuseum, Frankfurt am Main; © Arata Isozaki; Foto: Uwe Dettmar, Frankfurt am Main. This model demonstrates the extent to which the future city would rise mid-air above Tokyo. Reaching up into the sky and capable of organic evolution based on the city's needs for adaption, the clusters provide a striking new urban condition through the radical exploration of the vertical dimension.

Multiplicity (2010) by John Wardle Architects and Stefano Boscutti visualizes Melbourne in 2110 as a city of rising layers of cloud-like forms as the urban landscape grows upwards rather than outwards [figure 151]. A radical reimagining of where the boundaries of growth for the city and its population should be, the proposal speculates a hyper-density of the central business district. In this vision for the future city the air rights have been altered to support farming, food production and rainwater harvesting at the top level, solar-cell microfibre surfaces generate energy from sunlight and prevailing winds, and architectural facades have constantly adaptive skins.

Visions that extend what we understand to be the extant city, not matter how or to what extreme, still retain a grounded quality to them beyond the literal connection to the landscape since they exist within the boundaries of what we know to be plausible.

However, if the future city becomes untethered from the planet and is airborne, a very different kind of imaginative space is opened up. Flying cities are not a new idea. In Jonathan Swift's *Gulliver's Travels* (1726), the island city of Laputa floats in the sky, apparently able to levitate through magnetic forces. In the 1920s, the science fiction author Hugo Gernsback featured cities floating in the sky such as the one envisioned 10,000 years in the future as presented in a feature in *Science and Invention* (1922): 'The city the size of New York will float several miles above the surface of the earth, where the air is cleaner and purer and free from disease carrying bacteria.' On a similar trajectory was Georgii Krutikov's The Flying City (1928). This future city was imagined as a series of beehive living colonies floating in space, with atomic-powered aircraft envisioned to provide transit for the urban residents between their industrial work stations and their homes

Figure 151.
Layered Cities. Layered City. John Wardle Architects and Stefano Boscutti, Multiplicity, Melbourne 2110, 2010. This concept for increasing density of the existing city is based on new air and foundation rights, permitting new forms of development. This creates multiple cities on the original street grid, shifting the datum to provide different ground planes and urban topographies for energy and food production alongside rainwater harvesting.

[figure 152]. Inspired in equal measure by the sci-fi dreams of space travel and the revolutionary idealism that still permeated in the Soviet Union at the time, Krutikov provided a significant amount of detailed information about his city in numerous drawings. However, as Khan-Magomedov (2015) has shown, he was also well aware that such a radical proposal was speculative, enabling him to explore the possibilities of mobile architecture. It is also symbolic of utopian thought, the ultimate liberation (Stites 1989).

Never one to miss a bold vision, in 1960 Buckminster Fuller in collaboration with Shoji Sadao proposed Cloud Nine, one-mile-diameter geodesic spheres that would act as vast thermal airships, each able to accommodate thousands of people. The theory ran that once adequately heated by sunlight these 'mini-cities' would become airborne and be able to float freely in the earth's atmosphere, providing residents and passengers a migratory lifestyle. It was one of many projects developed by Buckminster Fuller as a partial solution to the ongoing depletion of non-renewable resources. Cloud Nine could be free-floating, manoeuvrable or tethered in relation to climatic and environmental conditions and was thus also conceived as being able to provide emergency shelters. More recently, Tomas Saraceno's Cloud Cities (2015) provides an invitation to explore the limits of our fragile human and terrestrial ecosystems [figure 153]. Pursuing the

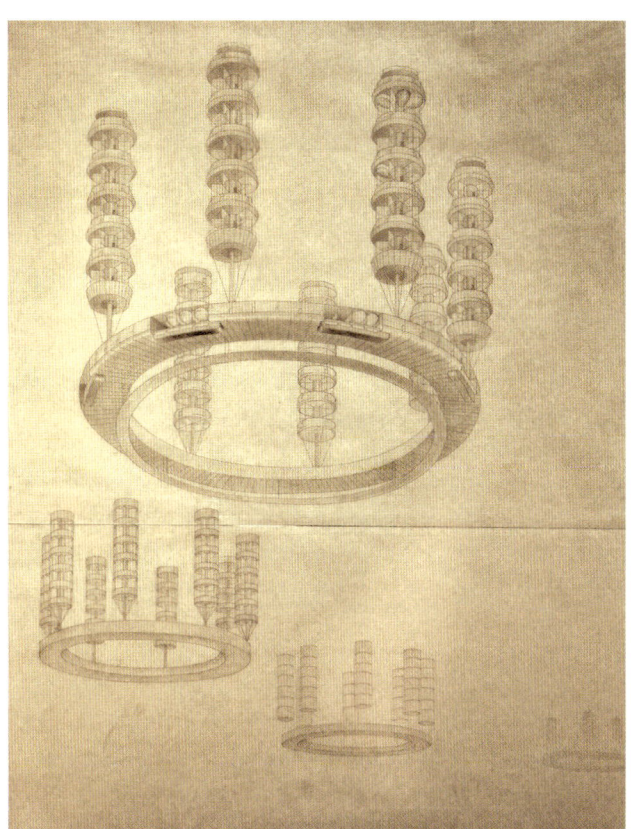

Figure 152. (left)
Layered Cities. Floating City. Georgii Krutikov, The Flying City, (VKhUTEMAS diploma project, 1928). © Schusev State Museum of Architecture. In this city in the sky, industrial and commercial spaces are located on the ground and residential quarters are suspended in the air. The architecture itself is not in motion, but it will mobilize its inhabitants, who reach their homes via individual flying capsules.

Figure 153. (below)
Layered Cities. Floating City. Tomás Saraceno, Biosphere 3, 2015, Collage. Courtesy the artist; Tanya Bonakdar Gallery, New York/Los Angeles; Pinksummer contemporary art, Genoa; Andersen's, Copenhagen; Esther Schipper, Berlin. © Studio Tomás Saraceno, 2015. This vision places the future city amongst the clouds as a series of geodesic spheres that float above the earth's surface without using fossil fuels. Forming part of Saraceno's larger body of work titled Aerocene, the proposal aims to illustrate how it is possible to become airborne in collective sustainable environments.

notion of Buckminster Fuller's precedent coupled with the latter's *Operation Manual for Spaceship Earth* (1968) which presented the planet as a vessel of finite resources requiring careful cultivation, Saraceno explains that the project 'imagines alternative possible scenarios for futures, conjuring an era in which humanity ceases to negatively impact our planet's fossil-fuel resources'.

Flying and other airborne cities have been a rich source of visions for future cities. Science fiction in particular has provided vivid speculations for how collective life might exist in the future. Many of these scenarios occur in deep space or on other planets. Off-earth communities have been engaged in numerous narratives as the quest to sustain human life within alien terrain provides exciting storylines, more recently reflecting deeper concerns about how we might continue to inhabit an increasingly hostile planet as climate change alters the earth. For example, in Christopher Priest's *The Inverted World* (1974) the city on an inhospitable planet escapes on self-laying railway track to stay ahead of atmosphere distortions. As a self-contained world, the city is kept separate from the outside world and its perils. By contrast, the future city in *Elysium* (2013) presents an off-earth community on a vast space station for the wealthy elite whilst the rest of humanity scrapes a living on a ravaged, overpopulated earth below. In this way it extrapolates issues of urban segregation and inequality.

Whilst typically the preserve of fiction, the construction of Biosphere 2 (1991) in Oracle, Arizona, was intended to be the second fully self-sufficient biosphere, after the earth itself. As a prototype, it was originally meant to demonstrate the viability of closed ecological systems to support and maintain life in outer space. Biosphere 2 was used only twice for its intended purpose, with both missions running into much publicized complications and unforeseen problems. Despite this outward failure to achieve its goals, considerable research advances and knowledge of closed ecological systems were produced. It is important to understand the context of the project as it emerged at the tail end of a particular strand of technological optimism as a means to solve all humanity's problems as Douglas Murphy (2016) has discussed. Ambitions to populate other planets have long held our imagination, and of the extraterrestrial options most viable, Mars's surface conditions and past presence of water make it likely to be least inhospitable in the solar system. Taking this motion forwards is Foster + Partners' Mars Habitat (2015). The project continues the practice's earlier explorations of designing architecture for extreme environments and extraterrestrial habitats. The vision consists of a 3D-printed modular settlement constructed by an array of pre-programmed, semi-autonomous robots before humans arrive [figure 154]. Whilst certainly not a city, the proposal outlines many of the principal tenets of adaptive systems for constructing environments in hostile contexts that may provide shelter for human life in the future. Given the vast distance from the earth and the ensuing communication delays, the deployment and construction are designed to take place with minimal human input, relying on rules and objectives rather than closely defined instructions. This makes the system more adaptive to change and unexpected challenges – a strong possibility for a mission of this scale. Although the predictions for living off-earth continue to capture headlines and the public imagination, the viability of future developments being of a sufficient scale to accommodate a significant proportion of the earth's population remains remote.

Figure 154.
Flexible Cities. Space City. Foster + Partners, Mars Habitat, 2015. © Foster + Partners. The visualizations appear synonymous with many sci-fi scenarios for extra-terrestrial inhabitation, yet this belies the multiple aspects of the project from delivery and deployment to construction and operations.

Urban life aquatic: floating and underwater cities

If extraterrestrial inhabitation is not where the seeds of future cities will be found, then we will need to reassess the possible futures of planet earth. In Richard Jefferies' *After London* (1885), an unspecified catastrophe has depopulated England and London has reverted to lake and poisonous swampland. During this early example of post-apocalyptic fiction, a lone figure surveys the former capital from a canoe, experiencing a London that has been literally swamped and requires a very different form of inhabitation. Instead of living with the aftermath of such climatic events, there have been various proposals for the future city to be aquatic, whether floating or underwater, as a means of supporting collective life. These visions are typically reflective of how we imagine cities to exist on firm terrain, transplanting gigantic agglomerations of architecture in order to treat the oceans as a new 'ground' condition upon which a city is built. A prime example is Kiyonori Kikutake's Marine City (1963). The vision for the future city here proposes tower units built on a number of irregularly shaped lands [figure

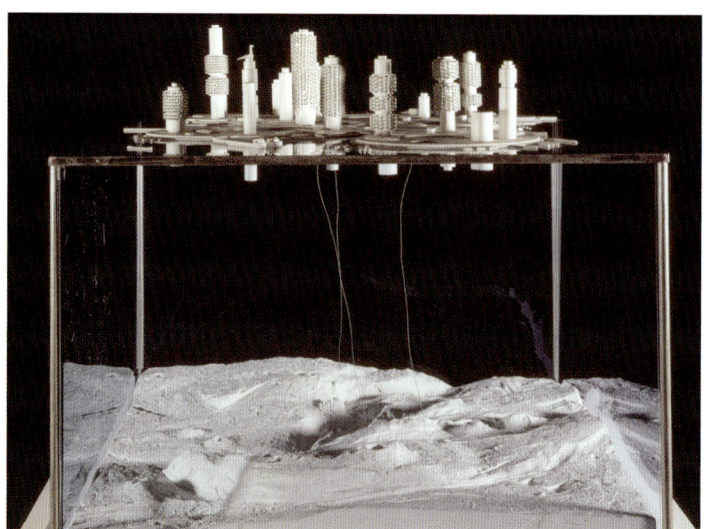

Figure 155.
Flexible Cities. Water City. Kiyonori Kikutake, Marine City, uncompleted project, 1963 Plexiglas, plaster, glass and metal, 57.1 × 58.5 × 58.5 cm Paris, Centre Pompidou, Musée national d'art moderne – Centre de création industrielle © Centre Pompidou, MNAM-CCI/Georges Meguerditchian/Dist. RMN-GP © Kiyonori Kikutake. The model shown here demonstrates the self-supporting nature of the proposal, a significant development from earlier iterations of the concept. Kikutake, along with his fellow Metabolists, believed that Floating Cities such as this were the solution to the growth problem of Tokyo as well as a means of escaping the megacity's heavy industrialization.

155]. A development of his earlier scheme, Ocean City, Unabara (1960), as well as a combination of two other projects from 1958, Tower Shape Community and Marine City, the vertical structures are now conceived as robust enough to stand up to heavy seas, so they no longer have platforms underneath them as in earlier iterations. This version forms a much clearer expression of the Metabolism notion of growth and change with its analogy to biological systems. Subsequent iterations of this future city vision by Kikutake featured mid-air connections between towers, enabling 3D circulation.

Around the same time, Paul Maymont was exploring similar possibilities in his Floating Paris (1965). Intended for the Paine de Montesson, west of the suburb of La Défense, monumental cone-like structures of extreme density hover over the wetland area [figure 156]. Each of these hyper-structures was envisaged to accommodate between fifteen and thirty thousand residents. Like many architects of his generation, Maymont's ideas were fuelled by the space-age preoccupations of living free of terrestrial dependence. Sharing common ground with Paolo Soleri's ecological megastructures that literally raise techno-settlements off the land, the scheme proposes a future city as a floating mosaic of objects linked by suspended motorways. A hollow central column in the gigantic cones would contain wiring and ducts;

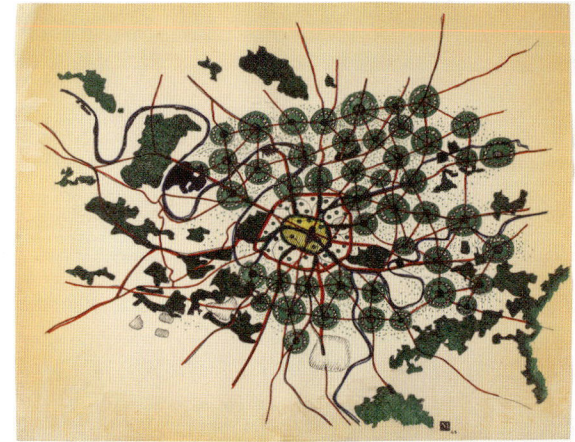

Figure 156.
Flexible Cities. Water City. Paul Maymont, Floating Paris, 1965. Map of Paris and its surroundings. 1962. Blueprint, 28.5 x 38.5 cm. Inv.: AM2010-2-869. Photo: Philippe Migeat, Musee National d'Art Moderne, Centre Georges Pompidou, Paris, France. Photo Credit: © CNAC/MNAM/Dist. RMN-Grand Palais / Art Resource, NY. This drawing illustrates the extent of the vision for the future city as a series of urban cores connected by a series of suspended infrastructural ribbons. Rather than one, solid landscape, the scheme proposes a network of settlements akin to vast lily pads.

Figure 157.
Flexible Cities. Water City. Charles Simonds, Floating City, an Arrangement, 1978. Photography François Lauginie, Collection Frac Centre-Val de Loire. Through a series of photomontages, the artist offers a poetic and dynamic vision of a utopian city upon the ocean. Carefully combining small wooden models with different backdrops, it forms an imaginative alternative to the car-dominated American landscape of the time.

the cables would unwrap to circulate energy and connectivity for the structure. Each conical city is arranged with suspended plazas, vertically stacked railroad systems, and housing and commercial areas. Maymont wrote of an 'urbanism entirely conceived by spaces that are easy to draw . . . and immediately graspable by the public' (as quoted in Wakeman 2016: 287). The implication was that the new Paris would go from the musings of illustration to actual built environment with ease.

Developing this concept further, in his Floating City (1978) project Charles Simonds envisions a new type of city based on mobility, exchange and its inhabitants' wishes [figure 157]. Rather than accepting the then-dominant principle of the zoned city with different areas linked to a specific function, in this proposal the artist sought to transfer the sites onto floating barges, designed with respect to different building typologies. The result is that the future city becomes one of endless mutation and reconfiguration as housing, industry, office buildings, green space and public buildings all move around, creating new relational possibilities. Emancipated from its relationship with the ground, Simonds' Floating City was also a radical counter proposal to the enduring American myth of land and property which permeated its society.

Questioning land use and exploring ways for the future city to be self-sufficient is at the core of CCCC-FHDI & AT Design Office's Zhujiangkou Island (2012) proposal [figure 158]. The project envisions a city comprising both above- and underwater environments supported by an array of sustainable infrastructures. It is expected to be self-sufficient, utilizing on-island food production, power generation and waste management systems. Movement throughout the city is proposed to be via electric cars as part of an integrated system of zero-carbon transport. These ambitions are brought under the provision of the city as spectacle as it will contain two gigantic buildings and ten theme parks and tourism facilities which perhaps reveal more about the contemporary mechanisms needed to make investment in such ambitious and speculative schemes viable.

Proposals such as these reconstruct the urban imagination as a holistic vision for collective life in a similar manner to many existing cities. Populations throughout history have necessarily moved to and from cities in the event of various climatic and environmental disasters. By contrast, the vision

Figure 158.
Regulated Cities. Water City. CCCC-FHDI & AT Design Office, Zhujiangkou Island, 2012. This Floating City proposes a four-square-mile structure comprising hexagonal modules connected by underwater tunnels that form a network of walkways and roads. The above- and underwater segments are envisioned to house all the major functions of a city underpinned by sustainability.

produced by Terreform ONE for their Future North: Ecotariums in the North Pole (2008) is founded on the premise that due to irreversible climatic effects there will be an urgent need to move the cities themselves [figure 159]. As a provocation, the project highlights the issues of movement facing millions of climate migrants who will need more hospitable contexts as the polar ice caps melt. Illustrating the shift of major urban centres including Hong Kong, London, Miami, New York, San Francisco and Tokyo, the vision consists of gigantic ecotariums in which entire cities are floated to the North Pole in response to expanded populations and flooding caused by global warming.

Floating Cities are a recurrent theme for future visions as drowned cities facilitate multiple ways of thinking through how existing cities will respond to significant flooding or as a mechanism to envisage new cities that would be resilient to such dramatic events.

They are valuable in that they contribute to the tangled interchange between fact and fiction concerning climate change. Whilst providing bountiful depths for the imagination to explore urban futures, they are also articulated in nonfictional accounts to highlight the challenges of surviving such transformations to our planet (Lynas 2008; Oreskes 2014). Thus far in this section we have encountered cities that address the future city within rising sea levels via the view from above. Where the ruination of existing cities occurs as they are drowned typically leads to aquatic life flourishing in the absence of humans or a new dynamic existing between them. These strategies of either floating or coexisting with flooded areas still retain the principle of living on the water as a new datum rather than living in it. The challenges of how future cities might be designed to be partially or completely underwater are considerable. The

Figure 159.
Ecological Cities. Water City. Terreform ONE, Future North: Ecotariums in the North Pole, 2008. The future cities of this vision are extant urban centres physically migrating to accommodate the huge populations escaping severe flooding and increased temperatures as a result of climate change. Deliberately polemical, the scheme aims to highlight how we perceive tomorrow's world and the implications of the challenges ahead.

submarine environment is equally hostile to human life as outer space and extraterrestrial contexts are (Kaji-O'Grady and Raisbeck 2005). And similar to these off-earth domains, underwater inhabitation has been an enduring theme of fiction and speculative designs for future cities. The series of experimental SEALAB habitats developed by the United States Navy in the 1960s aimed to prove the viability of underwater living, whilst the Futurama exhibit in General Motors' pavilion at the 1964 World's Fair in New York featured a submarine hotel complex, though the latter was a vision for life that whilst imaginative could not be as easily assimilated into everyday life as its predecessor in 1939.

More recently, National Geographic's *City Under the Sea* (2011) gave a vision for a submarine city of the future constructed as a response to global warming. The pseudo-documentary depicted a design of communal domes and living pods along the seabed. This renewed interest in underwater cities is also reflected in Ocean Spiral (2014) by Shimizu Corporation. The design proposes a floating 500-metre-wide sphere connected to a resource centre on the ocean floor via a fifteen-kilometre helix-shaped path [figure 160]. The buoyant dome is envisaged to accommodate business and residential zones for five thousand permanent residents whilst a research facility at the seabed will enable scientists to investigate ways to excavate and develop energy resources.

The threat of global warming and its rising sea levels has provided sufficient impetus for an array of different proposals and strategies to live on or in the planet's oceans. As with extraterrestrial visions for future cities, there remains a strong throwback to the notion of pioneering and colonization which

Figure 160.
Layered Cities. Water City. Shimizu Corporation, Ocean Spiral, 2014. © Image Courtesy of Shimizu Corporation, 2014. This underwater city proposed for five thousand permanent residents is typical of the imaginative schemes created by Shimizu Corporation. Beyond the seductive imagery, the company has stated the technology needed to build the structure and to sustain life below the surface of the ocean will be available by 2030.

frames the oceans as a hostile environment that must be conquered. Whilst many of these visions promote sustainable developments that would be self-contained and supported by renewable energy sources, they often overlook the dynamic qualities of the sea that is far from stable, becoming more acidic and increasingly warmer. These effects which have already caused significant devastation to marine life and ecosystems around the world have also propelled visions for future cities that seek to remediate such conditions such as the Biorock of Newton Fallis's Autopia Ampere [see figure 75, Chapter 3] or the protocell architectures of Rachel Armstrong [see figure 26, Chapter 1]. If the future of cities turns out not to be aquatic, then perhaps another option could be found under our feet.

Going underground in subterranean cities

Speculating on subterranean life has enabled various writers to draw on both the primal origins of cave dwelling as well as the dark imaginaries of being away from familiar surface-level conditions and ensconced in the netherworld. Jules Verne's *The Underground City (Les Indes noires)* (1877) captures some of the thrill and disconcertment of being in the subterranean world, whilst Jeanne DuPrau's *The City of Ember* (2003) explores the perils facing the inhabitants of a subterranean city, intended to enable their survival for centuries, as its supplies become exhausted and its energy generators decay. The extension of cities underground has a long history, often providing the hidden yet vital infrastructures to support urban life via energy cables, water and waste pipelines, telecommunication networks, and transportation systems. At the beginning of the twentieth century there were various visions for the future city, especially Manhattan as the ultimate metropolitan future, that began to excavate far below street level. In 1925, Harvey Wiley Corbett's vision for how New York would look in 1950 was based on addressing the increased overcrowding of the city and the need to remove streetcars and elevated trains. This multi-level future city had no cars visible at street level, proposing to bury all vehicular traffic underground. Far more extreme was Oscar Newman's Nukeproof Manhattan (1969). This future city vision proposed

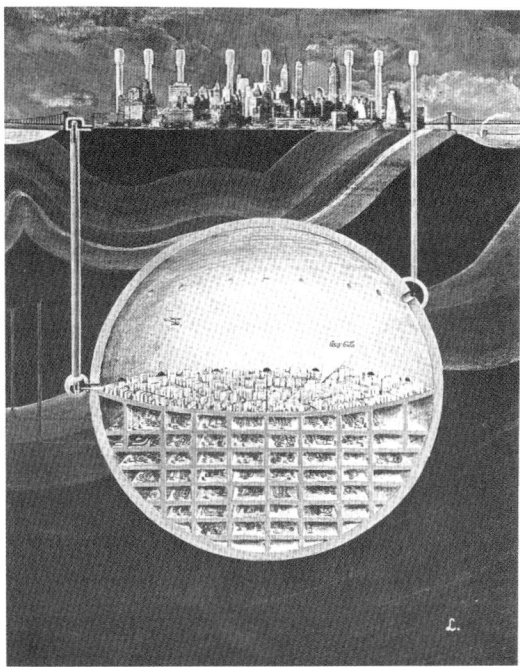

Figure 161.
Layered Cities. Underground City. Oscar Newman, Nukeproof Manhattan, 1969. This arresting image of the future city sequestered underneath New York City illustrates a radical vision of subterranean engineering to house the urban population safely away from the impact of nuclear war.

amidst the Cold War era of high-running tensions and fears concerning the outbreak of nuclear war, it warranted exploration as Newman (as quoted in *Sky and Stone* 1976: 192) elaborated: 'Manhattan could have a half-dozen such atomic cities strung under the city proper . . . the real problem in an underground city would be the lack of views and fresh air, but its easy access to the surface and the fact that, even as things are, our air should be filtered and what most of us see from our window's [sic] is somebody else's wall.'

Despite stimulating the imagination, the sheer difficulty of such an endeavour becomes readily apparent. Perhaps for this reason there have been comparatively few subterranean future cities proposed. However, the effects of climate change not least in terms of rapid desertification have encouraged some designers and writers to imagine situations where inhabitation at ground level is impossible. This forms the premise for Sietch (2009) by Matsys, who proposed a series of underground biomes as a vision for the future city and its infrastructures [figure 162]. As water becomes increasingly scare, the importance of banking it through vast aquifers and mixed-use caverns creates a massive subterranean network that employs a variety of symbiotic eco-services to sustain it. Matsys's vision draws considerable inspiration, intentionally or not, from both Frank Herbert's novel *Dune* (1965) and E. M. Forster's 'The Machine Stops' (1909) in which an underground cell architecture controlled by a supercomputer provides all the needs of the cell inhabitants.

the construction of a spherical city within Manhattan's bedrock, formed by the creation of vast underground caverns using nuclear explosions [figure 161]. Inside the underground sphere was envisaged a version of the city directly above along the medial which for all intents and purposes would appear as a regular city. Underneath this was a further underground city consisting of a honeycomb structure of multi-block-sized enclosures that would provide the means of production and energy needed to enable the new city to function. The proposal's scale is monumental, if indeterminate, but given the vast air filters that puncture through the existing Manhattan, the volume needed to be excavated is almost incalculable in that it would at the very least significantly disrupt the Hudson and East Rivers. Far-fetched certainly but

In contrast to the notion of sustaining collective life in one fixed location, the idea of future cities being nomadic and able to move to better climates or more suitable terrain has been a conceptual thread for a number of architects [for example see figure 24, Chapter 1]. However, the majority of these proposals retain the view of the city as a resource-hungry superorganism that simply mobilizes itself towards preferable situations as necessary. A counterpoint to such thinking is offered by Stephane Malka's The Green Machine (2014). Rather than taking from the immediate context and then moving on, this proposal regenerates dry and semi dry degraded land to address issues of desertification via a

Figure 162.
Layered Cities. Desert City. Matsys, Sietch, Nevada, 2009. This future city is essentially a Desert City borne of the scarcity of fresh water. As such, the proposal describes a network of subterranean biomes and infrastructure to sustain life amid the extreme arid landscape. The visualization is compelling, connecting serious ecological concerns and resonating with images from the covers of many science fiction books.

huge agricultural and industrial machine [figure 163]. Viewed from perspectives of global population and climate change, the territory of the desert has turned out to be a major stake in terms of human development and sustainability. This future city collects water through air condensations and uses solar power to drive itself over arid landscapes, ploughing and then injecting a mixture of water, natural fertilizer and cereal seeds as it passes. Hydroponic agricultural greenhouses along with livestock farms that also fertilize the earth support the city's inhabitants and supplement local populations.

The subterranean imaginary as a space for visions of future cities is not always founded on direct ecological imperatives. The Underground City proposed in Subterranean Singapore 2065 (2016) by Finbarr Fallon is predicated on the existing character of the nation which due to extreme climatic tendencies has been culturally interior with lots of air-conditioned environments, suggesting that a naturally cool underground environment might be attractive. In this future vision, artificial weather systems create an optimally habitable Underground City [figure 164]. However, the project is also a vehicle to question its own smooth 'official' narrative by exploring the principles and potential of underground dwelling by playing off the tensions and conflicts between the technological sublime and the largely hidden human labour that has actually produced it.

Perhaps inhabitation of the world beneath us needs completely rethinking. With the project Chthonopolis (2017), its architect Nic Clear seeks to radically question the traditional hierarchies of vertical space by inverting

Figure 163.
Flexible Cities. Desert City. Stephane Malka, The Green Machine, 2014. Studio Malka Architecture. This nomadic future city seeks to address the 120,000 km² of the planet's surface being lost to desertification and degradation of lands by acting as a mobile oasis to regenerate dry and semi-dry grounds. It envisions an autonomous and industrial city for revitalizing deficient ecosystems and the development of permaculture.

Figure 164.
Layered Cities. Underground City. Finbarr Fallon, Subterranean Singapore 2065, 2016. These stills from the architectural film project that offered a speculative proposal for large-scale underground living in land-scarce Singapore create an evocative atmosphere within vast super-frame structures that accommodate artificial weather systems to produce a temperate and stable climate for the city's inhabitants.

Figure 165. (facing page)
Layered Cities. Underground City. Nic Clear, Chthonopolis, 2017. A subterranean post-singularity city, named ZeroSix, is hypothetically located on the Gold Mine peninsula in the Thames Estuary, London. The physical model and sectional drawing shown here give an indication of the complex labyrinth that the city provides access to, stimulating discourse on traditional urban planning by subverting the typical relationships found in vertical hierarchies.

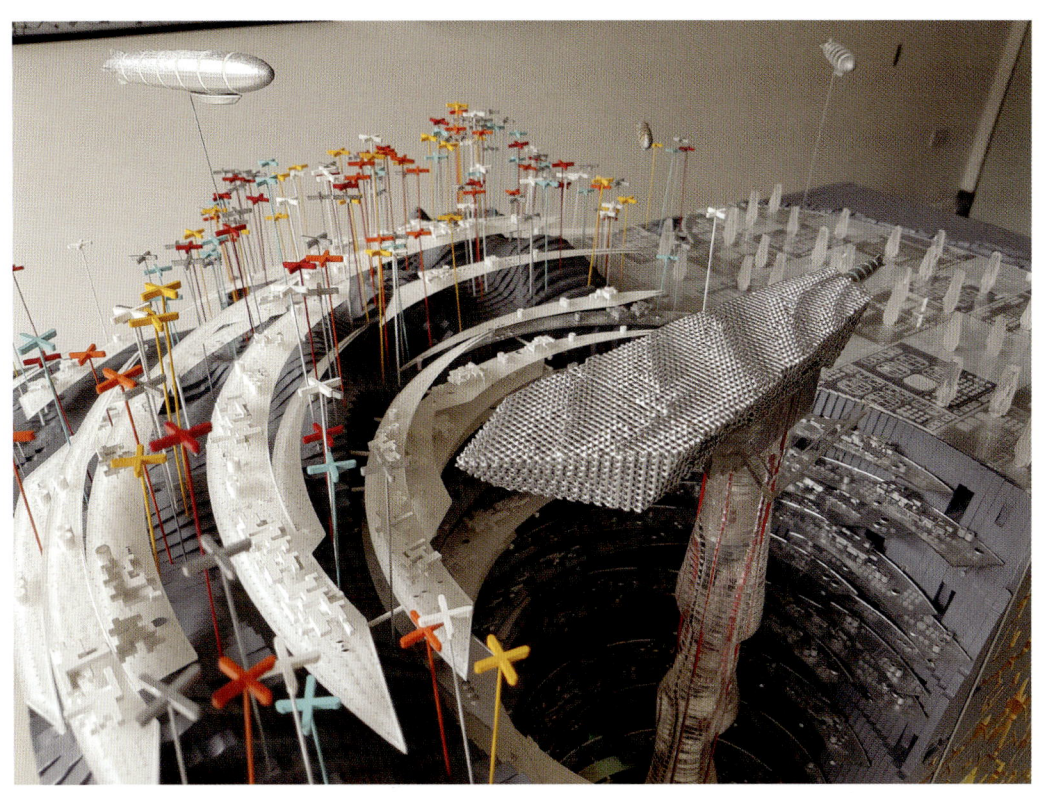

them. Imagining a utopian city, ZeroSix, founded on ludic principles, this future vision is built in an artificial crater 1-kilometre wide at the top and 1-kilometre deep [figure 165]. Envisaged as a city for around one million inhabitants and generated as a gateway to a vast labyrinthine network of underground spaces that form a huge computational system, the proposal explores the potential of a mixed reality for urban life.

The future cities envisioned as responses to the ways in which our planet may change are diverse in their approaches and the types of environment they aim to make habitable for human life. Although many of them address hostile terrain or situations, they are all based on overarching optimism for civil behaviour to remain as vital resources on earth such as fresh water and fossil fuels become increasingly scarce. That humanity might find itself plunged into the violent wasteland of the *Mad Max* trilogy (1979–1985) or be forced underground by a deadly virus in order to survive as in Terry Gilliam's *12 Monkeys* (1995) remains largely avoided in favour of more positive visions. However, if the global cataclysmic events that climate change appears set to potentially bring actually occur, then living with the aftereffects may lead us towards a very different future that is more nomadic and desperate as described in Cormac McCarthy's *The Road* (2006). That such barbarism is possible from our current standpoint seems abhorrent, and long may it remain so. What is apparent and increasingly urgent is the need to find radical alternatives to avoid the deep-rooted pathways of dependency that will limit our options for collective life in the future. The global imaginary for the planet as rendered in searing detail in *Wall-E* (2008) is a useful reminder of the wasteful nature of many modern urban societies and the bleak future that is its logical conclusion. The importance and priority of visions for global futures is therefore paramount.

Chapter 7

Tomorrow's Cities Today: Conclusions and alternative futures

Envisioning future cities

The purpose of this book is to bring much-needed critical attention to the subject of visions for future cities. Through the compilation and analysis of a wide array of visual materials, we have sought to do this as comprehensively as possible. Such an endeavour is significant given the plurality and diversity of visions produced for future cities throughout history and their complex interrelationships with how we view both the present and futures beyond. Given the nature of the topic and the degree to which visualizations can be interpreted and represented in entirely different ways due to the context they are used in, a neat summary is a daunting if near impossible task. This situation is further complicated by the proliferation of visions for future cities across culture and media that without careful scrutiny may not aid their understanding but do contribute a high level of background noise to the subject. However, the first principal contribution is to highlight the importance of visions for future cities and their role in bringing about positive change. How we envision future cities is framed by those we encounter in relation to a number of key factors: their methods of representation, their thematic content, the cultural context of their production, and, importantly, the situation in which they are subsequently viewed. In order to develop this understanding, visions for future cities have been examined in relation to specific themes. It has been demonstrated how the visualization of cities and their futures is crucial to their development and influence, whether constructed or imaginary. This was followed by an exploration of which different modes of representation have been used to provide expression for future cities and the dissemination of them across various media, sometimes to mass audiences. Three umbrella terms were then introduced and applied to illustrate various ideological threads and their evolution over time. Technological futures have been shown to be those visions that are driven by optimism in technology and are frequently deterministic through their conception of the city as a series of systems, networks and processes. Social futures provided a useful lens to bring together those visions for future cities that place greater emphasis on the human-scale of the city, emphasizing the lived experience of people, their relationships and interactions. Global futures have been evident in those visions where future cities explicitly articulate the environmental impacts of climate change and how they choose to adapt, resist or perish as a result of its effects. It is important to highlight the considerable complex interrelationships between these three types of futures. The nature of how visions are constructed through the employment of various characteristics, representational techniques, and cultural and historical associations means ideological and thematic overlap and blurring between them. Their inclusion in this book through its structure is deliberate and part of an ongoing attempt to rebalance and orientate perspectives on futures that are not driven by technology alone (Urry 2016). This is because these latter futures have established and maintained their dominance in futures thinking at the expense of occluding or discrediting other futures. From the current position, it is vital that the collective purview of futures is less limited and more open than this situation allows, thus the bringing in of both social and global futures as equally viable and significant.

The detectable wave of diverse visions that have emerged over the last decade or so is emblematic of the important shifts in awareness and knowledge concerning urban theory outside of the West (Edensor and Jayne 2012). This is a field that requires considerably more attention than is possible here. Accompanying this has been a detectable move towards visions that creatively promote sustainability and resilience rather than continue to support the previous foci on the economic development of industrialization and globalization. That is not to suggest this latter category of visions has disappeared but is now situated within a wider spectrum of future cities, somewhat diminished in its dominance in shaping cities of the future. The major disruptions throughout the twentieth century that led to a growth in knowledge and understanding of humanity's impact upon the planet have continued as the effects of climate change are bringing increasingly frequent challenges unevenly distributed across geographies. Amidst the many visions that seek to formulate responses to pressing environmental concerns are those that have ulterior motives. The disentanglement of conflicting forces sometimes presented under the guise of sustainability and resilience makes this task complicated and requires further scrutiny. It is perhaps useful, therefore, to examine the visions included from a different perspective as a means of gaining insight into the underlying patterns and trends that have occurred throughout history.

Patterns and trends of visions for future cities

One of the premises of this book is to provide a useful resource for catalysing new perspectives on, and rethinking the potential for, visions for future cities. In addition to the critical evaluation of the visual materials compiled and their connections via different thematic flows is their position within the six principal paradigms introduced at the start of this book: Regulated Cities, Layered Cities, Flexible Cities, Informal Cities, Ecological Cities, and Hybrid Cities. When organized in relation to a timeline, different relationships between the collated visions emerge when appreciated from a historical perspective [figure 166].

This enables the six principal paradigms to be understood as flows throughout the time period examined, illustrating connectivity and reoccurrence of ideologies, where applicable. It is evident that the historical needs for establishing a city that could be defensible are reflected in the prevalence of Regulated Cities. As cities became increasingly complex through processes of industrialization, the growth of Layered Cities is demonstrable. Technological futures have been instrumental in consolidating both of these categories whilst also augmenting them with Flexible Cities and Hybrid Cities through the optimism and belief in the city as a kit of parts, more recently overlaid with digital technologies. Social futures have complemented all of these four principal paradigms with the addition of Informal Cities, in their striving for new human-focused visions for cities. Both social futures and technological futures contain objectives for Ecological Cities within many of their examples, whether explicitly or implicitly, though their respective articulations for how to achieve these and the reasons why are very different. Global futures are imbued with aspects of all the principal paradigms but are unmistakably characterized as Ecological Cities through their architectural features and visual language. Care needs to be taken when evaluating the speculations for collective life support and human flourishing in spite of the challenging climatic and environmental transformations occurring and envisaged since their positive attributes may be undermined by unintended consequences. Possible scenarios include the further devastation of oceans through inhabitation, congestion of airspace, high energy consumption in desert climates, geological disruption through over-engineering underground spaces etc.

As we move further into the twenty-first century, the identifiable recurrence and growth of socially engaged visions for future cities that are coupled with environmental concerns suggest a positive shift away from those futures driven primarily by technological expectation. It is essential, however, to remain vigilant when attempting to draw neat conclusions from this form of synthesis. For example, this notable trend may be representative of greater societal and global ambitions of ecological and social sustainability for future cities. But an alternative reading might indicate that the branding of contemporary visions to align with political and economic agendas may hide other forces and discreet ideologies. Conceived in this manner, the category of Ecological Cities is likely to encompass a wide spectrum from legitimate and innovative strategies to deliver low- or zero-carbon development to proposals that have been subject to 'greenwashing'. Although this demonstrates the agency and plasticity of visualizations of future cities, it also raises complicated issues concerning the communication and interpretation of them. It necessarily raises further questions about where visions fit within methods that might support the process of becoming for futures.

What is evident from this timeline is the apparent reemergence of all six paradigms in the last ten years. This is particularly notable for Hybrid Cities, Ecological Cities and Layered Cities which seem to be undergoing a major rebirth. This is not particularly surprising when we consider the ubiquity of Smart Cities, environmental concerns, and the complexity of urban life and the systems that support it. That Informal Cities, Flexible Cities and Regulated Cities also seem to be experiencing a growth in representation again is perhaps an important signal of both the uncertainty of the present and our strong desire to look to the past for our futures, but also of the increasingly multifaceted and rapidly changing dynamics of contemporary cities and their contexts.

What is much harder to disentangle is the degree of blurring between these six paradigms and the allocation of the examples surveyed into one rather than several based on our visual analysis. In truth, as cities become even more vital to forming and sustaining collective life in the future, the language and visualization techniques used to create their visions become increasingly complicated, borrowing key terminology and visual motifs that make discerning a clear and discrete assignment to one specific paradigm difficult. Whilst, on the one hand, this demonstrates the flexibility of the taxonomy as a framework, on the other hand, it also highlights the need for more inquiry into such classifications through the application of its use in order to evolve more nuanced definitions and subdivisions. In this manner, the taxonomy presented in this book is done so to provide a foundation from which further research into the plurality and diversity of visions for future cities may be developed and stimulate alternative approaches.

Figure 166. Nick Dunn, Paul Cureton and Serena Pollastri, Timeline of principal paradigms, 2020.

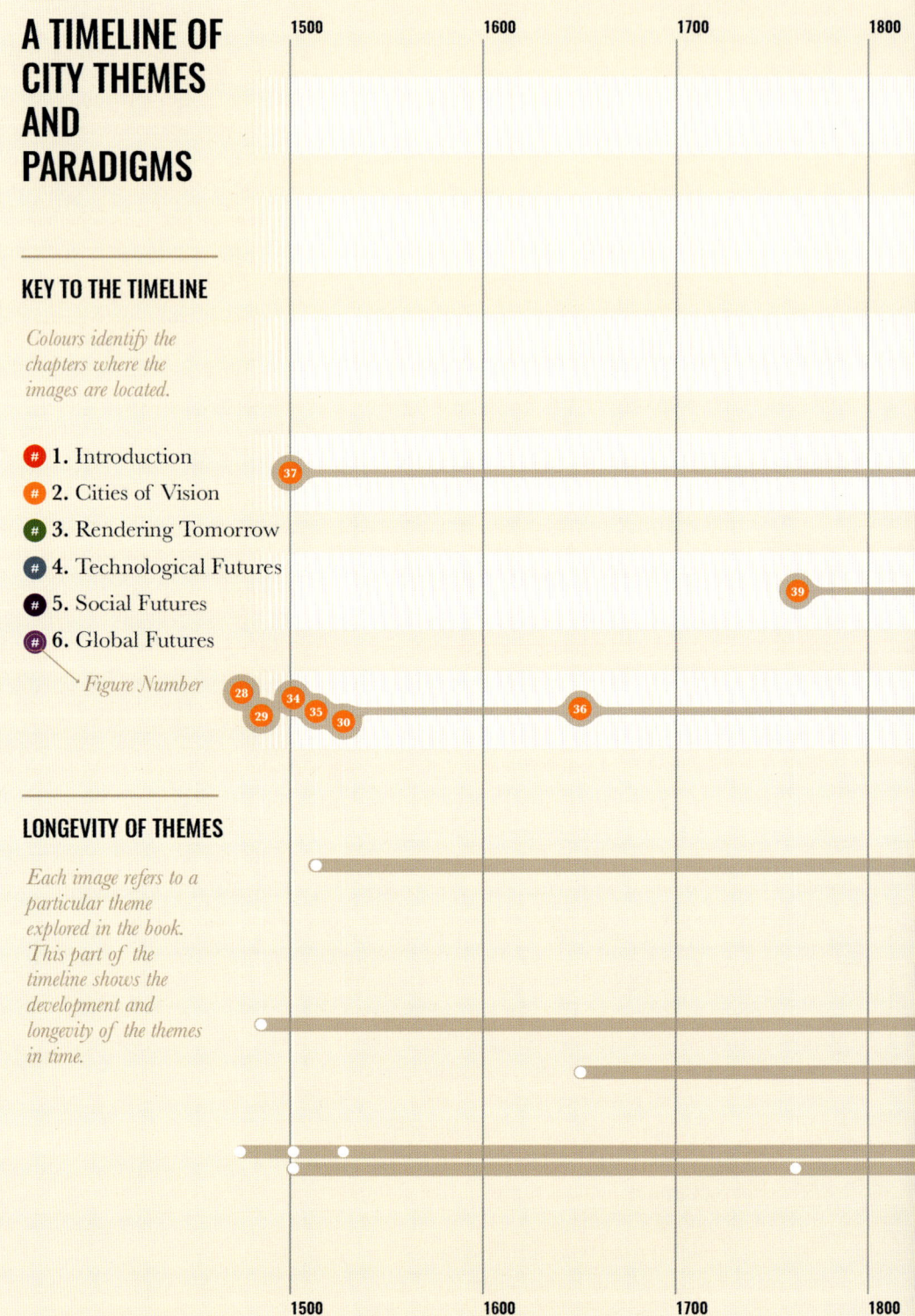

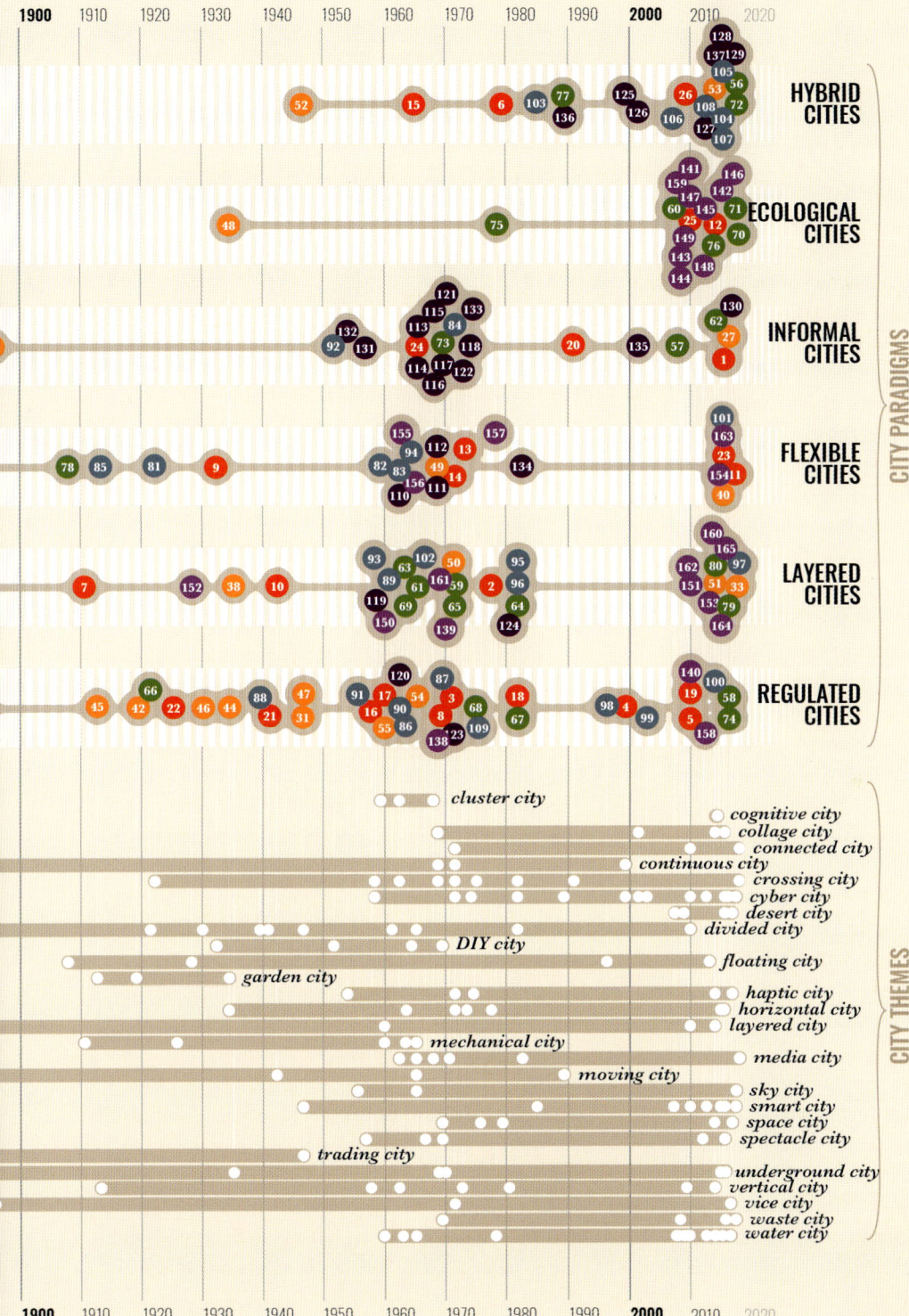

Collective visions for tomorrow's world

In providing methods to better understand visions for future cities, their values and influence, it has been shown that they are both expressive and instrumental in the way futures are articulated. There is no illusion here that visions alone will bring about the urgent and important changes needed if we are to secure and sustain a collective future that causes minimal or zero degradation to our planet and species beyond ourselves. Key to a way forwards is the engagement of methods to perform and mobilize visions into being. Futuring as a process can enable participatory and co-creation modes. Bringing in diverse assemblages of people into this process is critical to the conception and becoming of future cities. Therefore, it appears vital that we are able to create future cities that include and valorize plurality and agonism (DiSalvo 2010) especially in the visioning process (Pløger 2004). Such an approach as Pollastri et al. note (2017: S4375) not only challenges analytical and rational methods of examining the future by enabling controversies and diversities that characterize cities to emerge but also means that we may 'question assumptions, propose unthinkable alternatives and highlight unforeseen conflicts'. This 'staying with the trouble' (Haraway 2016) is critical if we are to acknowledge that such processes confront wicked problems and complex networks of heterogeneous stakeholders. Right now, as cities face new challenges and are re-examined for their potential to provide radical systemic revision and social restructuring, it is essential to reclaim visions of future cities as a means of questioning the present and demonstrating that what we think may be impossible is possible (Levitas 2013).

In terms of methods, there are three key issues emerging here that warrant further research. The first is how such visioning as creative agonism may be explored more fully to ensure it provides robust future cities that are able to capture and articulate the complexity of situations that dominant paradigms currently omit. This would support the urgent call made by John Urry (2016: 191): 'a planned future may not be possible, but a coordinated one may be the best show in town'. Second, having been able to formulate new future cities, is the examination of potential delivery mechanisms for the translation of vision into actions to achieve these futures (Rogers 2018). Third, an acknowledgement of the amount of time, energy and commitment that such a process requires is essential to its success, not only within the practices of the associated design disciplines, policy and governance organizations but also the need for it to be taken seriously academically. It is hoped that this book usefully contributes towards the latter. Futures, as with visions, will not be distributed homogeneously. Multiple futures will coexist, as there are currently multiple presents across different geographies and societal contexts, experienced differently by those in them (Sardar 2010; Savransky et al. 2017). There is much more work to be done in finding the most appropriate ways to engage as many people as possible in their respective futures.

Alternative futures next

There is, inevitably, much overlap across the many visions and ideologies featured in this book. It has been possible to see how some ideas emerge and echo over time, whilst others appear to lie conceptually exhausted in history. However, as we have seen, this does not mean such visions will not impact on the futures we may strive for. Any book, similar to the visions encountered for future cities, is defined by what it does not contain as much as by what it does. We have made a conscious decision to include as many unusual and obscure examples, alongside seminal and familiar ones, for how future cities have been imagined, including a significant number of examples from the last decade, as means of capturing the various ideologies at play concerning the future at this point in time. That people, having found a way to sustain collective life for humanity in the future, might look back on this book with the benefit of hindsight and wonder what all the debate was about would be encouraging, but the pathways there seem less obvious at this moment. What is clear, however, is that the seeds of these futures are likely already planted in the minds of those that will co-create them and, hopefully, in those generations that will follow.

To think of the future as something distant from us would be to underestimate our collective role in and responsibility for it. Visions are produced as ways of expressing the 'not-yet', and such imagery shapes our ideas of, and intentions towards, futures. In an era of rapid transformations and global uncertainties it would be easy to find solace through clarity and agreement rather than address the complexity of the task ahead of us. It is suggested here that articulating divergence is a crucial step in exploring radical alternatives and being able to fully appraise their respective values and limitations. Moving away from solution-orientated approaches to understand them as part of a considerably wider range of methods enables us to visualize and gain knowledge of the underlying similarities, tensions and contradictions. Through this process we have the ability to critically question assumptions about what futures are, who they are for, why they are desirable, and how and when they are to be brought into being. Without this sense of what options are available to us, the limited pathways that dominate our view obscure vital ways forward. This is the significance of visions for tomorrow's world and their relevance for our collective futures. The time to form them together is now.

REFERENCES

12 Monkeys (1995), [Film] Dir. Terry Gilliam, USA: Universal Pictures.

A Clockwork Orange (1971), [Film] Dir. Stanley Kubrick, USA: Warner Bros.

Abbott, C. (2007), 'Cyberpunk cities: Science fiction meets urban theory', *Journal of Planning Education and Research*, 27 (2): 122–31.

Abbott, C. (2016), *Imagining Urban Futures: Cities in Science Fiction and What We Might Learn from Them*, Middletown, CT: Wesleyan University Press.

Ache P. (2017), 'Vision Making in Large Urban Settings: Unleashing Anticipation?', in R. Poli (ed), *Handbook of Anticipation: Theoretical and Applied Aspects of the Use of Future in Decision Making*, 1–21, Cham, Switzerland: Springer.

Ahrens, J. and A. Meteling, eds (2010), *Comics and the City: Urban Space in Print, Picture and Sequence*, New York: Continuum.

Albrechts, L. (2015), 'Ingredients for a more radical strategic spatial planning', *Environment and Planning B: Urban Analytics and City Science*, 42 (3): 510–25.

Alexander, C. (1965), 'A City Is Not a Tree', *Architectural Forum*, 122(1): 58–62.

Alison, J., M-A. Brayer, F. Migayrou and N. Spiller, eds (2007), *Future City: Experiment and Utopia in Architecture*, London: Thames & Hudson.

Allen, S. (1999), *Points+Lines: Diagrams and Projects for the City*, New York: Princeton Architectural Press.

Allen, S. (2008), *Practice: Architecture, Technique and Representation*, 2nd edn, London: Routledge.

Ammon, F. R. (2016), *Bulldozer: Demolition and Clearance of the Postwar Landscape*, New Haven, CT: Yale University Press.

Anderson, D. (2015), *Imaginary Cities*, London: Influx Press.

Asimov, I. ([1951] 1955), *Foundation*, London: Voyager.

Aureli, P. V. (2013), 'More Money/Less Work: Archizoom', in Coles, A. and C. Rossi (eds), *EP Vol. 1 – The Italian Avant-Garde: 1968–1976*, Berlin: Sternberg, 146–64.

Azuma, R.T., 1997. 'A Survey of Augmented Reality'. *Presence: Teleoperators and Virtual Environments* 6: 355–385. https://doi.org/10.1162/pres.1997.6.4.355

Back to the Future: Part II, (1989) [Film] Dir. Robert Zemeckis, USA: Amblin Entertainment / Universal Pictures.

Bacon, F. ([1627] 2010), *The New Atlantis*, Ocean, WA: Watchmaker Publishing.

Baillie-Hislop, M. J. (2016), *Castle Builders: Approaches to Castle Design and Construction in the Middle Ages*, Barnsley: Pen & Sword Social History.

Ballard, J. G. (1962), *The Drowned World*, London: Gollancz.

Ballard, J. G. (1970), *The Atrocity Exhibition*, London: Jonathan Cape.

Ballard, J. G. (1975), *High Rise*, London: Jonathan Cape.

Ballon, H. and K. T. Jackson, eds (2008), *Robert Moses and the Modern City: The Transformation of New York*, New York: W. W. Norton & Company.

Banham, R. (1960), *Theory and Design in the First Machine Age*, London: Architectural Press.

Banham, R. (1976), *Megastructure: Urban Futures of the Recent Past*, New York: Icon.

Barbrook, R. (2007), *Imaginary Futures: From Thinking Machines to the Global Village*, London: Pluto Press.

Barker, R. and R. Coutts (2016), *Aquaculture: Buildings Designed to Live and Work with Water*, Newcastle upon Tyne: RIBA Publishing.

Barme, G. R. (2012), *The Forbidden City*, Cambridge, MA: Harvard University Press.

Batman (1989), [Film] Dir. Tim Burton, USA: Warner Bros.

Bel Geddes, N. (1940), *Magic Motorways*, New York: Random House.

Bellamy, E. (1888), *Looking Backward: 2000–1887*, Oxford: Oxford University Press.

Berardi, F. B. (2011), *After the Future*, Oakland, CA: AK Press.

Billing, R. (2011), *Tales from the Future*, Luxembourg: Publications Office of the European Union.

Bingham, N. (2013), *100 Years of Architectural Drawing: 1900–2000*, London: Laurence King.

Bjerstedt, A. (1982), *Future Consciousness and the School*, Malmo: School of Education, University of Lund.

Blade Runner (1982), [Film] Dir. Ridley Scott, USA: Warner Bros.

Blade Runner 2049 (2017), [Film] Dir. Denis Villeneuve, USA: Warner Bros.

Blomberg, K., ed (2015), *Haus-Rucker-Co: Architekturutopie Reloaded*, Berlin: Haus am Waldsee / Köln: Verlag der Buchhandlung Walther König.

Boudinot, R. (2012), *Blueprints of the Afterlife*, New York: Black Cat, Grove/Atlantic.

Boutwell, A. and M. Mitchell (1969), 'Planning on a National Scale', *Domus*, 470: 2–6.

Boyer, M. C. (2003), 'Aviation and the aerial view: Le Corbusier's spatial transformations in the 1930s and 1940s', *Diacritics*, 33 (3/4): 93–116.

Brand, S. (2010), *Whole Earth Discipline*, London: Atlantic Books.

Branzi, A. (2006), *No-Stop City – Archizoom Associati*, Orléans: HYX.

Brook, D. (2013), *A History of Future Cities*, New York: W. W. Norton & Company Inc.

Brook, R. and M. Dodge (2012), *Infra_MANC. Post-war Mancunian Infrastructures*, Manchester: bauprint

Brook, R. and N. Dunn (2011), *Urban Maps: Instruments of Narrative and Interpretation in the City*, Farnham: Ashgate.

Brooker, P. (2002), *Modernity and Metropolis: Writing, Film, and Urban Formations*, New York: Palgrave.

Brück, A. and A. Million (2018), 'Editorial: Visions for future cities', *Proceedings of the Institution of Civil Engineers – Urban Design and Planning*, 171 (4): 143–5.

Bruegmann, R. (2005), *Sprawl: A Compact History*, new edn, Chicago, IL: The University of Chicago Press.

Buckminster Fuller, R. (1968), *Operation Manual for Spaceship Earth*, Carbondale, IL: Southern Illinois University Press.

Buckminster Fuller, R. (1975), '2025, If. . .', *CoEvolution Quarterly*, Spring (5): 8–9.

Buckminster Fuller, R. and J. Snyder (2009), *Ideas and Integrities: A Spontaneous Autobiographical Disclosure*, Zürich: Lars Müller.

Buder, S. (1990), *Visionaries and Planners: The Garden City and the Modern Community*, New York: Oxford University Press.

Bulkeley, H. (2013), *Cities and Climate Change*, London: Routledge.

Burgess, A. (1962), *A Clockwork Orange*, London: William Heinemann.

Busbea, L. (2007), *Topologies: The Urban Utopia in France, 1960–1970*, Cambridge, MA: The MIT Press.

Campbell, K. (2011), *Massive Small: The Operating Programme for Smart Urbanism*, London: Urban Exchange.

Carson, R. (1962), *Silent Spring*, Boston, MA: Houghton Mifflin.

Černichov, J. G. (2009) *Graphic Masterpieces of Yakov Georgievich Chernikhov: Typefaces, Drawings, Ornaments*, Berlin: DOM Publishers.

CFTNU and E. Talen (2013), *Charter of the New Urbanism*, 2nd edn, New York: McGraw-Hill Education.

Chalk, W. (1963), 'Housing as a Consumer Product', *Archigram 3*, reprinted in *A Guide to Archigram 1961–74*, London: Academy Editions, 1994.

Christaller, W. (1933), *Die zentralen Orte in Süddeutschland*, trans. (in part) C. W. Baskin, Jena: Gustav Fischer.

City Under the Sea (2011), [Documentary] National Geographic, USA: National Geographic.

Clapson, M. (2013), 'Introduction: The Plan for Milton Keynes and Its Legacy', *The Plan for Milton Keynes*, London: Routledge.

Clear, N. (2009), 'A near future', *Architectural Design*, 79 (5): 6–11.

Cloverfield (2008), [Film] Dir. Matt Reeves, USA: Paramount Pictures.

Constant. (1974), 'New Babylon: Outline of a Culture' (1965), *New Babylon*, The Hague: Gemeentemuseum.

Corner, J., ed (1999), *Recovering Landscape: Essays in Contemporary Landscape Architecture*, New York: Princeton Architectural Press.

Crang, M. and S. Graham (2007), 'Sentient cities: ambient intelligence and the politics of urban space', *Information, Communication & Society*, 10 (6): 789–817.

Crash! (1971), [Film] Dir. Harley Cokeliss, UK: British Broadcasting Corporation.

Cruickshank, D. (2018), *Skyscraper*, London: Head of Zeus.

da Costa Meyer, E. (1995), *The Work of Antonio Sant'Elia: Retreat into the Future*, New Haven, CT: Yale University Press.

Cureton, P. (2020), *Drone Futures: UAS in Landscape & Urban Design*, London: Routledge.

Dahinden, J. (1972), *Urban Structures for the Future*, London: Pall Mall Press.

Dalrymple, W. and Y. Sharma (2012), *Princes and Painters in Mughal Delhi, 1707–1857*, New Haven, CT: Yale University Press.

Dator, J. (2009), 'Alternative futures at the Manoa School', *Journal of Futures Studies*, 14 (2): 1–18.

Davis, M. (1990), *City of Quartz: Excavating the Future in Los Angeles*, London: Verso.

Davis, M. (1998), *The Ecology of Fear: Los Angeles and the Imagination of Disaster*, New York: Metropolitan Books.

de Zegher, C. (1999), 'Another City for Another Life: Constant's New Babylon,' in *Drawing Papers 3*, New York: The Drawing Center.

Debord, G. (1974), 'De l'architecture sauvage', trans. T. Y. Levin as 'On Wild Architecture,' in E. Sussman, ed (1989), *On the Passage of a Few People through a Rather Brief Moment in Time: The Situationist International 1957–1972*, Cambridge/Boston, MA: The MIT Press/Institute of Contemporary Arts.

demerijn (2013), 'Retracing the Garden City,' *MO* (blog). April 3, 2013. https://merijnoudenampsen.org/2013/04/03/retracing-the-garden-city/.

Dessauce, M. (1999), 'On Pneumatic Apparitions', in Marc Dessauce (ed), *The Inflatable Moment: Pneumatics and Protest in '68*, New York: Princeton Architectural Press.

Dick, P. K. (1968), *Do Androids Dream of Electric Sheep?*, New York: Doubleday.

DiSalvo, C. (2010), 'Design, Democracy, and Agonistic Pluralism', *Design & Complexity*. Montreal. http://www.drs2010.umontreal.ca/data/PDF/031.pdf.

Dorrian, M. (2006), 'Cityscape with Ferris wheel. Chicago, 1893', in C. Linder (ed), *Urban Space and Cityscapes. Perspectives from Modern and Contemporary Culture*, London: Routledge.

Duany, A., J. Speck and M. Lydon (2010), *The Smart Growth Manual: New Urbanism in American Communities*, New York: McGraw-Hill Education.

Dune (1984), [Film] Dir. David Lynch, USA: Universal Pictures.

Dunn, N. (2012), *Digital Fabrication in Architecture*, London: Laurence King.

Dunn, N. (2016), *Dark Matters: A Manifesto for the Nocturnal City*, Winchester: Zero Books.

Dunn, N., P. Cureton and S. Pollastri (2014), *A Visual History of the Future*, London: Foresight Government Office for Science, Department of Business Innovation and Skills, HMSO.

DuPrau, J. (2003), *The City of Ember*, New York: Random House.

Eaton, R. (2002), *Ideal Cities: Utopianism and the (Un) Built Environment*, London: Thames and Hudson.

Edensor, T. (2017), *From Light to Dark: Daylight, Illumination, and Gloom*, Minneapolis, MN: University of Minnesota Press.

Edensor, T. and M. Jayne, eds (2012), *Urban Theory Beyond the West: A World of Cities*, Abingdon: Routledge.

Edgington, R. (2012), 'An "all-seeing flying eye": V-2 rockets and the promises of Earth photography', *History and Technology* 28 (3): 363–71. https://doi.org/10.1080/07341512.2012.722796.

Elysium (2013), [Film] Dir. Neill Blomkamp, USA: TriStar Pictures.

Escape from New York (1981), [Film] Dir. John Carpenter, USA: AVCO Embassy Pictures.

Evans, R. (1996), *Translations from Drawing to Building and Other Essays*, London: Architectural Association.

Farías, I. and T. Bender, eds (2011), *Urban Assemblages: How Actor-Network Theory Changes Urban Studies*, London: Routledge.

Ferriss, H. ([1929] 1986), *The Metropolis of Tomorrow*, reprint edn, New York: Princeton Architectural Press.

Fezer, J. and M. Schmitz (2012), *Lucius Burckhardt Writings. Rethinking Man-made Environments*, New York: SpringerWein.

Fisher, M. (2016), *The Weird and the Eerie*, London: Repeater Books.

Fishman, R. (1982), *Urban Utopias in the Twentieth Century*, Cambridge, MA: The MIT Press.

Forster, E. M. (1909), 'The Machine Stops', *Oxford and Cambridge Review*, 8, November.

Frampton, A., J. D. Solomon and C. Wong (2012), *Cities without Ground*, San Francisco: ORO Editions.

Frampton, K. (2007), *Modern Architecture. A Critical History*, 4th edn, London: Thames & Hudson.

Frase, P. (2016), *Four Futures: Life after Capitalism*, London: Verso.

Frazer, J. (1995), *An Evolutionary Architecture*, London: Architectural Association.

Gadanho, P. and G. D. Lowry (2014), *Uneven Growth: Tactical Urbanisms for Expanding Megacities*, New York: The Museum of Modern Art.

Galtung, J. (1982), *Schooling, Education and the Future* (Vol. 61). Malmo: Department of Education and Psychology Research, Lund University.

Gell, A. (1998), *Art and Agency: Towards a New Anthropological Theory*, Oxford: Clarendon Press.

Gernsback, H. (1922), *Science and Invention*, New York: Experimenter Publishing Co.

Gibson, G. (1984), *Neuromancer*, New York: Ace.

Gibson, G. (1986), *Count Zero*, New York: Arbor House.

Gibson, G. (1988), *Mona Lisa Overdrive*, New York: Bantam Books.

Gidley, J. M. (2017), *The Future: A Very Short Introduction*, Oxford: Oxford University Press.

Giedion, S. ([1948] 2013), *Mechanization Takes Command: A Contribution to Anonymous History*, Minneapolis, MN: University of Minnesota Press.

Gissing, G. ([1889] 2008), *The Nether World*, Oxford: Oxford University Press.

Glaeser, E. (2011), *Triumph of the City: How Our Greatest Invention Makes Us Richer, Smarter, Greener, Healthier, and Happier*, London: Penguin.

Gold, J. R. (2001), 'Under darkened skies: the city in science-fiction film', *Geography*, 86 (4): 337–45.

Goodman, D. (2008), *A History of the Future*, New York: Monacelli Press.

Goreau T. Hilbertz, W. (2005), 'Marine ecosystem restoration: costs and benefits for coral reefs', *World Resource Review*, 17 (3): 375–409.

Graham, S. (2016a), 'Vertical noir', *City*, 20 (3): 389–406.

Graham, S. (2016b), *Vertical: The City from Satellites to Bunkers*, London: Verso.

Greenfield, A. (2017), *Radical Technologies: The Design of Everyday Life*, London: Verso.

Groihofer, B. ed (2011), *Raimund Abraham [UN]BUILT*, 2nd edn, Vienna: Springer.

Grove, J. M., M. Cadenasso, S. T. Pickett, W. R. Burch and G. E. Machlis (2017), *The Baltimore School of Urban Ecology: Space, Scale, and Time for the Study of Cities*, New Haven, CT: Yale University Press.

Gyger, P. J. (2011), *Flying Cars: The Extraordinary History of Cars Designed for Tomorrow's World*, Sparkford: J. H. Haynes & Co Ltd.

Gyure, D. A. (2018), *Minoru Yamasaki: Humanist Architecture for a Modernist World*, New Haven, CT: Yale University Press.

Hagan, S. (2014), *Ecological Urbanism: The Nature of the City*, New York: Routledge.

Hall, P. (2014), *Cities of Tomorrow: An Intellectual History of Urban Planning and Design since 1880*, 4th edn, Hoboken, NJ: Wiley-Blackwell.

Halprin, L. (1963), *Taking Part Workshop Method*, Cambridge, MA: The MIT Press.

Haraway, D. (2016), *Staying with the Trouble: Making Kin in the Chthulucene*, Durham, NC: Duke University Press.

Hardy, D. (1991), *From Garden Cities to New Towns: Campaigning for Town and Country Planning 1899–1946*, London: Spon Press.

Hartmann, G. E. and J. Cigliano (eds) (2002), *Pencil Points Reader: A Journal for the Drafting Room, 1920–1943*, New York: Princeton Architectural Press.

Hays, K. M. and D. A. Miller (2008), *Buckminster Fuller: Starting with the Universe*, New Haven, CT / New York: Yale University Press / Whitney Museum of American Art.

Hénard, E. (1910), 'The Cities of the Future'. Available online: http://urbanplanning.library.cornell.edu/DOCS/henard.htm (accessed 22 August 2018)

Henderson, K., K. Lock and H. Ellis (2017), *The Art of Building a Garden City: Designing New Communities for the 21st Century*, London: RIBA Publishing.

Herbert, F. (1965), *Dune*, Philadelphia, PA: Chilton Books.

Hester, R. (1982), *Planning Neighborhood Space with People*, New York: Van Nostrand Reinhold Company.

Hetherington, K. (1997), 'In place of geometry: the materiality of place', *The Sociological Review* 45 (S1): 183–99. https://doi.org/10.1111/j.1467-954X.1997.tb03461.x.

Hewitt, L. and S. Graham (2015), 'Vertical cities: representations of urban verticality in 20th-century science fiction literature', *Urban Studies*, 52 (5): 923–37.

High Rise (2015), [Film] Dir. Ben Wheatley, UK: StudioCanal.

Hnilica, S (2012), *Metaphern für die Stadt: Zur Bedeutung von Denkmodellen in der Architekturtheorie*, Berlin: Gebr. Mann Verlag.

Hollands, R. G. (2008), 'Will the real smart city please stand up?' *City*, 12 (3): 303–20.

Hollis, L. (2013), *Cities Are Good for You: The Genius of the Metropolis*, London: Bloomsbury.

Howard, E. (1898), *To-morrow: A Peaceful Path to Real Reform*, London: Swann Sonnenschein & Co.

Huxley, A. ([1932] 2007) *Brave New World*, London: Vintage Books.

I Am Legend (2007), [Film] Dir. Francis Lawrence, USA: Warner Bros.

Ingold, T. (2007), *Lines: A Brief History*, London: Routledge.

Iossifova, D., C. N. H. Doll and A. Gasparatos, eds (2017), *Defining the Urban: Interdisciplinary and Professional Perspectives*, London: Routledge.

IPCC. (2013), 'Summary for Policymakers', in *Climate Change 2013: The Physical Science Basis.*

Contribution of Working Group I to the Fifth Assessment Report of the Intergovernmental Panel on Climate Change, [Stocker, T. F., D. Qin, G.-K. Plattner, M. Tignor, S. K. Allen, J. Boschung, A. Nauels, Y. Xia, V. Bex and P. M. Midgley (eds)]. Cambridge/New York: Cambridge University Press. https://doi.org/10.1017/CBO9781107415324.004

IPCC. (2018), *Global Warming of 1.5°C, an IPCC special report on the impacts of global warming of 1.5°C above pre-industrial levels and related global greenhouse gas emission pathways, in the context of strengthening the global response to the threat of climate change, sustainable development, and efforts to eradicate poverty*, Bonn: UNFCCC.

Jackson, M. and V. della Dora (2009), '"Dreams so Big Only the Sea Can Hold Them": Man-Made Islands as Anxious Spaces, Cultural Icons, and Travelling Visions', *Environment and Planning A: Economy and Space*, 41 (9): 2086–104.

Jacobs, J. [1961] (2011), *The Death and Life of Great American Cities*, 50th anniversary edn, London: Random House Inc.

Jallon, B., U. Napolitano and F. Boutté (2017), *Paris Haussmann: A Model's Relevance*, bilingual edn, Zürich: Park Books.

Jameson, F. (2007), *Archaeologies of the Future: The Desire Called Utopia and Other Science Fictions*, London: Verso.

Jazairy, E. H. (2011), *New Geographies, 4: Scales of the Earth*. Cambridge, MA: Harvard University Press.

Jefferies, R. (1885), *After London; Or, Wild England*, London: Cassell & Company, Ltd.

Jellicoe, G. (1961), *Motopia: A Study in the Evolution of Urban Landscape*, London: Studio.

Jerrold, B. (1872), *London: A Pilgrimage*, London: Grant & Co.

Just Imagine (1930), [Film] Dir. David Butler, USA: Fox Film Corporation.

Kaijima, M., J. Kuroda and Y. Tsukamoto (2001), *Made in Tokyo*, Tokyo: Kajima Institute.

Kaji-O'Grady, S. and P. Raisbeck (2005), 'Prototype cities in the sea', *Journal of Architecture*, 10 (4): 443–61.

Keen, B. (1990), *The Aztec Image in Western Thought*, New Brunswick, NJ: Rutgers University Press.

Kipper, G. and J. Rampolla (2012), *Augmented Reality: An Emerging Technologies Guide to AR*, Amsterdam/Boston, MA: Syngress,

Khan-Magomedov, S. O. (2015), *The Flying City and Beyond*, trans. C. Lodder, Chicago, IL: University of Chicago Press.

Kitchin, R. and J. Kneale, eds (2002), *Lost in Space. Geographies of Science Fiction*, London: Continuum.

Klemek, C. (2011), *The Transatlantic Collapse of Urban Renewal: Postwar Urbanism from New York to Berlin*, Chicago, IL: The University of Chicago Press.

Klingmann, A. (2007), *Brandscapes: Architecture in the Experience Economy*, Cambridge, MA: The MIT Press.

Knabb, K., ed (2007), *Situationist International Anthology*, revised edn, Berkeley CA: Bureau of Public Secrets.

Komninos, N., C. Kakderi, A. Panori and P. Tsarchopoulos (2018), 'Smart city planning from an evolutionary perspective', *Journal of Urban Technology*, 26 (2): 3–20. https://doi.org/10.1080/10630732.2018.1485368.

Koolhaas, R. ([1978] 1994), *Delirious New York: A Retroactive Manifesto for Manhattan*, new edn, New York: Monacelli Press.

Kostof, S. and R. Tobias. (1999), *The City Shaped: Urban Patterns and Meanings Through History*, new edn, London: Thames & Hudson.

Kuan, S. (2012), *Kenzo Tange: Architecture for the World*, Baden: Lars Müller.

Lakoff, G. and M. Johnson (2003), *Metaphors We Live By*, Chicago, IL: University of Chicago Press.

Lang, P. and W. Menking (2003), *Superstudio: Life without Objects*, Milan: Skira.

Larsson, M. (2011), 'Dune: Arenaceous Anti-Desertification Architecture', in Badescu, V. and R. B. Cathcart (eds), *Macro-Engineering Seawater in Unique Environments: Arid Lowlands and Water Bodies Rehabilitation, Environmental Science and Engineering*, Berlin: Springer, 431–63.

Latour B. (1986), 'Visualization and cognition: drawing things together', *Knowledge and Society Studies in the Sociology of Culture Past and Present*, 6: 1–40.

Latour, B. (2007), *Reassembling the Social: An Introduction to Actor-Network-Theory*, new edn, Oxford: Oxford University Press.

Law, J. and J. Urry (2004), 'Enacting the social', *Economy and Society*, 33 (3): 390–410.

Lefaivre, L. (2005), *Leon Battista Alberti's Hypnerotomachia Poliphili: Re-Cognizing the Architectural Body in the Early Italian Renaissance*, new edn, Cambridge, MA: The MIT Press.

Lefebvre, H. (1968), *Le Droit à la Ville*, Paris: Anthropos.

Lefebvre, H. (1970), *Le Révolution urbaine*, Paris: Gallimard.

Lefebvre, H. (1996), *Writings on Cities*, trans. and ed. E. Kofman and E. Lebas, Oxford: Blackwell.

Legeby, A. (2010), 'From housing segregation to integration in public space', *Journal of Space Syntax*, 1 (1): 92–107.

Levine, N. (2015), *The Urbanism of Frank Lloyd Wright*, Princeton, NJ: Princeton University Press.

Levitas, R. (2013), *Utopia as Method: The Imaginary Reconstitution of Society*, New York: Palgrave Macmillan.

Lewallen, C. M. and S. Seid (2004), *Ant Farm: 1968–1978*, Oakland, CA: University of California Press.

Lin, Z-J. (2007), 'From megastructure to megalopolis: formation and transformation of mega-projects in Tokyo Bay', *Journal of Urban Design* 12 (1): 73–92. https://doi.org/10.1080/13574800601072442.

Lustig, P. (2015), *Strategic Foresight: Learning from the Future*, Axminster: Triarchy Press Ltd.

Lydon, M. and A. Garcia (2015), *Tactical Urbanism*, 3rd edn, Washington, DC: Island Press.

Lynas, N. (2008), *Six Degrees: Our Future on a Hotter Planet*, London: Harper Perennial.

Lynch, K. (1960), *The Image of the City*, Cambridge, MA: The MIT Press.

Lynch, K. (1995), *City Sense and City Design: Writings and Projects of Kevin Lynch*, new edn, Cambridge, MA: The MIT Press.

Lynn, G. (1997), *Architecture after Geometry*, London: John Wiley & Sons.

Lynn, G. (1998), *Fold, Bodies and Blobs: Collected Essays*, Brussels: Ante Post.

Lyon, G. and C. Lin (2017), *No Small Plans*, Chicago, IL: Chicago Architecture Foundation.

Mad Max trilogy (1979–1985), [Film] Dir. George Miller, USA: Warner Bros.

Maki, F. (1964), *Investigations in Collective Form*, St. Louis, MO: School of Architecture, Washington University.

Maniaque-Benton, C. et al. (eds) (2016), *Whole Earth Field Guide*, Cambridge, MA: The MIT Press.

Mansfield, H. (1990), *Cosmopolis: Yesterday's Cities of the Future*, New Brunswick, NJ: Center for Urban Policy Research.

Marcus, A. and D. Neumann, eds (2008), *Visualizing the City*, London: Routledge, London.

Mathews, S. (2007), *From Agit-prop to Free Space: The Architecture of Cedric Price*, London: Black Dog.

Mattie, E. (2000), *World's Fairs*, New York: Princeton Architectural Press.

McCarthy, C. (2006), *The Road*, London: Vintage.

McQuaid, M., ed (2002), *Envisioning Architecture: Drawings from the Museum of Modern Art*, New York: The Museum of Modern Art.

Merrifield, A. (2013), 'The urban question under planetary urbanization', *International Journal of Urban and Regional Research*, 37 (3): 909–22. https://doi.org/10.1111/j.1468-2427.2012.01189.x

Metropolis (1927), [Film] Dir. Fritz Lang, Germany: UFA.

Miller, M. (1989), *Letchworth: The First Garden City*, Chichester: Phillimore & Co Ltd.

Miller, M. (2008), *Hampstead Garden Suburb: Arts and Crafts Utopia?* Chichester: Phillimore & Co Ltd.

Miller, M. (2010), *English Garden Cities: An Introduction*, Swindon: Historic England.

Minden, M. and H. Bachmann (2002), *Fritz Lang's* Metropolis: *Cinematic Visions of Technology and Fear*, Rochester, NY: Camden House.

Minority Report (2002), [Film] Dir. Steven Spielberg, USA: 20th Century Fox.

Mitchell, W. J. (1979), *Computer Aided Architectural Design*, New York: Van Nostrand Reinhold Company.

Mittner, D. (2018), *New Towns: A Study on Urban Design*, Berlin: JOVIS Verlag.

Moir, E., T. Moonen and G. Clark (2014), *What Are Future Cities? Origins, Meanings and Uses*, London: Foresight Future of Cities Project and the Future Cities Catapult.

Montfort, N. (2017), *The Future*, Cambridge, MA: The MIT Press.

Montgomery, C. (2013), *Happy City: Transforming Our Lives through Urban Design*, London: Penguin.

Moody, W. D. (1911), *Wacker's Manual of the Plan of Chicago: Municipal Economy*, Chicago, IL: Henneberry Co.

More, T. ([1516] 2012), *Utopia*, London: Penguin.

Morris, W. ([1890] 1993), *News from Nowhere*, London: Penguin.

Morshed, A. (2002), 'The cultural politics of aerial vision: Le Corbusier in Brazil (1929)', *Journal of Architectural Education*, 55 (4): 201–10.

Mumford, E. (2002), *The CIAM Discourse on Urbanism 1928–1960*, new edn, Cambridge, MA: The MIT Press.

Mumford, L. (1968), *The City in History: Its Origins, Its Transformations, and Its Prospects*, London: Harcourt Brace International.

Mumford, L. and L. Winner ([1934] 2010), *Technics and Civilization*, reprint edn. Chicago, IL: University of Chicago Press.

Mundy, B. E. (1998), 'Mapping the Aztec capital: the 1524 Nuremberg map of Tenochtitlan, its sources and meanings', *Imago Mundi*, 50 (1): 11–33. https://doi.org/10.1080/03085699808592877.

Murphy, D. (2016), *Last Futures: Nature, Technology and the End of Architecture*, London: Verso.

Murray Bell, L. and G. Goodwin, eds (2012), *Writing Urban Space*, Winchester: Zero Books.

MVRDV. (1998), *FARMAX: Excursions on Density*, Rotterdam: 010 Publishers.

Neuman, M. and A. Hull (2009), 'The futures of the city region', *Regional Studies*, 43 (6): 777–87.

Neumann, D. ed (1996), *Film Architecture: From Metropolis to Blade Runner*, Munich: Prestel.

Neville, H. (1668), *The Isle of Pines*. Available online: http://www.gutenberg.org/files/21410/21410-h/21410-h.htm (accessed 19 July 2018).

Oldfield Ford, L. (2011), *Savage Messiah*, London: Verso.

Olthuis, K. and D. Keuning (2010), *Float!: Building on Water to Combat Urban Congestion and Climate Change*, Amsterdam: Frame Publishers.

Oreskes, N. (2014), *The Collapse of Civilization: A View from the Future*, New York: Columbia University Press.

Orwell, G. ([1949] 2013), *Nineteen Eighty-Four*, London: Penguin Books.

Oshima, K. T. (2009), *Arata Isozaki*, ed, A. Isozaki, London: Phaidon Press.

Pallasmaa, J. (2011), *The Embodied Image: Imagination and Imagery in Architecture*, Chichester: John Wiley & Sons.

Parsons, G. (2017), *Siena, Civil Religion and the Sienese*, New York: Routledge.

Pawley, M. (1975), 'We Shall Not Bulldoze Westminster Abbey: Archigram and the Retreat from Technology', in *Oppositions*, 7, reprinted in K. Michael Hays (ed), *Oppositions Reader*, New York: Princeton Architectural Press, 1998.

Pérez-Gómez, A. (2000), *Architectural Representation and the Perspective Hinge*, new edn, Cambridge, MA: The MIT Press.

Perng, S.-Y. (2016), *Code and the City*, London: Routledge.

Pløger, J. (2004), 'Strife: urban planning and agonism', *Planning Theory*, 3 (1): 71–92.

Polak, F. (1973), *The Image of the Future*, trans. E. Boulding, San Francisco: Jossey-Bass.

Pollastri, S., C. Boyko, R. Cooper, N. Dunn, S. Clune and C. Coulton (2017), 'Envisioning urban futures: from narratives to composites', *The Design Journal*, 20(Suppl. 1): S4365–77.

Pollastri, S., N. Dunn, C. Rogers, C. Bokyo, R. Cooper and N. Tyler (2018), 'Envisioning urban futures as conversations to inform design and research', *Proceedings of the Institution of Civil Engineers – Urban Design and Planning*, 171 (4): 146–56.

Porritt, J. (2013), *The World We Made*, London: Phaidon.

Priest, C. (1974), *The Inverted World*, London: Faber & Faber.

Ramadan, Z. (2018), 'The gamification of trust: the case of China's "social credit"', *Marketing Intelligence & Planning*, 36 (1): 93–107.

Riedel, J. (1906), *Tuinsteden,* Utrecht: J. van Boekhoven.

Rodchenko, A. (1921), '"Slogans" and "Organizational Programme" of the Workshop for the Study of Painting in State Art Colleges', in *Artistic-Constructive Education*, no. 4, Moscow.

Rogers, C. (2018), 'Engineering future liveable, resilient, sustainable cities using foresight', *Proceedings of the Institution of Civil Engineers – Civil Engineering*, 171 (6): 3–9.

Rydin, Y. and L. Tate (2017), *Actor Networks of Planning: Exploring the Influence of Actor Network Theory*, London: Routledge.

Sadler, S. (1998), *The Situationist City*, Cambridge, MA: The MIT Press.

Sadler, S. (2005), *Archigram – Architecture without Architecture*, Cambridge, MA: The MIT Press.

Sardar, Z. (2010), 'Welcome to postnormal times', *Futures*, 42 (5): 435–44.

Savage, M. and A. C. Clarke (1995), *The Millennial Project: Colonizing the Galaxy in Eight Easy Steps*, reprint edn, Boston, MA: Little, Brown.

Savransky, M., A. Wilkie and M. Rosengarten (2017), 'The Lure of Possible Futures. On Speculative Research', in A. Wilkie, M. Savransky and M. Rosengarten (eds), *Speculative Research: The Lure of Possible Futures*, 1–17, New York: Routledge.

Schulz, J. (1978), 'Jacopo de' Barbari's view of Venice: map making, city views, and moralized geography before the year 1500', *Art Bulletin* (60): 425–74.

Schumacher, P. (2009), 'Parametricism – A New Global Style for Architecture and Urban Design', in N. Leach and H. Castle (eds), *Digital Cities AD Architectural Design*, 14–23, Chichester: John Wiley & Sons Ltd..

SeaSteading. (n.d.), *Homesteading the High Seas*. Available online: http://gramlich.net/projects/oceania/seastead1.html (accessed 16 July 2018).

Shaviro, S. (2016), *Discognition*, London: Repeater Books.

Silent Running (1972), [Film] Dir. Douglas Trumbull, USA: Universal Pictures.

Sky, A. and M. Stone (1976), *Unbuilt America: Forgotten Architecture in the United States from Thomas Jefferson to the Space Age,* New York: Abbeville Press.

Slaughter, R. A. (1997), 'Developing and applying strategic foresight', *ABN Report,* 5 (10): 13–27.

Söderström, O., T. Paasche and F. Klauser (2014), 'Smart cities as corporate storytelling', *City* 18 (3): 307–20.

Sorkin, M. (2004), 'Sex, Drugs, Rock and Roll, Cars, Dolphins, and Architecture', in C. M. Lewallen and S. Seid (eds.), *Ant Farm: 1968–1978,* 4–13, Oakland, CA: University of California Press.

Spuybroek, L. (2004), *NOX: Machining Architecture,* London: Thames and Hudson.

Spuybroek, L. (2016), *The Sympathy of Things: Ruskin and the Ecology of Design,* 2nd edn, London: Bloomsbury Academic.

Steinberg, P. E., E. Nyman and M. J. Caraccioli (2012), 'Atlas swam: freedom, capital, and floating sovereignties in the Seasteading vision', *Antipode,* 44 (4): 1532–50.

Sterling, B. (2005), *Shaping Things,* Cambridge, MA: The MIT Press.

Srivastava, S. (2014), *Entangled Urbanism: Slum, Gated Community, and Shopping Mall in Delhi and Gurgaon,* Oxford: Oxford University Press.

Stites, R. (1989), *Revolutionary Dreams: Utopian Vision and Experimental Life in the Russian Revolution,* Oxford: Oxford University Press.

Sutherland, I. E. (1963), 'Sketchpad: A Man-Machine Graphical Communication System'. *Proceedings of the AFIPS Spring Joint Computer Conference,* Washington, D.C.

Suvin, D. (1972), 'On the poetics of the science fiction genre', *College English,* 34 (3): 372–82.

Swift, J. ([1726] 2010), *Gulliver's Travels,* London: Penguin.

Tafuri, M. (1969), 'Per una Critica dell'ideologia architettonica', *Contropiano,* 1 (January–April 1969): 31–79; trans. Stephen Sartarelli as 'Toward a critique of architectural ideology', in *Architectural Theory since 1968,* K. Michael Hays (ed), 6–35, Cambridge, MA: The MIT Press, 1998.

Tafuri, M. ([1973] 1976), *Architecture and Utopia: Design and Capitalist Development,* trans. B. Luigia La Penta, Cambridge, MA: The MIT Press.

Talbot, B. (2007), *Alice in Sunderland,* London: Jonathan Cape.

The Age of Stupid (2009), [Film] Dir. Franny Armstrong, Spanner Films / Dogwoof Pictures.

The Fifth Element (1997), [Film] Dir. Luc Besson, USA: Columbia Pictures.

The Matrix (1999), [Film] Dir. The Wachowskis, USA: Warner Bros.

The Pruitt-Igoe Myth (2011), [Documentary] Dir. Chad Freidrichs, USA: First Run Features.

Thiel, P. (1997), *People, Paths, and Purposes: Notations for a Participatory Envirotecture,* Seattle: University of Washington Press.

Thompson, J. B. (1984), *Studies in the Theory of Ideology,* Cambridge: Polity.

Toffler, A. (1970), *Future Shock,* New York: Random House.

Tschumi, B. (1995), *The Manhattan Transcripts: Theoretical Projects,* London: St. Martin's Press/Academy Editions.

Turner, F. (2006), *From Counterculture to Cyberculture: Stewart Brand, the Whole Earth Network, and the Rise of Digital Utopianism,* Chicago, IL: The University of Chicago Press.

Turner, F. R. (1996), *The Maunsell Sea Forts: A Potted History of the WW2 Thames Estuary Forts,* Kent: F. R. Turner.

UN DESA Population Division (2018), *World Urbanization Prospects: The 2018 Revision, Key Facts,* New York: United Nations.

UNFPA (2007), *State of World Population 2007: Unleashing the Potential of Urban Growth,* New York: United Nations Population Fund.

Urry, J. (2016), *What Is the Future?* Cambridge: Polity Press.

van Es, E., G. Harbusch, B. Maurer, M. Pérez, K. Somer and D. Weiss, eds (2014), *Atlas of the Functional City: CIAM 4 and Comparative Urban Analysis,* Bussum, The Netherlands: THOTH Publishers / gta Verlag.

van Schaik, M. and O. Mácel, eds (2005), *Exit Utopia: Architectural Provocations 1956–1976,* Munich/Delft: Prestel/Institute of History of Art, Architecture and Urbanism.

Vaneigem, R. ([1967] 2003), *The Revolution of Everyday Life,* trans. D. Nicholson-Smith, London: Rebel Press.

Vaneigem, R. (1961), 'Internationale situationniste' no. 6 (August 1961), 33–7; trans. T. McDonough as 'Comments Against Urbanism,' in T. McDonough (ed.), *The Situationists and the City,* London: Verso, 2009.

Vanstiphout, W. and M. Provoost (2007), *WiMBY! Hoogvliet: The Future, Past and Present of a Satellite Town,* Rotterdam: NAi Publishers.

Varnelis, K. (2006), 'Programming after program: Archizoom's No-Stop City', *Praxis*, 8: 82–91.

Verne, J. (1877), *The Underground City*, London: Sampson Low.

Vesely, D. (2006), *Architecture in the Age of Divided Representation: The Question of Creativity in the Shadow of Production*, Cambridge, MA: The MIT Press.

Vivrett, W. K. (1971), 'Planning For People: Minnesota Experimental City,' in Shirley Weiss, ed., *New Community Development Vol. 1: Planning, Process, Implementation, and Emerging Social Concerns*, Chapel Hill, NC: University of North Carolina.

von Eckardt, W. (1965), 'The case for building 350 new towns', *Harper's Magazine*, December, 85–8 & 91–4.

Voros, J. (2003), 'A generic foresight process framework', *Foresight*, 5 (3): 10–21.

Wakeman, R. (2016), *Practicing Utopia: An Intellectual History of the New Town Movement*, Chicago, IL: University of Chicago Press.

Waldheim, C. (2016), *Landscape as Urbanism: A General Theory*, Princeton, NJ: Princeton University Press.

Waldheim, C., ed, (2006), *The Landscape Urbanism Reader*, New York: Princeton Architectural Press.

Wall-E (2008), [Film] Dir. Andrew Stanton, USA: Walt Disney Studios Motion Pictures.

Weisman, A. (2007), *The World Without Us*, New York: St. Martin's Press.

Wells, H. G. ([1905] 2005), *A Modern Utopia*, London: Penguin.

Wendort, R. (2001), 'Piranesi's double ruin', *Eighteenth-Century Studies*, 34 (2): 161–80.

WHO and UN-Habitat (2016), *Global report on urban health: equitable healthier cities for sustainable development*, Geneva: World Health Organization. Available online: http://www.who.int/iris/handle/10665/204715 (accessed 11 September 2018).

Wigley, M. (2001), 'Paper, scissors, blur', in C. de Zegher and M. Wigley (eds.), *The Activist Drawing: Retracing Situationist Architectures from Constant's New Babylon to Beyond*, New York: The Drawing Center/Cambridge, MA: The MIT Press.

Wilcoxon, R. (1968), *A Short Bibliography on Megastructures*, Monticello, IL: Council of Planning Librarians Exchange Bibliography.

Williams, R. (2014), *Keywords: A Vocabulary of Culture and Society*, 2nd edn, London: Fourth Estate.

Wilson, R. A. (2016), *Prometheus Rising*, Grand Junction, CO: Hilaritas Press.

Wines, J. (1988), *De Architecture*, New York: Rizzoli.

Wittkower, R. (1998), *Architectural Principles in the Age of Humanism*. 2nd edn, Chichester: John Wiley & Sons.

Wolfflin, H. (1984), *Renaissance and Baroque*, trans. K. Simon, new edn, London: Collins.

Wright, E. O. (2010), *Envisioning Real Utopias*, London: Verso.

Wright, F. L. (1945), *An Autobiography*, London: Faber & Faber.

Yusoff, K. and J. Gabrys (2011), 'Climate change and the imagination', *Wiley Interdisciplinary Reviews: Climate Change*, 2 (4): 516–34.

Zamyatin, Y. ([1921] 2007), *We*, trans. N. Randall, London: Vintage Classics.

INDEX

Page references in *italics* denote figures; page references in **bold** denote tables.

A

Abercrombie, Patrick, *12*, 44
Abraham, Raimund, 86, *86*
Abu Dhabi, 105, *106*
actor-network theory (ANT), 38
After London (Jefferies), 161
The Age of Stupid (film), 143
Agglomeration, David George Emmerich, *92*
Aircraft Carrier City, Hans Hollein, *54*
Albert, Allen D., *10*
Alexander, Christopher, 45
Ali Khan, Mazhar, *34*
Allen, Stan, 31
Altered Carbon (Netflix), 55, *56*
Amaravathi, 106, *107*
American Institute of Steel Construction, 63
Amico, V., 40
Analemma Tower, Clouds Architecture Office, *76*
Anderson, Michael, *110*
Ant Farm, 71, 122, *123*, 123–4
  Convention City, 71, *123*
  Dolphin Embassy, 71, 123, *123*, 124
  Freedomland, 123
Ant Farm, WORKac &, 3-C CITY: Climate, Convention, and Cruise, *74*

Anti-desertification, Magnus Larsson, 61, *62*
Apollo 17, 52
Aqualta, Studio Lindfors, 154, *155*
Archigram, 93, 118, 119, 120, 122
Architectural Association, 59
Architectural Fantasies (Černichov), *39*
Architectural Principles in the Age of Humanism (Wittkower), 37
Architecture and Utopia (pamphlet), 114, *115*
Architecture Mobile (Friedman), 81
Archizoom, 5, *115*
arcology, 87
Arcosanti, Arizona, 52
Armstrong, Rachel, *28*, 166
Asimov, Isaac, 73, 104
Association for Organic Architecture, 146
Atelier Bow-Wow, 140, *140*
Atlanpole, Hans Kollhoff, *141*
The Atrocity Exhibition (Ballard), 90
augmented reality (AR), 59
AUJIK, Spatial Bodies, *58*
Auto-Expander, Zünd Up, 122, *122*
Autopia Ampere, Newton Fallis, 71, *73*, 166

B

Babel IIB, Arcology, Paolo Soleri, 87, *87*
Back to the Future (film franchise), 141
Back to the Future: Part II (film), *141*
Bacon, Francis, 34

Ballard, J. G., 59, 90, 156
Banham, Reyner, 60, 83, *84*, 145
Barbari, Jacopo de', bird's eye of Venice, 38, *38*
Barthes, Roland, 139
Bartolini, Ernesto, 5
Bataille, Georges, 139
Batman (film), 63, 95
Bayer, Kayce, *64*
Bel Geddes, Norman, 48, 88
Bellamy, Edward, 41
Belleri, Daniele, *50*
Bennett, Edward, 62, *64*
Berardi, Franco 'Bifo', 56–7
Berlin TV Tower, *35*
Besson, Luc, 97
BIG, Loop City, 148, *149*
Biorock™, 71, *73*, 166
Biosphere 2, 160
Biosphere 3, *159*
Blade Runner (film), 55, 85, 94, 95, 96, 99, 104
Blade Runner 2049 (film), *96*
Blessed Ambrogio Sansedoni, *32*
Blockchains City, 153, *153*
Blow-Out Village, Peter Cook, 119
Boscutti, Stefano, 157, *158*
Boutwell, Alan, 144, *145*
Brand, Stewart, 52
Branzi, Andrea, 5
Brasília, Brazil, Lúcio Costa and Oscar Niemeyer, *18*
Brave New World (Huxley), 55, *61*
British Royal Commission, 43

Broadacre City, Frank Lloyd Wright, 47, *47*
Broad Sustainable Building, Changsha, 156
Brutalist movement, 123
Brutalist Vertical City, *60*
Buckminster Fuller, Richard, 18, 29, 48, 50, 52, 92, 101, *102*, 147, 158, 160
Bulgarian Communist Party, 6
Burckhardt, Lucius, 138
Burgess, Anthony, 60
Burnham, Daniel, 62, *64*
Burton, Tim, 63

C

Candilis, Georges, 92
Carpenter, John, 68
Carson, Rachel, 61
Casabella (magazine), 115
CCCC-FHDI & AT Design, Zhujiangkou Island, 163, *164*
Centre Georges Pompidou, 118
Chalk, Warren, 118
Chanéac, Jean-Louis, 126, *127*
Chan K Q Audrey and Iskm (Studio aVOID), *13*
Charles V, 31
Chernikhov, Yakov, Architectural fantasy, *39*
Chicago Architecture Foundation, 61, 62, *64*
China, *100*
  Great Wall of, 114
  Social Credit System, 109
China, A Vertical Forest on Mars?, *77*
Christaller, Walter, 45
Chtcheglov, Ivan, 56
Chthonopolis, Nic Clear, 168, *170*
Cities of Vision, 20
  imaginary cities, 29, 31, 34, 37–8
  industrial cities, 40–1
  mechanized life, 41–5, 47–8
  urbanism from road and beyond, 48, 50–4
Citivues International, Inc., bird's eye view of Manhattan, *67*

city categories, **22**
The City in History (Mumford), 37
City in Space, Bernhard Hafner, *63*
A City Is Not a Tree (Alexander), 45
The City of Ember (DuPrau), 166
'City of Things' perspective, Manuel Herz Architects, *70*
City Under the Sea (documentary), 165
Clear, Nic, 168, *170*
climate change, envisioning, 154, 156
A Clockwork Orange (Burgess), 60, *61*
Cloud Iron, El Lissitzky, 156
Cloud Nine, Buckminster Fuller and Shoji Sadao, 158
Cloverfield (film), 63
Cluster City, **22**
  Cumbernauld New Town, Geoffrey Copcutt, *90*
  Instant City, Archigram, *119*
  Raumstadt, Eckhardt Schulze-Fielitz, *82*
Clusters in the Air (Cluster City), Arata Isozaki, 156, *157*
Cognitive City, **22**
  HYPER-REALITY, Keiichi Matsuda, *141*
Cohen, Thierry, 154, *155*
Cold War, 52
Collage City, **22**
  Generations of Tokyo Architecture, Atelier Bow-Wow, *140*
  Hundred Mile City, Peter Barber Architects, *40*
  Lagos 2081, Ikiré Jones, *2*
  Re-ruined Hiroshima Project, Arata Isozaki, *50*
  Strelka Unsettled, *50*
Colonna, Francesco, *Hypnerotomachia Poliphili*, *35*
Comprehensive (Continuous) City, Mike Mitchell and Alan Boutwell, 144, 145, *145*
computer-aided design (CAD), 58, 128
computer-generated imagery (CGI), 140
Concrete Quarterly (journal), 60

Congrès Internationaux d'Architecture Moderne (CIAM), 45
Connected City, **22**
  Europa EuroGrid, OMA/AMO, *147*
  Stratiform Structure Module, Kiyonori Kikutake, *85*
Constant Nieuwenhuys, 112, *113*, 118
Continuous City, **22**
  Le Dodici Città Ideali, Superstudio, *5*
  Manifesto New New York, Superstudio, *114*
  Masterplan Strijp Philips, Eindhoven, *5*
  No-Stop City, Archizoom, *115*
  Utopia (More), 36
Continuous Monument, Superstudio, 113–14
Contropiano (journal), 114
Convention City, Ant Farm, 71, 123
Cook, Peter, 93, *93*, 119
Copcutt, Geoffrey, 90, *90*
Corbett, Harvey Wiley, 166
Cortés, Hernando, 33
Costa, Lúcio, 18
Count Zero (Gibson), 73
Covarrubias, Luis, 33
Crash! (film), 90
Crickmer, Courtenay, *42*
Crossing City, **22**
  Anderson Isometric Maps, *66*
  bird's eye view of Manhattan, *67*
  'City of Things' perspective, Manuel Herz Architects, *70*
  Comprehensive City, Mike Mitchell and Alan Boutwell, *145*
  Earthscratcher for Century City, DR_D, *21*
  Intrapolis, Walter Jonas, *125*
  New Babylon, Constant, *113*
  New Welfare Island, Rem Koolhaas, *69*
  Spatial City, Yona Friedman, *82*
Crystal Palace, 10
Cullen, Gordon, 48
Cumbernauld New Town, 90, *90*

Cyber City, **22**
- Agglomeration, David George Emmerich, *92*
- Akira – Destruction of Neo-Tokyo, *19*
- Altered Carbon, *56*
- *Blade Runner* (film), *95*
- *Blade Runner 2049* (film), *96*
- Cybertopia, Egor Orlov, *25*
- Dolphin Embassy, Ant Farm, *123*
- *Ghost in the Shell* (film), *78*
- Heathrow City, Hawkins\Brown, *132*
- Metacity/Datatown, MVRDV, *130*
- Minecraft, *19*
- *Minority Report* (film), *98*
- One North Masterplan, Zaha Hadid Architects, *131*
- Spatial Bodies, AUJIK, *58*

cyberpunk city, Neo-Tokyo, *19*
Cybertopia, Egor Orlov, *25*

D

Dahinden, Justus, 124, 126, *126*
Darkened Cities, 154, *155*
Dator, Jim, 6
Da Vinci, Leonardo, 40, 90
Davis, Mike, 96
Daybreak Express (Pennebaker), *40*
The Death and the Life of American Cities (Jacobs), 48
Debord, Guy, 135, *136*
Defence Meteorological Satellites Program, 53
Delhi, panorama of, *34*
Delirious New York (Koolhaas), 66, 69
Derrida, Jacques, 139
Desert City, **22**
- Blockchains City, EYRC Architects + Tom Wiscombe Architecture, *153*
- dune anti-desertification, Magnus Larsson, *62*
- Green Machine, Stephane Malka, *169*
- Sietch, Matsys, *168*

De Soissons, Louis, *42*
Dessauce, Marc, 123
de Vauban, Sébastien Le Prestre, 40
Dharavi Masterplan, Foster + Partners, 150, *150*
Dick, Philip K., 96
Dickens, Charles, 43
Divided City, **22**
- E.P.C.O.T. Masterplan, *17*
- *Escape from New York* (film), 68
- Futurama exhibit, Norman Bel Geddes, 88
- Imaginary drawings, Zoning ordinances, Hugh Ferriss, *67*
- Memorial House of Bulgarian Communist Party, 6
- *Motopia* (Jellicoe), 89
- Plan of Paris, France, *41*
- Ville Radieuse, Le Corbusier, *46*

DIY City, **22**
- Auto-Expander, Zünd-Up, *122*
- Chicago World Fair, Allen D. Albert, 10
- La Cité Mobile, Charles Péré-Lahaille, *91*
- Plug-in City, Archigram, *93*
- *Do Androids Dream of Electric Sheep?* (Dick), 96
- Dolphin Embassy, Ant Farm, 71, *123*, 123–4

Domenig, Günther, 63, 83, *84*
Doré, Gustave, 42, *43*
Dorrian, Mark, 98
The Drowned World (Ballard), 59, *59*, 156
Dubai, drone photography, *99*
Dune (Herbert), 61, 167
DuPrau, Jeanne, 166
Dymaxion Map, Richard Buckminster Fuller, 147
Dynamic City, 45

E

Ecological Cities, 174
- 3-C CITY: Climate, Convention, and Cruise, WORKac & Ant Farm, *74*
- Aqualta, Studio Lindfors, *155*
- Autopia Ampere, Newton Fallis, *73*
- Blockchains City, EYRC Architects + Tom Wiscombe Architecture, *153*
- Broadacre City project, Frank Lloyd Wright, *47*
- 'City of Things' perspective, Manuel Herz Architects, *70*
- Dharavi Masterplan, Foster + Partners, *150*
- dune anti-desertification, Magnus Larsson, *62*
- Future North, Terreform ONE, 164, *165*
- Hydro-Net, Iwamoto Scott, *151*
- Loop City, BIG, 148, *149*
- Nature-City, WORKac, *152*
- Oystertecture, SCAPE / MoMA Rising Currents Exhibition, *27*
- Post Carbon City State, Terreform ONE, *72*
- Postcards From the Future, Robert Graves and Didier Madoc-Jones, *154*
- Resilient by Design, Hassell and MVRDV, 148, *149*
- taxonomy, 23
- timeline, **176**–7
- Uxcester Masterplan, URBED, *14*
- Villes éteintes (Darkened Cities), Thierry Cohen, *155*

Eliopolis, Aldo Loris Rossi, 3
El Lissitzky, 156
Elysium (film), 160
Emmerich, David George, 92, *92*
Environment Transformers, Haus-Rucker-Co, 120
Envisioning Real Utopias (Wright), 15
E.P.C.O.T. (Experimental Prototype Community Of Tomorrow), *17*
Escape from New York (film), 63, 68
European Union, Institute for Security Studies, 40
Evans, Robin, 57–8
An Evolutionary Architecture (Frazer), 71

Expo 67, United States Pavilion, Richard Buckminster Fuller, 101, *102*
EYRC Architects + Tom Wiscombe Architecture, 153, *153*

F

Fallis, Newton, Autopia Ampere, 71, *73*, 166
Fallon, Finbarr, 168, *170*
FARMAX (MVRDV), 129
Ferriss, Hugh, 45, 47, 63, *67*
Feuerstein, Günther, 116, *116*
The Fifth Element (film), 96, *97*
5th Studio, 133, *133*
Fisher, Sidney R., *91*
Fishman, Robert, 47
Flatwriter, 81
Flexible Cities, 174
    Aerotopia, Chan K Q Audrey and Iskm (Studio aVOID), *13*
    bird's eye of Venice, Jacopo de' Barbari, *38*
    Chicago World Fair, Allen D. Albert, *10*
    City Club, Milton Keynes, Andrew Mahaddie, *16*
    Cybertopia, Egor Orlov, *25*
    Der Bau der Luftkolonie, Wenzel Hablik, *79*
    Floating City, Charles Simonds, *163*
    Floating Paris, Paul Maymont, *162*
    Green Machine, Stephane Malka, *169*
    Hundred Mile City, Peter Barber Architects, *40*
    Macau, Southeast China, Paul Tsui, *100*
    Manifesto New New York, Superstudio, *114*
    Marine City, Kiyonori Kikutake, *162*
    Mars Habitat, Foster + Partners, *161*
    MK in 1990, Helmut Jacoby, *15*
    New Babylon/Paris, Constant, *113*
    No-Stop City, Archizoom, *115*
    Parc de la Villette, Bernard Tschumi, *139*
    Plug-in City, Archigram, *93*
    Raumstadt, Eckhardt Schulze-Fielitz, *82*
    Spatial City, Yona Friedman, *82*
    Stadt Ragnitz, Eilfried Huth and Günther Domenig, *84*
    taxonomy, 23
    timeline, **176–7**
Floating City, **22**, 70–1
    Analemma Tower, Clouds Architecture Office, *76*
    Biosphere 3, Tomás Saraceno, *159*
    Der Bau der Luftkolonie, Wenzel Hablik, *79*
    Floating City, Charles Simonds, 163, *163*
    The Fifth Element (film), *97*
    The Flying City, Georgii Krutikov, *159*
Floating Paris, Paul Maymont, 162, *162*
Flooded London, 59, 154, *154*
Flying City, Georgii Krutikov, 157, *159*
Forest City, 15
Forget Your Past project, *6*
Forshaw's London Community map, Patrick Abercrombie, *12*
Forster, E. M., 59, 167
Fort Worth City Walk Map, *138*
Foster + Partners, 105, 106, 150, 160, *161*
Foundation (Asimov), 104
France, plan of Paris, *41*
Frassinelli, Piero, *5*
Frazer, John, 71
Freedomland, Ant Farm, 123
Friedman, Yona, 81, *82*, 91
Fun Palace, Cedric Price, 117, *117*, 118
Futurama exhibit, Norman Bel Geddes, 48, 88, *88*, 89
future cities
    description of, 7–8, 10–11
    envisioning climate change for rethinking, 154, 156
    highways and skyways, 87–90
    how to study, 17
    as machine, 83, 86–7
    patterns and trends of visions for, 174–5
    representing, 55–7
    studying visions of, 11–12, 14–16
    taxonomy of, 22–4, 26, 28
    techno clarity and off-world, 70–1
    visions for, 2
    visualization of, 1–2, 10, 17, 21
future city, definition of, 7
Future New York, Moses King, *65*
Future North, Terreform ONE, 164, *165*
Future of Cities Foresight Project, xix
futures, plurality and diversity of, 6
Future Shock (Toffler), 117
futures methods, 4
futurism, 56

G

Garden City, **22**, 43, 44
    movement, *42*, 42–4
    Silkscreen Plan of Griffith, Walter Burley Griffin, *45*
    Welwyn Garden City Masterplan, Louis De Soissons, *42*
    Westelijke Tuinsteden Expansion Plan, Cor van Eesteren, *44*
Garden City concept, 14
Garden City Trust, 14
Garland, Kenneth, 7
GEAM (Mobile Architecture Study Group), 92
General Motors, 88, *88*
geodesic dome, Midtown Manhattan, Richard Buckminster Fuller, *18*
Gernsback, Hugo, 157
Ghost in the Shell (film), 55, *78*, 95
Giant Billiard project, Haus-Rucker-Co, 120
Gibson, William, 59, 73
Gidley, Jennifer, 4
Gilliam, Terry, 172
Gissing, George, 42

Global Futures, 20
   ecological infrastructures and regional responses, 144–8, 150–3
   envisioning climate change for rethinking, 154, 156
   floating and underwater cities, 161–6
   going underground in subterranean cities, 166–8, 172
   planetary problems and us, 143–4
   sky isn't the limit, 156–8, 160
   urban life aquatic, 161–6
Global North, 11
Global South, 20
Global Strategic Trends programme, Ministry of Defence in UK, 40
global warming, 151, 154, 164–5
Goldfinger, Ernő, 60
Goreau, Thomas, 71, 73
Gothic Arch, Piranesi's, 39
Graf Zeppelin (German airship), 10
Graham, Stephen, 94, 156
Grankina, Olena, 50
Graves, Robert, 154, *154*
Great Exhibition of the Works of Industry of All Nations, 10
Green Float, Shimizu Corporation, 73, *79*
Green Machine, Stephane Malka, 167, *169*
Griffin, Walter Burley, 45
Griffith, Sir Arthur, 45
Gulliver's Travels (Swift), 37, 157

H

Hablik, Wenzel, *79*
Hadid, Zaha, 130
Hafner, Bernhard, *63*
Hagan, Susan, 29
Halprin, Lawrence, 138, *138*
Hancock, James Gulliver, *103*
Hanczyc, Martin, 28
Haptic City, **22**
   Fort Worth City Walk Map, Lawrence Halprin, *138*

Guide psychogéographique de Paris, Guy Debord, *136*
Labyrinth City, Léon Krier, *128*
No Small Plans (Lyon and Lin), *64*
Peep Pop City, You + Pea, *135*
Perceptual Form of the City, Kevin Lynch, *137*
Häusermann, Claude, 126, *127*
Häusermann, Pascal, 126, *127*
Haus-Rucker-Co, 116, 120, *121*
Haussmann, Georges-Eugène, 41, *41*
Hawkins\Brown, 131, *132*
Heathrow City, Hawkins\Brown, 131, *132*
Hénard, Eugène, 7, *8*
Herbert, Frank, 61, 167
Herron, Ron, *26*, 119
Herz, Manuel, *70*
Hester, Randolph, 138
Hetherington, Kevin, 38
High Rise (Ballard), 60
High Rise (film), 59, 60, *60*
Highrise of Homes, SITE, 127, *129*
Hilbertz, Wolf, 71, *73*
Hnilica, Sonja, 57
Hollein, Hans, 54, 69, 116
Holliday, Clyde T., 52
Hopkins, Don, 102
Horizontal City, **22**
   Broadacre City, Frank Lloyd Wright, *47*
   City Club, Milton Keynes, Andrew Mahaddie, *16*
   Eliopolis, Aldo Loris Rossi, *3*
   Lower Manhattan Expressway (LoMex), Paul Rudolph, *49*
   MK in 1990, Helmut Jacoby, *15*
   Paris 2050: A Smart City, Vincent Callebaut Architectures, *105*
   Stour City, 5th Studio, *133*
   Universal City, Raimund Abraham, *86*
Howard, Ebenezer, 42, 43
How Cities Work (Hancock), *103*
HSE Graduate School of Urbanism, *13*
Huang, Kevin, *76*

Hundred Mile City, Peter Barber Architects, 40
Huth, Eilfried, 63, 83, *84*
Huxley, Aldous, 55
Hybrid Cities, 174
   Abu Dhabi, *106*
   Altered Carbon, 56
   Analemma Tower, Clouds Architecture Office, *76*
   Back to the Future: Part II (film), *141*
   E.P.C.O.T. Masterplan, *17*
   Future Cities (Garland and Jefferis), 7
   Future Venice, Neil Spiller, Rachel Armstrong and Martin Hanczyc, 28
   Ghost in the Shell (film), *78*
   Heathrow City, Hawkins\Brown, *132*
   How Cities Work (Hancock), *103*
   HYPER-REALITY, Keiichi Matsuda, *141*
   Jakarta Jaya – The Green Manhattan, SHAU Architects, 107, *108*
   Mega Cities Project, *53*
   Metacity/Datatown, MVRDV, *130*
   One North Masterplan, Zaha Hadid Architects, *131*
   Paris 2050: A Smart City, Vincent Callebaut Architectures, *105*
   Seed Capital Area Masterplan, Amaravathi, *107*
   Stour City, 5th Studio, *133*
   taxonomy, 24
   timeline, **176–7**
   V2 Rocket, Launched White Sands, *52*
Hybrid City, SimCity, *102*
Hydro-Net, Iwamoto Scott, 150, *151*
HYPER-REALITY, Keiichi Matsuda, 141, *142*
Hypnerotomachia Poliphili, Francesco Colonna, 34, *35*

I

I Am Legend (film), 63
The Image of the City (Lynch), 136
imaginary cities, 29, 31, 34, 37–8
Imagination Lancaster, xix
industrial cities, 40–1
industrialization, mechanized life, 41–5, 47–8
Inflatocookbook, Ant Farm, 123
Informal Cities, 174
    Auto-Expander, Zünd-Up, *122*
    Centre Beaubourg Competition Paris, Jean-Louis Chanéac and Claude & Pascal Häusermann, *127*
    Dolphin Embassy, Ant Farm, *123*
    Earthscratcher for Century City, D_RD, *21*
    Flooded London, Squint/Opera, *59*
    Fort Worth City Walk Map, Lawrence Halprin, *138*
    Fun Palace for Joan Littlewood, Cedric Price, *117*
    Generations of Tokyo Architecture, Atelier Bow-Wow, *140*
    Guide psychogéographique de Paris, Guy Debord, *136*
    Instant City, Archigram, *119*
    La Cité Mobile, Charles Péré-Lahaille, *91*
    Lagos 2081, Ikiré Jones, *2*
    London: A Pilgrimage (Jerrold), *43*
    No Small Plans (Lyon and Lin), *64*
    Parsec City, Onyx, *75*
    Peep Pop City, You + Pea, *135*
    Perceptual Form of the City, Kevin Lynch, *137*
    Pneumacosmic Formation, Haus-Rucker-Co, *121*
    Radio City, Justus Dahinden, *126*
    Salzburg Superpolis, Günther Feuerstein, *116*
    Stratiform Structure Module, Kiyonori Kikutake, *85*
    taxonomy, 23
    timeline, **176–7**
    United Plastic Nation, Noel Schardt + Bjoern Muendner, *30*
    Walking City on the Ocean, Ron Herron, *26*
innovations, towards gleaming, 80–1
Instant City
    Archigram, *119*
    Cook, Peter, 119
Institute for Social Futures, xix
Intergovernmental Panel on Climate Change (IPCC), 143
Internet of Things, 109
Intrapolis, Walter Jonas, 124, *125*
The Inverted World (Priest), 160
Investigations in Collective Form (Maki), 83
The Isle of Pines (Neville), 34
Isozaki, Arata, *50*, 156, 157
Iwamoto Scott, 150, *151*

J

Jacobs, Jane, 48, 133
Jacoby, Helmut, 15
Jakarta Jaya – The Green Manhattan, SHAU Architects, 107, *108*
Jansson, Jan, 37
Jefferies, Richard, 161
Jefferis, David, *7*
Jellicoe, Geoffrey, 48, 89, *89*, 98
Jencks, Charles, 57
Jerrold, William Blanchard, *43*
Jeyfous, Olalekan, *2*
Joachim, Mitchell, *72*
Johnson, George Clayton, *110*
Jonas, Rosa Maria, *125*
Jonas, Walter, 124, *125*
Jones, Ikiré, *2*
Jorn, Asger, 135
Joseph, M. K., 141
Just Imagine (film), 63

K

Kahn, Albert, 48
Keilig, Morton, 59
Keiller, Patrick, 40
Kelp, Günther Zamp, 120
Kerrigan, Christian, *28*
Keynes, Milton, 15, 16
Kikutake, Kiyonori, 51, *85*, 161, 162, *162*
King, Moses, 65
Klutsis, Gustav, 45
Kollhoff, Hans, 141
Koolhaas, Rem, 66, 69
Kosmaj Project, *35*
Krier, Léon, 127, *128*
Krutikov, Georgii, 157, *159*
Kubrick, Stanley, 60, *61*
Kurokawa, Kisho, 51

L

Labyrinth City, Léon Krier, 127, *128*
La Cité Mobile, Charles Péré-Lahaille, *91*
Lagos 2081 A.D., Ikiré Jones, *2*
Lakoff, George, 57
Landscape Architecture, 71
Landscape Urbanism, 57
Lang, Fritz, *7*, *24*, 45
Lani, Lapo, *5*
La Révolution urbaine (Lefebvre), 104
Larsson, Magnus, 61, *62*
Latour, Bruno, 70
Laurana, Luciano, *32*
Layered Cities, **22**, 45, 89, 174
    Agglomeration, David George Emmerich, *92*
    Anderson Isometric Maps, *66*
    Architectural fantasy, Yakov Chernikhov, *39*
    Biosphere 3, Tomás Saraceno, *159*
    bird's eye view of Manhattan, *67*
    Blade Runner (film), *95*
    Blade Runner 2049 (film), *96*
    Buckminster Fuller with model of US Pavilion for Expo 67, *102*
    Chthonopolis, Nic Clear, *170*
    The Cities of the Future, Eugène Hénard, *8*
    City in Space, Bernhard Hafner, *63*
    A Clockwork Orange (film), 61, *61*
    Clusters in the Air (Cluster City), Arata Isozaki, *157*

Layered Cities, *continued*
    Eliopolis, Aldo Loris Rossi, *3*
    The Flying City, Georgii Krutikov, *159*
    Forshaw's London Community map, Patrick Abercrombie, *12*
    Future New York, Moses King, *65*
    The Gothic Arch, Giovanni Piranesi, *39*
    Highrise of Homes, SITE, *129*
    Intrapolis, Walter Jonas, *125*
    Lower Manhattan Expressway (LoMex), Paul Rudolph, *49*
    Mazhar Ali Khan, panorama of Delhi, *34*
    Metropolis (film), *24*
    Motopia (Jellicoe), *89*
    Multiplicity, John Wardle Architects and Stefano Boscutti, *157*, *158*
    New City (La Citta Digital Nuova), Antonio Sant'Elia, *85*
    Nukeproof Manhattan, Oscar Newman, *167*
    Ocean Spiral, Shimizu Corporation, *166*
    Re-ruined Hiroshima Project, Arata Isozaki, *50*
    Sietch, Matsys, *168*
    Spatial Bodies, AUJIK, *58*
    Strelka Unsettled, *50*
    Subterranean Singapore 2065, Finbarr Fallon, *170*
    taxonomy, 23
    timeline, **176–7**
    Urban Renewal in New York, Hans Hollein, *69*
    Uxcester Masterplan, URBED, *14*
    Vector habitat, Luigi Pellegrin, *146*
    View of an Ideal City, or The City of God, *32*
    Lean Urbanism, 57
Le Corbusier, 45, *46*, *47*, *48*, 145
Le Droit à la Ville (Lefebvre), 104, 111
Lefaivre, Liane, 34, *35*
Lefebvre, Henri, 73, 104, 111
Lin, Chris, 64
Linear Cities, 86, *86*
Littlewood, Joan, 117
Liveable Cities programme, xix
Logan's Run (film), 109, *110*
London
    climate change, 154
    Flooded London, Squint/Opera, *59*
    Greater London Plan, *12*
    master plan by M.A.R.S. Group, *23*
London: A Pilgrimage (Jerrold), 42, *43*
Looking Backward (Bellamy), 41, 59
Lord, Chip, 122
Lovag, Antti, 126
Lower Manhattan Expressway (LoMex), *49*
Lynch, David, 61
Lynch, Kevin, 136, *137*
Lynn, Greg, 59
Lyon, Gabrielle, 64

M

McCarthy, Cormac, 172
McDowell, Alex, 97, 98
McDowell, Malcolm, 61
'Machine Stops, The' (Forster), 59, 167
Mad Max (film trilogy), 172
Madoc-Jones, Didier, 154, *154*
Magic Motorways (Bel Geddes), 88
Magnon, Philippe, *82*, *85*, *136*
Mahaddie, Andrew, *16*
Maki, Fumihiko, 51, 83
Malka, Stephane, 167, *169*
Manchester heliport, *91*
Manhattan, 62–3, 66, 69
    architecture model, 69
    bird's eye view of, *66*, *67*
    'City of Things' perspective, Manuel Herz Architects, *70*
    Escape from New York (film), *68*
    Future New York, Moses King, *65*
    Post Carbon City State, Terreform ONE, *72*
Manhattan Transcripts, 140
Margheri, Giulio, *50*
Marine City, Kiyonori Kikutake, 161, *162*
M.A.R.S. Group, *23*
Mars Habitat, Foster + Partners, 160, *161*
Masdar Development, Foster + Partners, 105, *106*
Masterplan Strijp Philips, Eindhoven, *5*
Mathews, Stanley, 118
The Matrix (film), 140
Matsuda, Keiichi, *141*, 142
Matsys, 61, 167, *168*
Mawdsley, Devin, *64*
May, Ernst, 44
Maymont, Paul, 162, *162*, 163
Mcharg, Ian, 71
Mechanical City, **22**
    Aircraft Carrier City, Hans Hollein, *54*
    The Cities of the Future, Eugène Hénard, *8*
    Dome over Manhattan, Richard Buckminster Fuller, *18*
    Future New York, Moses King, *65*
    Metropolis (film), *24*
    Urban Renewal in New York, Hans Hollein, 69
Media City, **22**
    'Our New Age', Athelstan Spilhaus, *125*
    Parc de la Villette, Bernard Tschumi, *139*
    Pneumacosmic Formation, Haus-Rucker-Co, *121*
    Radio City, Justus Dahinden, *126*
    Salzburg Superpolis, Günther Feuerstein, *116*
Mega Cities Project, Paris, *53*
megastructures, 81, 83, 126
Melbourne, Multiplicity, 157, *158*
Merrifield, Andy, 73
Metabolism, 51
Metabolists, 51, 83, 156
Metacity/Datatown, MVRDV, 129, 130, *130*
Metropolis (film), 7, *24*, 45, 85

The Metropolis of Tomorrow (Ferriss), 45
Michels, Doug, 122, 124
Midtown Manhattan, geodesic dome, *18*
Mihov, Nikola, *6*
Millennial Project (Savage and Clarke), 70
Milton Keynes Development Corporation, *15, 16*
Minecraft, *19,* 25
Minnesota Experimental City (MXC), 124*, 125*
Minority Report (film), 97, *98,* 109
Mitchell, Mike, 144, *145*
Mitchell, William, 58
Miyazaki, Hayao, *79*
A Modern Utopia (Wells), 42
Mona Lisa Overdrive (Gibson), 73
Monument to the Third International, 45
Moody, Walter D., 62, *64*
Moore, Nicolas, *50*
More, Thomas, 34, *36*
Morris, William, 41
Moses, Robert, 48
Motopia (Jellicoe), 48, 89, *89,* 98
Moukarzel, Bachir, *99*
Moving City, **22**
    Back to the Future: Part II (film), *141*
    Forshaw's London Community map, Patrick Abercrombie, *12*
    View of Strasbourg, Jan Jansson, *37*
    Walking City on the Ocean, Ron Herron, *26*
Muendner, Bjoern, *30*
Multiplicity, John Wardle Architects and Stefano Boscutti, 157, *158*
Mumford, Lewis, 31, 37, 38
Murphy, Douglas, 160
MVRDV, 129, *130,* 148, *149*
The Mystery of Edwin Drood (Dickens), *43*

N

Naked City, 135
National Intelligence Council, 40
nation-state, concept of, *30*
Neo-Tokyo, *19*
The Nether World (Gissing), 42
Neuromancer (Gibson), 59, 73
Neville, Henry, 34
The New Atlantis (Bacon), 34
Newman, Oscar, *60,* 166
News from Nowhere (Morris), 41
New Shanghai, Stefano Boeri Architetti, *77*
New Town movement, 44
new urbanism, 11, 57, 127
New Welfare Island Project, Rem Koolhaas, 69
New York City, Rising Currents exhibition, *27*
New York World's Fair, 48
Niemeyer, Oscar, *18*
1984 (Orwell), 55, *61*
Nolan, William F., *110*
No Small Plans (Lyon and Lin), 61, *64*
No-Stop City, Archizoom, 115, *115*
Novak, Marcus, 59
Nukeproof Manhattan, Oscar Newman, 166, *167*

O

Ocean Spiral, Shimizu Corporation, 165, *166*
Okhitovich, Mikhail Aleksandrovich, 48
OMA/AMO, Eneropa Eurogrid, 147, *147*
Onyx, Parsec City, *75*
Operation Manual for Spaceship Earth (Buckminster Fuller), 160
Orlov, Egor, *25*
Ortner, Laurids, 120
Ortner, Manfred, 120
Orwell, George, 55, *61*
Osborn, Fredrick, *42*
OTEC (ocean thermal energy conversion), 71
Our New Age, Athelstan Spilhaus, *125*

P

Parc de la Villette, Bernard Tschumi, 139, *139*
Paris, Mega Cities Project, 53
Paris 2050: A Smart City, Vincent Callebaut Architectures, *105*
'Parliament of Things', Bruno Latour, *70*
Parsec City, Onyx, *75*
Pask, Gordon, 118
Pawley, Martin, 120
Péré-Lahaille, Charles, *91*
Peep Pop City, You + Pea, 133, *135*
Pellegrin, Luigi, 146, *146*
Pencil Points (Regan), 57
Pennebaker, D. A., *40*
Persson, Markus 'Notch', *19*
Piano, Renzo, 118
Pichler, Walter, 116
Pinter, Klaus, 120
Piranesi, Giovanni Battista, *39*
Plan for Tokyo, Kenzo Tange, *51*
Plan of Voisin, Le Corbusier, *46*
Plug-In City, Peter Cook, 93, *93*
Pneumacosm, 120, *121*
Polak, Fred, *4*
Porritt, Jonathon, 143
possible futures, *6*
Postcards From the Future, Robert Graves and Didier Madoc-Jones, 154, *154*
preferred futures, *6*
Price, Cedric, 117
Priest, Christopher, 160
probable futures, *6*
The Pruitt-Igoe Myth (documentary), 57
Pushwagner, *Soft City*, 8, *9*, 62

Q

Quarmby, Arthur, 126

R

Radebaugh, Arthur, 89, *89*
Radio City, Justus Dahinden, 124
Ragghianti, Carlo, 83

Raumstadt, Eckhardt Schulze-Fielitz, *82*
reality tunnels, 57
Reed, Deon, *64*
Regan, Oliver, 57
Regulated Cities, 43, 45, 174
    Aircraft Carrier City, Hans Hollein, *54*
    Babel IIB, Arcology, Paolo Soleri, *87*
    Blessed Ambrogio Sansedoni, *32*
    Brasília, Brazil, Lúcio Costa and Oscar Niemeyer, *18*
    China, A Vertical Forest on Mars?, Stefano Boeri Architetti, *77*
    City of Manchester Heliport, R. Nicolas, *91*
    Comprehensive City, Mike Mitchell and Alan Boutwell, *145*
    Cumbernauld New Town, Geoffrey Copcutt, *90*
    Destruction of Neo-Tokyo, *19*
    Dome over Manhattan, Richard Buckminster Fuller, *18*
    Dubai, *99*
    Europa EuroGrid, OMA/AMO, *147*
    Escape from New York (film), *68*
    The Fifth Element (film), *97*
    Futurama exhibit, Norman Bel Geddes, *88*
    High Rise (film), *60*
    Hypnerotomachia Poliphili, Francesco Colonna, *35*
    Imaginary drawings, Zoning ordinances, Hugh Ferriss, *67*
    industrial cities, 40–1
    Island Capital of the Aztecs, *33*
    Labyrinth City, Léon Krier, *128*
    Le Dodici Città Ideali, Superstudio, *5*
    Logan's Run (film), *110*
    master plan for London, 23, *23*
    Masterplan Strijp Philips, Eindhoven, *5*
    Memorial House of Bulgarian Communist Party, *6*
    Minecraft, *19*
    Minority Report (film), *98*
    New Welfare Island, Rem Koolhaas, *69*
    'Our New Age', Athelstan Spilhaus, *125*
    plan of Mexico, *33*
    Plan of Paris, France, *41*
    Plan for Tokyo, Kenzo Tange, *51*
    Silkscreen Plan of Griffith, Walter Burley Griffin, *45*
    Soft City, Pushwagner, *9*
    taxonomy, 23
    timeline, **176–7**
    Universal City, Raimund Abraham, *86*
    Utopia (More), *36*
    View of an Ideal City, or The City of God, *32*
    View of Strasbourg, Jan Jansson, *37*
    Ville Radieuse, Le Corbusier, *46*
    Welwyn Garden City Masterplan, Louis De Soissons, *42*
    Westelijke Tuinsteden Expansion Plan, Cor van Eesteren, *44*
    Zhujiangkou Island, CCCC-FHDI & AT Design Office, *164*
Rendering Tomorrow, 20
    digital faith and forgotten fingertips, 57–9
    global urbanized surfaces, 73
    Manhattan, 62–3, 66, 69
    representing the future city, 55–7
    techno clarity and off-world future city, 70–1
    writing cities, 59–62
Re-ruined Hiroshima Project, Arata Isozaki, *50*
Resilient by Design, Hassell and MVRDV, 148, *149*
Richter, Dagmar, *21*
Rising Currents Exhibition, 27
RMF FM Media Complex, *71*
The Road (McCarthy), 172
Robinson in Space (Keiller), 40
Rodchenko, Alexander, 56
Rogers, Richard, 118
Rosling, Ryan, *96*
Rossi, Aldo Loris, *3*
Rottier, Guy, 91
Royal Institute of British Architects, 7
Rudakevych, Ostap, 76
Rudolph, Paul, *49*
Rumsey, David, *66*, *67*
Russian Constructivism, 139

S

Sadler, Simon, 118, 120
Saint-Exupéry, Antoine de, 101
Salzburg Superpolis, Günther Feuerstein, 116, *116*
Sanders, Rupert, *78*
Sant'Elia, Antonio, 83, *85*
Saraceno, Tomás, Cloud Cities, 158, *159*
Savage, Marshall T., 70
Savorgnan, Giulio, 40
SCAPE, Oystertecture / MoMA Rising Currents Exhibition, 27
Schardt, Noel, 30
Schreier, Curtis, 122
Schulz, Jurgen, 38
Schulze-Fielitz, Eckhardt, 81, *82*
Schumacher, Patrik, 59
Science and Invention (Gernsback), 157
Scott, Ridley, 95
SEALAB habitats, United States Navy, 165
SeaSteading Institute, 70
Second World War, 44, 48, 89
Seed Capital Area Masterplan, Amaravathi, 106, *107*
SHAU Architects, 107, *108*
Shaviro, Steven, 94
Shimizu Corporation, 73, *79*
A Short Bibliography on Megastructures (Wilcoxon), 83
Sidewalk Labs, 133
Silent Running (film), *71*
Silent Spring (Carson), 61
SimCity, 101, *102*
Simonds, Charles, 163, *163*
SITE (Sculpture In The Environment), 127, *129*

Situationist International (SI), 112, 135, 136
Situationists, 135, *136*
Sketchpad (Sutherland), 58
Sky City, **22**
    Aerotopia, Chan K Q Audrey and Iskm (Studio aVOID), *13*
    City of Manchester Heliport, R. Nicolas, *91*
    City in Space, Bernhard Hafner, *63*
    Fun Palace for Joan Littlewood, Cedric Price, *117*
Slaughter, Richard, 4
Smart Cities, 31, 104, 129
Smart City, **22**
    Abu Dhabi, *106*
    How Cities Work (Hancock), *103*
    Jakarta Jaya – The Green Manhattan, SHAU Architects, *107*, *108*
    Loop City, BIG, 148, *149*
    Mega Cities Project, *53*
    Nature-City, WORKac, *152*
    Seed Capital Area Masterplan, Amaravathi, *107*
    SimCity, *102*
    V2 Rocket, Launched White Sands, *52*
smarter city, term, 105
Smithson, Alison, 60
Smithson, Peter, 60
Social Credit System, China, 109
Social Futures, 20
    architecture and its dissolution, 116–20
    continuous city for new society, 111–16
    disruption, hybridity and augmentation, 139–42
    exploding plastic urban, 120, 122–4
    new experiences of city, 135–6, 138
    new forms and organizations, 124, 126–30
    people and city, 111
    recent formulations for futures, 131, 133–4
Soft City (Pushwagner), 8, 9, 62

Soleri, Paolo, 52, 87, *87*, 145
Solten, Jerzy, 92
Sono, Masayuki, *76*
Sorkin, Michael, 124
Space City, **22**
    China, A Vertical Forest on Mars?, Stefano Boeri Architetti, *77*
    Future Cities (Garland and Jefferis), *7*
    Mars Habitat, Foster + Partners, *161*
    Parsec City, Onyx, *75*
Spatial Bodies, AUJIK, *58*
Spatial City, Yona Friedman, 81, *82*
Spectacle City, **22**
    Babel IIB, Arcology, Paolo Soleri, *87*
    Buckminster Fuller with model of U.S. Pavilion for Expo 67, *102*
    Logan's Run (film), *110*
    Macau, Southeast China, Paul Tsui, *100*
    Villes éteintes (Darkened Cities), Thierry Cohen, *155*
Spielberg, Steven, *98*
Spilhaus, Athelstan, 124, *125*
Spiller, Neil, 28
Sproull, Bob, 59
    Stadt Ragnitz, Eilfried Huth and Günther Domenig, *63*, 83, *84*
Steinberg, Phillip, 70–1
Sterling, Bruce, 94
Stevin, Simon, 40
    Stratiform Structure Module, Kiyonori Kikutake, 83, *85*
Strelka Unsettled, *50*
Studio Ghibli, *79*
Studio Lindfors, Aqualta, 154, *155*
Subterranean Singapore 2065, Finbarr Fallon, *170*
Sullivan, Louis, 63
Superstudio, *5*, 112, 113, 114, *115*
sustainability, new urbanism, 11
Sutherland, Ivan, 58–9
Suvin, Darko, 94
Swift, Jonathan, 37, 157

T

Tactical Urbanism, 57
Tafuri, Manfredo, 114, 115
Tange, Kenzo, 51, *51*, 52
Tatlin, Vladimir, 45, 56
taxonomy, future cities, 22–4, 26, 28
Technological Futures, 20
    architects dreaming of electric sheep, 94, 96–9
    being 'smart', 104–7, 109
    cities of moving parts, 91–3
    city as machine, 83, 86–7
    culture of technological desires, 101, 103
    highways and skyways to future, 87–90
    megastructures and endless cities, 81, 83
    towards gleaming innovations, 80–1
Tenochtitlan, Island Capital of the Aztecs, *33*
Terreform ONE, *72*, 164, *165*
Thiel, Philip, 138
3-C CITY: Climate, Convention, and Cruise, WORKac & Ant Farm, 71, *74*
Toffler, Alvin, 117
To-morrow: A Peaceful Path to Real Reform (Howard), 43
Tomorrow's Cities Today, 20
    alternative futures, 178–9
    collective visions for tomorrow's world, 178
    envisioning future cities, 173–4
    patterns and trends of visions for future cities, 174–5
    timeline of themes and paradigms, **176–7**
Trading City, **22**
    bird's eye of Venice, Jacopo de' Barbari, *38*
    Blessed Ambrogio Sansedoni, *32*
    Island Capital of the Aztecs, *33*
    Mazhar Ali Khan, panorama of Delhi, *34*
    plan of Mexico, *33*

Tschumi, Bernard, 139, *139*
Tsui, Eugene, 156
Tsui, Paul, *100*
Tuned Suburb, Ron Herron, 119
12 Monkeys (film), 172

U

Ultima Tower, Eugene Tsui, 156
Underground City, **22**, 168
    Architectural fantasy, Yakov Chernikhov, *39*
    Chthonopolis, Nic Clear, *170*
    The Gothic Arch, Giovanni Piransei, *39*
    Hypnerotomachia Poliphili, Francesco Colonna, *35*
    Nukeproof Manhattan, Oscar Newman, *167*
    Subterranean Singapore 2065, Finbarr Fallon, *170*
    Vector habitat, Luigi Pellegrin, *146*
The Underground City (Verne), 166
UN DESA Population Division, 11, 144
United Plastic Nation, Noel Schardt + Bjoern Muendner, *30*
Universal City, Raimund Abraham, 86, *86*
Urban Fiction, exhibition, 116
urbanism, car-led and beyond, 48, 50–4
urbanization, industrial cities, 40
urban project, 5
Urban Renewal in New York, Hans Hollein, *69*
Urban Structures for the Future (Dahinden), 126
URBED, 14, 44
Urry, John, xix, 14, 178
user's needs, concept, 5
US Pavilion, Richard Buckminster Fuller, 101, *102*
Utopia (More), 34, *36*
utopian city, concept of, 3

V

V2 Rocket, Launched White Sands, NASA, *52*
van Eesteren, Cor, *44*
van Herpt, Roel, *50*
Vasari, Giorgio, *32*
Vector Habitat, Luigi Pellegrin, 146, *146*
Verne, Jules, 166
Vertical City, **22**, 81
    Brasília, Brazil, Lúcio Costa and Oscar Niemeyer, *18*
    Centre Beaubourg Competition Paris, Jean-Louis Chanéac and Claude & Pascal Häusermann, *127*
    Dubai, *99*
    Future Venice, Neil Spiller, Rachel Armstrong and Martin Hanczyc, *28*
    Highrise of Homes, SITE, *129*
    New City (La Citta Digital Nuova), Antonio Sant'Elia, *85*
    Stadt Ragniz, Eilfried Huth and Günther Domenig, *84*
Vice City, **22**
    A Clockwork Orange (film), *61*
    High Rise (film), *60*
    London: A Pilgrimage (Jerrold), *43*
video game, Minecraft, 19
Villeneuve, Denis, 96
Ville Radieuse (The Radiant City), Le Corbusier, 45, *46*
Ville Spatiale, Yona Friedman, 81, *82*
Vincent Callebaut Architectures, 104, *105*
virtual reality (VR), 59
vision, 29
    method of futurist, 4
    study, of future cities, 11–12, 14–16
A Visual History of the Future (Dunn et al.), 22
visualization
    future cities, 1–2, 10, 17, 21
    representing the future city, 55–7
    role of, 12, 14
von Eckardt, Wolf, 90
Voros, Joseph, 4

W

Wachsmann, Konrad, 92
Wacker's Manual (Moody), 62, 64
Walking City on the Ocean, Ron Herron, *26*
Wall-E (film), 172
Waste City, **22**
    Dharavi Masterplan, Foster + Partners, *150*
    Hydro Net, Iwamoto Scott, *151*
    Post Carbon City State, Terreform ONE, *72*
    Soft City, Pushwagner, *9*
Water City, **22**
    3-C CITY: Climate, Convention, and Cruise, WORKac & Ant Farm, *74*
    Aqualta, Studio Lindfors, *155*
    Autopia Ampere, Newton Fallis, *73*
    Floating City, Charles Simonds, *163*
    Floating Paris, Paul Maymont, *162*
    Flooded London, Squint/Opera, *59*
    Future North, Terreform ONE, *165*
    Marine City, Kiyonori Kikutake, *162*
    Ocean Spiral, Shimizu Corporation, *166*
    Oystertecture, SCAPE / MoMA Rising Currents Exhibition, *27*
    Plan for Tokyo, Kenzo Tange, *51*
    Postcards From the Future, Robert Graves and Didier Madoc-Jones, *154*
    Resilient by Design, Hassell and MVRDV, 148, *149*
    United Plastic Nation, Noel Schardt + Bjoern Muendner, *30*
    Zhujiangkou Island, CCCC-FHDI & AT Design Office, *164*
We (Zamyatin), 59

Webber, Melvin, *15*
Weisman, Alan, 156
Wells, H. G., 41
Welwyn Garden City, *42*, 44
Wendorf, Richard, *39*
Westelijke Tuinsteden Expansion Plan, Cor van Eesteren, *44*
What is the Future? (Urry), 14
Wigley, Mark, 112
Wilcoxon, Ralph, 83
Wines, James, 127, *129*
Wittkower, Rudolf, 37

Wolfson Economics Prize, *14*
WORKac, Nature-City, 152, *152*
WORKac & Ant Farm, 3-C CITY: Climate, Convention, and Cruise, *74*
world fairs, 10
The World We Made (Porritt), 143
The World Without Us (Weisman), 156
Wright, Erik Olin, 15
Wright, Frank Lloyd, 47, 48, 146
Wright, Will, *102*

Y
Yamasaki, Minoru, 57
You + Pea, Peep Pop City, 133, *135*

Z
Zaha Hadid Architects, 130, *131*
ZeroSix, 172
Zevi, Bruno, 146
Zhujiangkou Island, CCCC-FHDI & AT Design Office, 163, *164*
zoning, concept, *5*
Zünd-Up, 122, *122*